THE
NATURE
SPECIALIST

A Complete Guide to Program and Activities

Lenore Hendler Miller

American Camping Association®

Photos by Steve Desantis.
Original cover drawing with dragonfly by Herman Zaage.
Cover design by Tom Dougherty.

Printed in the United States of America

American Camping Association
5000 State Road 67 North
Martinsville IN 46151-7902
317/342-8456 American Camping Association Business Office
800/428-CAMP American Camping Association Bookstore

Library of Congress Cataloging-in-Publication Data

Miller, Lenore Hendler.
    The nature specialist : a complete guide to program and activities /
by Lenore Hendler Miller. — Rev. ed.
        p.cm.
     Includes index and bibliography.
     ISBN 0-87603-087-8
     1. Nature study. I. Miller, Lenore Hendler. II. Nature history — Outdoor books.
QH51.M55   1986   86-10832
                                                                  CIP

TABLE OF CONTENTS

Acknowledgements

A teacher is first and foremost, a pupil. What we learn from our many teachers throughout our lives becomes an integral part of our own total body knowledge. Thus, it is sometimes impossible to pinpoint the exact time, place and person who imparted a specific bit of information. A teacher then draws on that total body of knowledge to pass this recycled information on to other pupils. My teachers and sources of inspiration have been numerous. I should like to acknowledge all of them who shared their knowledge with me and thereby inspired me to share mine with children and others. The list is long and perhaps incomplete, but I humbly thank all of them, named and unnamed.

Harry Betros, Olivia Hansen, and Rudolph Lindenfeld of High Rock Park, Staten Island. Phyllis Busch, Ruth Yarrow, Catherine Pessino, Rose and Elliott Blaustein, John Kominski, Joseph Saccente, Carlton Beil, Jean Porter, Helmut Schiller, Jerry Schierloh, Michael Weilbacher, Verne Rockcastle, Helen Ross Russell.

And for allowing me to share their expertise: Andy Angstrom, Ted Gilman, Pam and Win Carter, Bob Dorrance, Jack and Carol Padalino, Linda Palter, Ira Kanis, Louise Davis, Elmer Heberling, Leslie Markus, Estelle Bard, and Don Cook, Sallie Ruppert, Mary Shakespeare, George Barr, Eneas Sloman, Elaine Alberts, Eileen Doocey, Sam Holmes, James Lipton, Collen Seeley, Mary Vorndran, Clyde Lammey, Tom Wolfe, E. L. Palmer, Roger Tory Peterson, George Petrides, James Yaitch.

To Todd Gershowitz, for sparking the idea of this project; to my husband, Stan, for his patience and assistance; my sons Andrew and Bill who are my sounding boards; typist, Iva Loftman; artist, Herman Zaage; photographer, Steve de Santis.

A special note of thanks to Ben and Barbara Appelbaum, who gave me my first job as a camp nature specialist; to Alex Savitz, principal, who convinced me to share my knowledge by writing; and to the directors of Camps Blue Ridge/Equinunk, Joyce Greenwald and Gert and Marty Gelobter, for their continued support and encouragement.

This book is lovingly dedicated to the person who fostered and enhanced the role of nature specialist in his camp, Chief Edward Lehrer.

Preface

The job of the Nature Specialist in a children's summer camp is one rich in rewarding experiences for the specialist, as well as for the campers. In this role, the nature lover can be amateur scientist-botanist, ornithologist, ethologist, entomologist, zoologist—for a few weeks every summer.

In my more than ten years of experience as a Nature Specialist in camp, I have tried and tested many approaches and activities. This manual is the outgrowth of these experiences, organized in such a way that a novice may utilize it to maximize the effectiveness of the program.

No one can guarantee instant success in any venture. However, approaching the job of nature specialist with a desire to do one's best and to spread an environmental message, and using the material presented in this book, should make the job pleasant and successful.

INTRODUCTION

Summertime is the ideal time for nature study, and camps are the ideal places for it. Located in the country, camps are places where a more relaxed attitude prevails, where children gather for recreation and are exposed daily to the natural world. Camps present a great opportunity for the person who loves nature and the outdoors to share this love with children and help develop in them a proper attitude toward the natural world, one of admiration, awe and respect.

If the nature room is attractive, exciting, inviting; if the specialist is enthusiastic and available, then nature can become one of the most successful camp programs. Kids who used to think, "Ugh! Nature!" will start saying, "Wow! Nature!" It may take a while, even more than an entire summer. But, over the years, its success can grow. With it, will grow a conservation ethic, respect for life and the wilderness, a realization of the interdependence of living and non-living things and one's own role in the environment.

The specialist must always be aware that camp is *not* the classroom; it is a recreational setting. This is not to say that learning doesn't take place in such a setting; on the contrary, more nature learning can be crammed into eight weeks than in an indoor setting. Besides common good manners of listening and respect for the leader and each other, there should not be silence. Activities should emphasize fun while learning. Achievements and contests may be added as challenges to spark and add excitement.

Some basic guidelines:

1. Safety first, in and out of doors.
2. Always leave the group with a desire for more.
3. Keep yourself available and open.
4. Be especially attentive to the non-athletic camper.
5. Never force a camper to do anything he/she isn't comfortable with; encourage the campers to try.

There are many benefits to gain for yourself, too. A successful program will have a permanent impact on children, as well as an impact on conservation. Year after year, you will gain the satisfaction of building a more responsive audience.

Related Outdoor Activities

Some camps combine nature study and other outdoor/adventure programs. The same person may be doing both aspects of outdoor programming. This manual, however, is more narrowly focused and does not address itself to instruction in backpacking, adventure, mountain-climbing, canoeing, etc. Please refer to the other excellent resource materials and organizations for instruction and assistance. Common sense dictates that a person unfamiliar with such activities should not lead them. However, a person who *can* do both is a highly desirable staff member.

The nature specialist may be called upon to lead day-hikes, start campfires, accompany overnight hikes (a great place and time to do many darkness activities) and should become familiar with the skills (compass and map reading, etc.) needed to carry these out.

A Word to Camp Directors

A quality nature program should be a part of *every* camp experience for *every* camper. Getting close to nature is one of the major reasons for the existence of summer camps. Some camps seem to have let this aspect of camp slip away. But in this era of high tech and urbanization, the need for nature in camp becomes even more necessary than in the past when people lived on farms or in rural settings, where their daily lives brought them close to nature. Camp can be one of the places where people renew their ties to the earth and its resources. The nature program in camp fulfills an important role in this renewal.

What is a quality nature program and how does it come about?

A good nature program is the result of many interacting factors. The two major factors are the camp, its directors and policies and the other is the nature specialist.

The directors must see a need for and want a quality program and also need to put their resources behind it. They must seek out the best specialists and be willing to pay them well so that they can attract and retain the best. In their own minds, the directors must see Nature as a program that is as important to camp as the other key positions and programs. Nature cannot be an afterthought or a minor; it should be on a par with the crafts, waterfront and athletic specialties. This idea should be brought out in hiring practices, site provisions and in promoting the camp to prospective campers and their parents.

The camp must also provide a suitable facility where the nature specialist can set up a nature center and conduct activities. The directors should provide a budget to equip the facility, not a lavish budget for expensive and elaborate devices, but one that is adequate for the program to be successful.

The specialist should not be overwhelmed by numbers of children either. Outdoor and indoor nature activities require small groups so that each camper can see and hear. The ideal number of campers at one time per specialist is about 8 or 10. The maximum number a specialist should be asked to handle at one time is 15 or 16. Any more than this leaves kids out, unless the general counselor staff takes a very active role. Rainy days can double the number if indoor facilities allow for this.

The attitude of the camp director filters down to all staff members and to every employee. All workers at camp should demonstrate a reverence for living things and the environment. There should be a consciousness about not polluting, or wasting, or destroying. Camps should set the model in living in harmony with nature. This philosophy should be imparted to the entire staff at orientation, in brochures and in practice.

The nature specialist is the other key factor in conducting a successful nature program. The most important qualities the specialist must bring to the job are a love of nature, an enthusiastic approach and a sincere desire to impart that love and enthusiasm to people. The specialist doesn't need to be a nature expert and to be able to name every tree, flower or bird. Indeed, one would have to spend decades immersed in academia to master all of these. There are many excellent field guides and resource books available to find out that information. The specialist must be able and willing to have a "let's try to find out" attitude. Each new day and new sight in nature must spark the "WOW!" so that this marveling is passed on to the campers. The specialist must realize that to children, most sights are new sights—and it may also be the child's "once in a lifetime." If the specialist possesses a curiosity about the world, that attribute will also carry over to campers.

The combination of a camp that cares deeply about nature and is committed to it, plus the specialist who possesses curiosity, enthusiasm and love of nature along with the desire to impart these to children, will result in a high quality nature program for any camp.

Before You Go; Getting Ready

Whatever the opening date of camp, the naturalist must start to prepare before that time, especially if the nature program is beginning from scratch. Materials must be ordered, specimens accumulated, the program developed.

As the nature specialist, you need to develop in yourself, a mind-set, so that as you look around, you continually think, "How can I use such-and-such in my program? Can I recycle that baby food jar or old panty hose (tissue box, toilet roll, oatmeal box—whatever) in some way to make something for program or display?"

Many natural objects are more readily visible in the winter and early spring before the foliage of summer covers them. Such things as galls, nests, bagworms, cocoons, praying mantis egg cases, etc., should be collected and stored in a cool place (so they don't hatch). Your local pest exterminator may be an excellent source of specimens since he may be called upon to remove baldface hornets' or wasps' nests (only in winter). Call beforehand; ask to have it saved for you.

In the spring, you should start your leaf collection before insects damage the leaves. Dry, press and laminate or clear-plastic the leaves. Try to locate an owl tree for a source of owl pellets. Contact the local zoo or pet shop for shed snake skins or other cast-offs.

You'll need to order seeds, if you'll be doing any planting or gardening. Seeds could be shipped to camp or to you (see "Plants/Gardening" in Section II).

If you expect to be caring for animals, mid-winter is the time to contact your source of animals to place your order. By pre-ordering, you have a better chance of selecting choice animals.

If you expect to use tree-rings for display or for an activity, ask the camp director to contact the maintenance staff and request that they cut a felled tree trunk into sections of

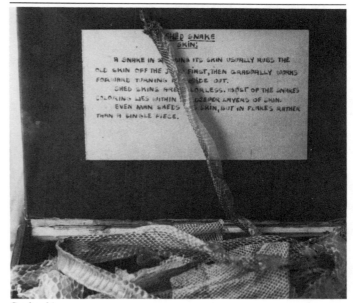

Snake skins.

about 1½-2 inches thick so that campers may observe the growth rings. A thicker section is good for display; the thinner ones for individual use.

Preview filmstrips for possible use. Look through school and library catalogs for lists and samples. Examine books at the same time.

Enhance your own knowledge. Check out courses, one-day workshops, conferences, weekends. Many are offered in every area in a variety of places (see Appendix for list of suggestions). Get on the mailing lists of local nature centers. Contact the local chapter of the Audubon Society; find out what they offer that may interest you. Check your local newspaper for interpretive tours and guided walks, conducted by various organizations, such as Urban or National Park Rangers. Be sure to equip yourself with a notebook, or better still, a portable cassette that will record the

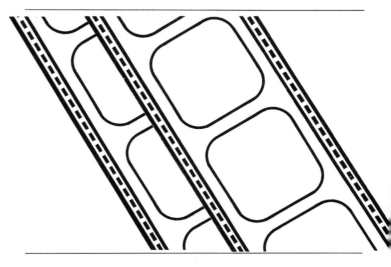

information for later playback and more leisurely absorption. Subscribe to magazines such as *Ranger Rick;* membership in National Wildlife Federation and Audubon will bring you their magazines (and the membership is tax-deductible). The New York State *Conservationist* and other state publications are also an excellent resource.

If you are planning to create dried or pressed flower pictures, you may wish to begin that process beforehand (pansies make especially lovely pictures).

As summer approaches, visit your school or local public library. You will have to make special arrangements to borrow books for the duration of the summer. You will also have to arrange for the use of any equipment you are borrowing. It is best to inventory all such material (including books, filmstrips) before leaving. Then, upon arrival, you can check against your inventory to make certain you have everything.

Obtain recordings or tapes of bird calls from your nearest nature center, university or local library. After obtaining permission, tape these onto a blank cassette. This is especially valuable if you plan to call owls on a night hike (see Night Hikes Section IV). If any of the filmstrips you'll be using are accompanied by records, re-record on cassette tape for ease in handling and storage.

You should request a copy of your programmed schedule (from the head counselor or camp director) so that you may pre-plan some of the activities. If you are gardening, seeds

have to be planted ahead of time—either at camp, or by you (see Plants/Gardening, Section II). Birdhouses must be made and put up in the spring. Summer is too late for most species to seek out and claim a birdhouse territory. Perhaps you might ask a scout troop or shop class to construct some for you. Cut out pictures and newspaper clippings that are pertinent to nature study. Prepare sets of cut out silhouettes of animals for many uses. (See Section V, pages 133-138.)

Investigate and decide how you and your materials will get to camp. Will you transport them in your own car? Is the

car big enough? Try UPS or other delivery service.

If you are going to a particular camp for the first time, it would be wise to spend at least a weekend there, if possible, before the season begins. Familiarize yourself with the layout, explore the trails, and scout the surrounding area for special sites (waterfalls, fossil sites, streams).

Check with the camp director regarding the availability of special equipment, e.g., mimeo, spirit duplicator, laminator. If these are not available, you may have to bring pre-printed items with you.

Equipment, Materials and Supplies

While there is no doubt that a well-equipped nature shack enhances the nature program, supplies need not be elaborate. Beyond some basic supplies that you must certainly have, other materials may be accumulated in stages over the years, be homemade (either by yourself or the camp carpenter or arts and crafts shop), or be borrowed from various sources.

A generous budget will allow you to provide adequate equipment; a smaller budget may necessitate economies. If you are given the responsibility of purchasing materials, shopping around for the best possible price will allow whatever funds you are given to go further.

Keep in mind that materials and equipment may be handled by children and should either be sturdy or placed off limits to campers (e.g., an expensive microscope—only you or a designated adult may adjust). There are many inexpensive, yet worthwhile, items that are specifically designed for handling by children. Try one out; and, if you find it satisfactory, order it. Order the catalogs of companies listed in the Appendix and look through them carefully; you will find many ideas for projects and activities. In addition, many of the larger scientific supply companies regularly publish information bulletins which have useful suggestions you can adapt for camp.

Most schools have audio-visual and lab equipment that you may be able to borrow for the summer. If your budget doesn't allow for the purchase of a good microscope ($200-$500), try to borrow one from your local college. There are many other items which may be borrowed: filmstrip projectors, cassette recorders/players, filmstrip viewers, microviewers, kits, filmstrips, books, film loops and loop projectors. An important word about borrowing any materials and/or equipment: keep scrupulous records of what was borrowed and from where or whom must be kept. Be absolutely certain to return the material in the condition in which it was lent to you. That requires inventorying and keeping a watchful eye on the equipment. Neglecting to do so will cause unnecessary aggravation and expense and may negate your chances of borrowing again in the future. People may borrow things from you at camp; keep a note of what was borrowed, so that you do not lose anything.

During the year, keep your eyes open for sales that may allow you to purchase items in quantity at decent prices. Flea markets and garage sales are good sources of items that may be useful. When the family outgrows its desire for that cute little gerbil, they'll put up their expensive cage set for sale, and you can buy it at a fraction of its cost. Wholesale outlet stores may also have items you could use such as small bowls, picture frames, and drapery rings.

Another very valuable source of equipment and material is your own recyclable discards. Strawberry or tomato boxes, onion or orange mesh bags, egg cartons, plastic containers, empty card boxes with clear plastic lids, baby food jars, spray can tops, gallon jars, and even Dynamint dispensers may all be turned into decorative and/or useful nature program items that children will like. This illustrates another important lesson that comes from utilizing old materials: a throw-away psychology is not the only way. Many children, especially those from privileged homes, have developed habits of disposing of half-used items without any regard for the environmental damage generated by the overwhelming amounts of garbage. An entire lesson could be built around ways to re-use things (see *Million-Year-Picnic* in Activities, Section III).

On the pages following are lists of basic supplies, categorized by type. Select and buy only equipment you will actually use. Read the section on displays and activities to help you decide.

Animal Supplies

Aerator pump, tubing, and bubble stone
Animal trap(s)—Havahart (See Appendix)
Bird cage
Buckets
Cages—small mammal, mouse, snake
Chick water fountain—metal, plastic
Chicken brooder—with heat/light source
Chicken house—with roost
Dip nets—assorted sizes
Feed troughs—for larger animals
Fish net, line, hooks
Food—fish, turtle, bran flakes, bird seed
Gravel
Hose

Arts and Crafts Materials

Incubator (homemade, bought)
Insect cages (homemade—see Section V, page 127.
Large animal houses—goats (shed), rabbits
Small animal water bottles, feeding bottles
Tanks—fish tanks, bowls (2, 5, 10 gallon), plastic tanks, reptile tanks

Arts and Crafts Materials

Brayers (rollers)
Bridal netting
Brushes—assorted sizes
Carbon paper (for tracing)
Clay—non-hardening, hardening
Colored chalk
Crayons
Dowel sticks
Dried flowers, ferns
Fabric—felt, burlap and others
Ink pads
Light sensitive paper—blueprint or ozalid
Marking pens—assorted colors; fine and thick
Nature seals or stamps
Paints—water colors, jars or powders, palettes (sets)
Paper—white construction (8½ x 11) colored construction (small, large), oak tag, velour paper, tracing, colored tissue paper
Paste, glue (white), silicon, rubber cement
Plaster of Paris
Pompoms—fluff balls; eyes—movable; fluffy feathers
Pop sticks
Printer's ink—washable, tubes, assorted colors
Scissors—for children's use
Spray paints—colors, clear
Tracing paper

Games/Puzzles

Animalia
Assorted cut-outs, mobiles, models (Check catalogs, museum shops.)
Audible Audubon
Audubon card sets—Birds, Flowers, Mammals, Trees
Hidden Kingdom Animal Rummy—Safari, Ltd.
Jigsaw Puzzles—Birds of America*
Monarch Game

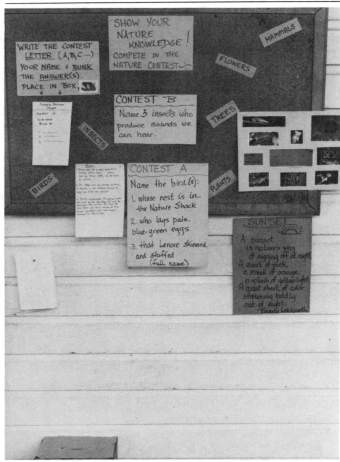

Nature knowledge

National Wildlife Old Maid*
Photograph Flash Card Sets—Birds, Wildflowers, Evergreens (Carolina Biological)
Predator—Prey Game—by Ampersand
Songbird Dominoes*
Wildlife Concentration*
Wildlife in Your World*
Wildlife Lotto*
"Yotta Know" Series—Mammals, Birds

Available from National Wildlife Federation.

Gardening Supplies

Gardening gloves
Hand trowels
Hoes
Hose
Insect repellent spray
Nail brush
Planting medium—potting soil, Jiffy pots or pellets, vermiculite
Pruning or garden shears
Rakes

Rope, string
Stakes—for tomatoes and other plants
Watering can(s)
Weed puller

Miscellaneous

Alcohol
Ammonia
Aquarium cement
Batteries, bulbs
Bleach
Book ends
Bowls—assorted, metal or glass
Candles—regular, votive
Charcoal
Clear Contact paper
Clear nail polish

Miscellaneous materials

Clothes pins—spring, other
Compasses
Cotton—sterile and non-sterile
Cotton balls or cosmetic puffs (much cheaper)
Extension cord(s); electrical adaptors (3 prongs to 2)
Field bag or carrying box
Filter paper—coffee
Foil wrap
Food coloring
Food flavoring—spices, essences, oils. (Try a crafts store which sells candle-making supplies or a health food store.)
Funnels
Glycerine (get at drug store)
Gravel
Hair dryer
Hole puncher
Knife—a good pocket knife (Swiss Army type)
Lubricating oil
Magnets
Matches—strike anywhere
Medicine droppers—dozen or more
Moth flakes or balls
Nails—assorted sizes; hammer
Nature stamps—National Wildlife Foundation

Paper plates, plastic spoons, foil trays
Paper toweling
Paraffin
Plastic baggies
Plastic cups, paper cups, small (1 ounce) medicine cups
Plastic food storage bags—medium; also Ziplocs
Plastic shoe boxes
Plastic wrap (Saran)
Poker chips
Pruning shears
Razor blades—single edge
Reflective tape, magnetic tape, cloth tape
Rubber gloves—few pair, including one heavy-duty
Sandpaper
Screening—metal
Sewing supplies—needles, thread, pins, thimble
Silica gel, corn meal, Borax (for drying)
Sponge(s)
Sprayer/mister
Steel wool
Strainers—several assorted sizes
Straws—paper, plastic
String
Tongs—1 large, 1 small
Toothpicks
Turkey baster
Tweezers—dozen
Velcro
Vinegar
Waxed paper
White enamel pan(s)
Wire—assorted rolls and gauges; wire clippers
Yarn—assorted colors

Office/Stationery Supplies

Clip boards—2 large; several small (homemade or masonite with clip)
Cork or bulletin board
Envelopes
File boxes
Index cards—several sizes, lined, unlined
Masking tape
Notebook
Paper clips
Paper fasteners
Push pins
Rubber bands
Scissors—big, good
Scotch tape
Squeeze clips
Staple gun, staples
Stapler, staples
Thumb tacks

Recyclable Discards

Baby food jars
Bleach bottles

Card or stationery boxes with clear plastic lids
Chopsticks
Cigar boxes—wood, cardboard
Corks
Dynamint or Tic-Tac boxes
Egg cartons—plastic, cardboard
Glass cigar holders
Glass sheets—from old picture frames (Tape edges for safety.)
Jars—especially large, glass. Ask your local deli to save the gallon size for you.
Margarine and other plastic containers

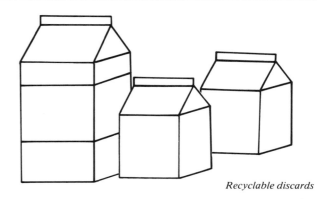

Recyclable discards

Mesh bags—type used to hold onions, oranges
Milk cartons—can get at camp
Paint color strips
Plastic pill bottles with snap caps
Small plastic cups (Chinese mustard)
Soft drink bottle tops (handy way to give glue to each camper)
Stockings, panty hose
Styrofoam—any kind: packing material or trays used to pack meats
Toilet paper, paper toweling tubes
Tomato or mushroom box (with handles)
Toothbrushes—synthetic, animal bristles
Twist'ems

Scientific/Lab Equipment

Binoculars—2-3 good ones, others may be cheaper
Blacklight (for collecting night insects)
Botany press
Butterfly tweezers
Cobalt chloride paper
Dissecting kit, wax pan
Enamel, white pans
Formaldehyde or other preservative
Insect nets—some good, rest homemade (see Appendix)
Insect killing jar, spreading board
Insect pins, softening box, relaxing fluid
Lens paper, lens cleaner (Xylol)
Litmus paper (can be homemade, see Activities)

Magnifying lenses—a good one for yourself; inexpensive ones for children, bug boxes with lens

Microscope(s)—at least one very good one, more if possible

Microviewers—plastic, plus Micro-Slide sets:

1. Life in a pond
2. Egg to Tadpole to Frog
3. Egg to Chick
4. How Living Things Breathe
5. From Flower to Fruit
6. Plants That Are Not Green
7. How Seeds Travel
8. Parts of an Insect
9. Pond Life

Plankton net (may be homemade, see Appendix)

Riker mounts

Slides, cover slips; well slides, prepared slides

Telescope

Test tubes—holder, brush

Thermometers

Setting Up the Shack

When you visit the camp prior to the opening for the season, you will see the facility you have to work with. If conditions are far from ideal, don't despair—make the best of it and work within the existing framework. During camp, prove yourself, and then request improvements for next summer. If your director realizes that you and your program are worthwhile, the director will be willing to make an investment of time and money.

At the least, your facility should have running water and electricity. You'll need to rely on your ingenuity and be able to improvise. The camp director should provide you with a description of the facility so you may begin to plan.

You will have to clean out any winter damage—squirrels, mice, raccoons, chipmunks and others may have used the shack for shelter. *Do not be too hasty in your cleaning;* there may be an interesting lesson or display in the traces animals have left behind. These may form the basis for an entire activity (see *Animal Traces* in Activities, Section III). Mice, especially, do some fascinating things in hoarding and nesting.

Display posters, plants (carnivorous plants make an interesting display), set up animals and specimens. Use a staple gun or nails. If you have access to a laminating machine, use it to seal the posters which will then last longer and be protected. Print informative charts. Set up various centers, elg., birds, insects, trees, plants, fungi and lichens, mammals. In this way the room will have some sense of order.

Try to obtain an outdoor set up—tables (on horses, or otherwise), benches, etc.—a place where both you and the campers can work. Set up a wild bird feeder, away from the area, but still in view. Birdhouses need to be put up well beforehand, in spring. Be sure any outdoor pens are set up and ready before you introduce any animals. If you are doing chick incubation and bringing eggs with you, see section on *Hatching Eggs*. Shelves, walls, cabinet doors can be filled with pictures from *National Wildlife, Audubon* and/or *Ranger Rick* magazines. Hang mobiles or models from beams, lighting fixtures or from the roof rafters. Display children's work.

Print signs that encourage campers to explore and touch sturdier items or, admonish them *not* to touch other, more fragile specimens with appropriate signs. Make them gimmicky, e.g., "SH . . . Earthworms at work." Put a bulletin board outside; change the display periodically (every week or more often) so that campers can maintain their interest in nature even when the room is closed or you are not around. Write timely and newsworthy announcements that call atten-

Display posters

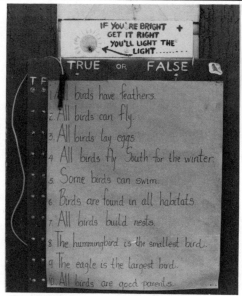

Electrical games

tion to nature happenings around camp, e.g., "The baby robins in the nest in the maple tree near the dining hall are sticking their necks over its edge. Tiptoe over and watch them." You might feature a "Bird of the Week" or "Tree of the Week" or wildflower or insect, etc., with appropriate pictures and information.

Create some electric games such as tree identification, birds, mammals or another changeable exhibit that is manipulative to spark interest (see Appendix). Maybe there's a hole in a wall; put a "feely" inside; change every 3 or 4 days. Set up a library with books for reference and browsing. Include *Ranger Rick* and other magazines. Put out microviewers and slide sets, along with instructions for their use. With proper instruction, Audible Audubon may also be displayed for campers to utilize.

Display collected specimens in an organized and suitable way. Bird's nests, insect exoskeletons, shed snake skins, wasp's nests, flowers—all should be displayed in a way to maximize their features while protecting them from damage. Use push-pins, styrofoam, empty card boxes with clear tops, or large glass jars. Find a large, downed branch of a tree, or have a piece cut from the woods. Set it up on a table and/or in a corner. Put nests on it. Hang children's work from its branches (poetry, drawings, leaf rubbings). Or, let campers cut out and hang paper leaves, if tree is dead. Perhaps each leaf could have a "use" of trees written on it. Or, more contemplative campers might want to write a piece, such as "If Trees Could Tell a Story . . ."

Other display ideas might include: stuffed birds or other animals, giant jigsaw puzzles, posters with "lift-up" questions (with answers underneath), or big murals, perhaps showing a habitat that kids could draw or add to or paste on. Use clothespins to suspend items from strings or rope. Luggage tags may also be used for labeling or use a tape-label machine. Egg cartons can be used as small specimen holders. Print a chart using one (or more) of the pledges (see Appendix), so that campers may have these principles in view. You may prepare aquaria or terraria (see Activities section), but it is better to have the campers do it as an activity. Depending on the amount of display material and size of the facility, you will need 1-2 *full* days to set up. Program could begin on the third day.

Starting the Program

Be all ready to go! Camp season is usually 8 weeks, and some have 2-week, 3-week, or one-month programs. So, there is little real opportunity to develop a concept slowly as one might do in a classroom setting.

Consequently, most periods or sessions should be self-contained, unless you are working on something more complex and difficult, as with older campers or adults. Crafts or other activities may be completed in the bunk, if unfinished, unless the materials are only available at the nature shack.

Some camps work on a 45-minute session, others have one-hour periods. Some provide double periods (1½-2

Display specimens

hours). Some camps insist that all children go to all activities; some permit total freedom of choice. Most camps balance and include some optional times. Prepare and plan your activities accordingly. For example, if the period is 45 minutes, you may have to do most of your activities within the immediate vicinity of your shed. Or, you could plan to meet your group at a pre-arranged time and place, e.g., if your group has swim just before nature, you might have them meet you at the lake and do some activities there. You would carry your supplies—nets, cups, scopes, lenses, guide books, etc., with you to the waterfront.

The best way to start is to start. Meet your group and state the rules you want them to abide by. Try to begin with an activity that will capture their interest and make them eager to return for more, e.g., *What Is It?* (see Activities section). The rules should be very small in number, but should be enforced. If you explain the reason for each rule, you will gain the campers' cooperation. Rules include:

1. No sticky candy (attracts flies).
2. No bare feet (dangerous).
3. No fingers in mouth (shack has animals, is not always clean).
4. No jumping, shouting or running about (scares animals).
5. Do not touch or remove anything without asking permission first (fragile, dangerous).

Rules generally are made for the safety of campers and to treat the animals humanely. They also protect items that are rare or valuable from overhandling and/or damage.

Some camps run on 1-to 3-week cycles with campers changing at the end of each cycle. Adjustments should be made in the scheduling of programs to provide a concentrated, yet complete series of nature activities. In a 1-week cycle, a nature period should take place *every* day for *every* camper, perhaps in 1-hour sessions. This might necessitate expanding the nature staff to accommodate all of the children. The nature specialist, then, would construct, devise and supervise the program with nature counselors doing the actual leading of activities so that their aims (and the children) don't get lost in the shuffle.

For 2-week cycles, the nature period should be programmed for every *other* day. Again, this might require additional personnel to effectively carry it out. For a 3-week cycle, nature could be programmed every third day. Use the sample schedules in back of Section III to plan programs.

Plants/Gardening

Gardening (flower and/or vegetable) is a very desirable project to undertake. Although many campers may know that food does not really come from supermarket canned and frozen foods, they do not fully appreciate the role of natural systems and the labor that goes into food production. First-hand experiences with vegetable gardening help to close that knowledge gap. After a session of pulling weeds, they should appreciate the farmers' labor while not taking for granted the soil and green plants that are their food source.

Several problems may exist, but they are all surmountable if the proper planning is instituted and with the support of camp directors who see the desirability of this aspect of the program. First, you must have the cooperation of year-round workers (caretaker and his staff). The garden must be turned over and started well before the arrival of kids and staff at camp. Some seeds will have to be started indoors or in a cold frame. After the danger of frost has passed, seedlings will need to be transplanted out-of-doors. Depending on the size of the plot and its nearness to your facility, the grounds crew may have to supplement whatever care you are able to give. They may need to roto-till, mulch and thin plants. After camp is over, the garden will also have to be prepared for over-winter and the next year's farming.

You will also need the cooperation of the kitchen staff since they may have to prepare what is harvested. Be sensitive about not giving these people extra work. Make certain whatever you bring in is washed and ready for cooking. Kids love to do this; some never get the chance to help out in the kitchen at home. There's a special camaraderie that is engendered when a group of campers and counselors gather around to wash and snap green beans or prepare other vegetables. If there is enough for the entire camp, be sure to announce at the meal that the vegetable or fruit being served was picked and prepared by bunk or cabin so-and-so. Sometimes the yield is too small for everyone to partake. Then, those groups would eat it; or, give every table a miniature portion for sampling.

What to Plant

When ordering seed from catalogs in late winter or early spring, two major criteria will govern your selections:

a) *Will the campers eat it?* Don't plant turnips or rutabagas! Try to select vegetables they will eat. Some campers will need lots of encouragement to try certain vegetables, but tasting should be encouraged. You may get new converts, e.g., raw green beans taste better than cooked ones. The vegetables which can be grown in camp with most success are green beans (bush), sugar snap peas (they never even get to the kitchen, but are eaten straight from the vine), cucumbers, zucchini, leaf lettuce, small tomatoes, peppers and radishes.

b) *Will it mature in time?* When selecting varieties of vegetables, note the number of days for maturity. Some vegetables which you might think would be good need a long growing season and could not mature within the time limit of the camp season. Therefore, choose the variety of vegetable with the shortest growing season so that children can harvest before camp is over.

Sugar and regular snap peas require a fence to climb on. You can purchase one (from the seed company) or you can fashion one from stakes (tall) and string. Whichever, it's worth the money or effort because the resulting produce is so marvelously crunchy and delicious. The sugar snap peas need to be planted outdoors very early in spring—even while the ground is frozen, since they require a cold period before germinating. Tomatoes need staking; be sure to order *bush* beans, not pole beans, because pole beans need to be staked. You may also want to plant marigolds as natural insect repellents.

About Campers and Weeding

You must be careful about devoting just the right amount of time to weeding. Weeding may start out as fun for children, but after a while, especially in hot weather, it becomes hard work. After all, this is camp, and they are there for fun and learning, not hard work. On the other hand, if children only harvest the finished produce without spending any time weeding or staking, then they have misunderstood the essential aim of the lessons to be learned from gardening. This practice only serves to reinforce the improper attitude that food can be taken for granted, that it is out there waiting to be plucked, with no work expended. You must attempt to strike a balance; every group should take one turn at chores, one at harvesting. Also, make certain no one group strips and/or devours the entire garden crop in one swoop. You might want to have a child named "Wonder Weeder of the Week!"

Campers weeding at Camp Tawingo, CN.

You might consider gardening in containers if you do not want to take on a regular garden plot. Consult the many booklets provided by the Department of Agriculture or the Cooperative Extension Services.

Another worthwhile gardening project to undertake is to investigate and use natural methods, instead of chemical pesticides, to destroy insects who invade the garden and damage crops. Organic gardeners have always used a variety of natural insect repellents. Plants such as marigolds interspersed between tomato plants is a well-known technique. Consult organic gardening books and magazines for other suggestions. There are also several commercial distributors of predatory insects. They offer such biological controls as lacewings, ladybugs, praying mantises and others that they breed and sell to farmers and gardeners. Send for their brochures (see Appendix for names).

Other Learnings While Gardening

In addition to those mentioned earlier, gardening presents many learning situations:

1. Nutrition and food. Eating well-balanced meals. The importance of fruits and vegetables in one's daily diet.
2. What is a weed? Is *this* a weed? Why are weeds so successful? Why do we pull out weeds? How did the weeds get there in the first place?
3. What insects are on these plants? What are they doing? Why do they eat these plants? Who preys on them? What is the role of earthworms?

Another source of foods (besides the kitchen) in camp are those plants that grow wild. Many people are knowledgeable about what wild plants are edible; but, unless you are absolutely certain of what is and what is not, do not try this with children. Wild berries are easily learned and identified and enjoyed by most children. Look for and pick blueberries, wild strawberries, raspberries, blackberries. If many are found, enough can be picked to put in pies, muffins and pancakes. You could also make jelly as an activity. Wild mushrooms may be delicious but some species are so deadly that, as far as camp is concerned, it's far too dangerous to try.

Sample seed order:

Barcarolle Lettuce
Bush Garden Beans—Remus or Blue Lake
Bitsy VF Hybrid Tomato
Bush Cuke—Pickle
Extra Early VFNT Tomato
French Breakfast Radishes
Lettuce Crispy Sweet
Marigold Janie (mixed)
Melon Golden Crispy Hybrid or
    Canteloupe Busheloupe
Peak Sugar Snap
Simpson Lettuce
Spinach Melody Hybrid
Squash—Gourmet Globe
Sweet Pepper
Tomato Whopper VFNT
Tiny Tim Tomatoes
Zucchini—Seneca Gourmet

In addition, order Blossom Set Aerosol (a hormone that speeds up flowering, fruiting). Seed companies are constantly improving their breedings, and the hybrids and varieties change from year to year. Read and use the catalogs. Also, be aware that there are seed companies that specialize in the less popular seed varieties. These companies provide a valuable service in keeping the diversity of the genetic pool and by providing an alternative and essential back-up stock should pestilence wipe out the popular genetic strains. For more information, contact the Seed Savers Exchange, 203 Rural Avenue, Decorah, IA 52101.

Planting Seeds and Propagating Plants

Growing plants provide a decorative touch while teaching about plant life. The camp season doesn't allow much time to start a plant from seed, but interested youngsters could take one home. Use jiffy pellets or peat pots for seeds or seedlings. Marigolds are easy to grow. Use the tops of spray cans with holes punched around top rim for a miniature hanging planter and make a hole on the bottom for drainage.

Do some plant experiments (light, gravity, water, fertilizer).

Plant some seeds you find, of wildflowers, perhaps.

Planting pot

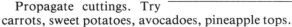

Propagate cuttings. Try carrots, sweet potatoes, avocadoes, pineapple tops.

Plant herbs.

Plant an avocado seed.

Make a mini-greenhouse with a milk carton and Saran Wrap.

Plant seeds on blotters or paper towels between pieces of glass so that root development can be shown.

Bring a live Aloe Vera plant. Demonstrate its use as a healing plant.

Bring greenery into the nature shack.

Sprouts

Alfalfa sprouts and mung bean sprouts are the best for camp use. Buy the seeds in the produce section of a supermarket, or order from a seed company through its catalog.

Materials:

Large glass jar, gallon size, if possible (institutional mayonnaise jar), with wide neck, cheesecloth, rubber bands.

Procedure:

Put ¼ cup of seeds into jar. Fill about ¾ full with lukewarm water and cover jar with cheesecloth held on by rubberbands around the neck. Shake vigorously for one minute.

Pour out water right through the cheesecloth. Fill again with cold water, shake, and pour out again. This wetting/washing process should be done two or three times a day until the sprouts are ready to be eaten (3-4 days). Place the jar on its side for sprouts to grow.

You may either keep in a dark place (for white sprouts—the mung beans are good white) or in indirect sunlight for green sprouts (alfalfa sprouts are good when green). Share for eating; if very popular, set up one jar each day to keep a constant supply. The darkness/white, sunlight/green, of course, demonstrates photosynthesis. Rinse in a bowl and allow the hulls to float away before serving. However, the best part of sprouts is the eating!

Planting seeds

Animals

Why is it desirable to keep animals in camp? There are many reasons why the nature program in camp should involve live animals. First of all, animals bring pleasure to children, especially if, as pets, they are tame and friendly. Petting and cuddling them, caring for them, and observing them is an extension of one's humanity. (In fact, animals are now used for therapeutic purposes in hospitals and nursing homes.) Secondly, city and suburban children rarely have the opportunity to be close to animals (though many own dogs or cats) and this closeness promotes a greater respect for them. Third, there are many first-hand lessons to be derived from having animals around.

What kinds of animals belong in a camp setting? The kinds of animals that could be kept in camp depend on the facilities available. Larger animals (rabbits, chickens, ducks, geese, goats, lambs, calves) require an outdoor pen or series of pens or a well-fenced corral. Pens must be close enough to a water source so that a hose is available. Waterfowl, like ducks, require a place to swim—a small in-ground pool, a children's plastic wading pool or a fenced-off portion of a pond or lake. Goats are browsers (not grazers) and like a source of weeds and shrubs to munch on. All animals need an enclosed (at least on 3 sides), roofed shelter from rain and cold. It is cruel to keep any animal confined in a cage that is too small or one that cannot be easily cleaned.

Other Tips

1. Try to buy or order *young* animals only.
2. Open an account (in camp's name) with the local animal feed/supply store. They also have good information booklets.
3. If the wood used in the camp carpentry shop is not chemically treated, have the wood shavings and sawdust saved for you to use as litter for small animals. If in doubt, commercial litter may be healthier for the animals.
4. Contact the Agricultural Extension Office of the state for additional information.

Smaller animals may be kept indoors in small cages or tanks. Small mammals include gerbils, hamsters, mice (bred for tameness—laboratory mice make good pets), and guinea pigs. Reptiles and amphibians include snakes, toads, frogs, turtles, tadpoles, lizards, chameleons, anoles, salamanders. Among the very best animals to keep in camp are the invertebrates, including insects. Ants, earthworms, butterflies and moths (as caterpillars and pupae), mealworms, crickets, and spiders are easy to care for and fascinating to study. Fish, crayfish and other pond and lake animals may be kept in tanks (with a bubbler for oxygen). An important rule to remember for all animals found, caught and kept in camp is that wild animals are *wild,* not tame, not domesticated, not pets, not naturally friendly or comfortable with humans. Many abandoned or injured animals (birds, rabbits or others) may be brought to you. You may attempt to care for them; you may succeed or not (see books re: animal care in *The Nature Library* section of the Appendix and the feeding table at end of this section). Healthy animals may also be captured by you or by campers. Animals may be kept for a reasonable length of time (hours or days), looked at, fed for a while, but then must be released into their habitat. This is especially true if the animals refuse to eat. Some wild animals are very timid and react poorly when handled; some even die from fright. Others respond well to care—I hand-fed an injured bullfrog tadpole, and kept it in an oxygenated tank filled with pond water for 6 weeks until it changed into a frog and could be released into a lake. You may have to convince a camper to release the little newt or toad which was found; some compromise can be found—keep it for a time, then release it.

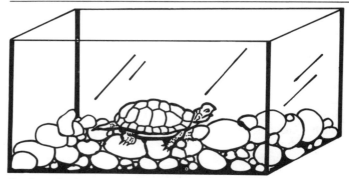

Keeping animals at camp

Sources of Camp Animals

1. Farms—if possible, the best sources of many animals are local farmers. Inquiries should be made early in the year.
2. Newspapers—check out local ads in those newspapers that are free in area supermarkets, or buy the area newspaper and check the classified columns.
3. Keep an eye out for signs on the roads "Rabbits for Sale," etc.
4. See Appendix for listing of names and addresses of animal suppliers (hatcheries).
5. Your own neighborhood pet shop.
6. The various zoos and/or privately owned petting zoos may have excess animals that they will sell to you.
7. Classified ads from your local newspaper.
8. Yellow pages of various rural areas. (Try Information number for that area code.)
9. Colleges and universities that use animals for research purposes may be a good source, especially if you know a faculty member.
10. Inquire at the local animal feed store. Speak to the manager who may be able to tell you about local farmers or animal raisers who would be willing to sell, lend or rent animals. Or, ask if you might put up a notice requesting them.

As a general rule, order the animals as soon as you know which ones you will need or want. This gives the supplier an opportunity to handle them, wean them or breed them. You'll want animals bred and raised for tameness and docile qualities and that may require early handling (before camp begins). The animal quarters should be set up as soon as possible after arriving at camp (or even before camp begins), so that the animals may be obtained as soon as possible. Small animals can ride in a box in a car (rabbits and smaller). Goats and lambs will need a pick-up truck filled with hay. Some animal suppliers may deliver them; others will require that you arrange to pick them up. Some (baby chicks, ducks) may be mailed. Clear this matter up beforehand with the supplier and the camp director.

Campers may also want to bring certain animals from home because parents will not be available to care for them, or for some other reason. Once again, depending on facilities and camp policy, this may or may not be feasible. (Naturally, pet dogs or cats would not be permitted. Two excellent books that offer realistic suggestions for the care of animals are: 1) *The Complete Care of Orphaned or Abandoned Baby Animals* by C. E. Spaulding and Jackie Spaulding, published by Rodale Press; and 2) *Small Pets of the Woods and Field* by Buck.

The local residents who work in various capacities at camp may provide another source of help. Many may be part-time farmers and have knowledge about animal care.

A potential problem that may arise is that campers love the animals *too* much. They tend to overhandle them and overwhelm the animals (especially the cuddly ones) with affection; children may vie for the chance to be with them. As a result, the nature specialist may have to set up and enforce rules concerning the handling of animals (e.g., only 2 or 3 campers allowed in the pen at one time). It may also be necessary to keep the pen(s) locked so that you are able to supervise. Thus, no one can get to animals unless you are there. (Sometimes, animals may be used for practical jokes and you need to be aware of this possibility.)

Campers may be directly involved with the animals in various ways:

1. Have a "Name-the-Animal" contest for any or all of the animals. Choose a name selected by campers. Award a prize to winner(s)—or the fact that you chose that camper's name suggestion may be reward enough. Publish it in the camp newsletter, being sure to mention who named each animal.
2. Campers may wish to be involved in the day-to-day feeding and care. Set up a schedule, perhaps rotating, to accommodate the many campers who will want to participate. To eliminate repetition of describing the responsibilities to each new person or group of caretakers, print (and laminate) the specific instructions on cardboard or oak tag. Have all materials needed to carry out the job accessible. Thus, you can just give each camper the correct card and they can go to work. Fitting this into a daily schedule does present logistical problems and should be discussed prior to camp with the director and/or head counselor. The time just before or just after breakfast might be best; animals must be fed in the morning. This may conflict with cabin clean-up time; campers may either be excused from chores that day (or week) or do their cabin job quickly first, then report to the nature shack to carry out that job, or the reverse—doing the nature job first, then their cabin responsibility. Campers should not use this as a means of getting out of chores, however.

Sometimes, a particular camper may be having problems adjusting to camp (especially a first-time camper), and the nature shack and its animals may provide a place where the camper can find a pressure-free situation. Animals do not criticize nor insult. Of course, the nature shack cannot eliminate the symptoms creating the camper's unhappiness, but it may help the camper to overcome the difficulties in a non-threatening, non-competitive setting. For the child who doesn't exactly fit the mold, the nature shack and its program may save the summer from becoming a total disaster. Not every camper is athletic or good at sports and nature may be one area where this particular child shines. The nature specialist must be sensitive to this and appointing such a camper as an "assistant," making the camper responsible for the care and feeding of animals, will help the child and perhaps allow the camper to stay in camp.

One cannot order and keep animals in camp without considering what to do with them when camp is over. Kids will invariably ask that question as the summer draws to a close. There are several choices and the ultimate disposal of all the animals must be decided well before camp ends. Among the alternatives are the following:

1. Send the animal home with campers—such small animals as guinea pigs, hamsters, gerbils, rabbits, and mice may be sent home (in cartons or boxes), providing the parent is contacted and *written* (or phone) permission is given. You cannot depend on a camper telling you that the parent will not mind. You must also ascertain whether the child's house can accommodate the animal. Rabbits can live in New York City apartments, but the wisdom of doing so is questionable. Is there sufficient room? Will the animal live indoors or out? Is there a place to buy feed? The campers can also bring the animals back to camp the next summer. One guinea pig made the trip for 4 consecutive summers, returning to its winter home after camp.

2. Resell to the supplier from whom you purchased the animal (or you may arrange to lease the animal in the first place). Sometimes the farmer will buy the animal back from you; check it out when you order or buy it. Goats and sheep fall into this category.

3. Ask some of the local residents if they know anyone who might want to buy or take the animal. Certain animals (sheep) are expensive on the open market and you may be able to sell to local farmers, a mutually beneficial arrangement.

4. The poultry may also be left for local residents or members of the kitchen staff to slaughter and dress. Ducks, geese and chickens are good food presents to people who will appreciate them. (Rabbits may also be included.) One word of caution: If the animal is to be destined for someone's freezer or table, do not inform the campers. They find the idea very upsetting. To the kids, these creatures were pets, and it is inappropriate to discuss the philosophy at this point.

5. Some local residents may want the poultry for their egg-laying. Ask around. Put up signs in the local general store. Many of the White Leghorn hens hatched at camp from fertile eggs are now providing their owners with fresh eggs.

6. Releasing them into the wild. Domesticated animals cannot survive without human help. Others, however, can and should be released. That includes reptiles (not ones from warm climates), frogs, toads, crickets—in short, anything captured in camp. When releasing reptiles and amphibians, put them *exactly* where you found them or else they are likely to die, since their ranges and territories are very specific. Some insects (like wax moths) should *not* be released as they parasitize beehives. Other animals and insects, too, that are not indigenous to the area should not be released as they may not have any natural enemies and may cause ecological damage. Any animal which is ordered from a biological supply house will usually have a written warning about releasing it. Be sure to heed that warning as it is illegal to release such an animal and may prove to be ecologically disastrous. In the past, some people were unintentionally careless and we now pay the price of trying to cope with introduced species that have become major pests: gypsy moths, starlings, Japanese knotweed, etc. Discussing all of this with older campers can be a very worthwhile lesson—which ones may be safely released, which destroyed and why.

7. Mealworm beetles can come home if they have a classroom that will want them. It is possible to keep an original culture of mealworms alive for years. They can be used in a classroom in winter and or camp in the summer. White mice may be kept the same way—try to find a willing teacher in your district. You'll be doing each other a favor and saving the expense of buying new animals every year. (They're quite prolific!)

8. Butterflies and moths that may not yet have emerged at summer's end require special treatment. If it is a desirable species (check out guide books thoroughly), then place it out of doors in such a way that when it does emerge, it can fly away. (See "Insect Cage" section in Appendix for instructions.)

9. One year, we were able to secure mallard ducklings (a wild species). At summer's end, we placed bands around their legs (chicken rings, really) and released them on the lake. It was reported that they flew away as winter approached and returned the next spring, although they did not remain in the area. Technically, it is illegal in some states to keep mallards; only certified persons may actually band birds. Contact the local Audubon Society person or the district conservation officer (game warden) for guidelines.

Hatching Fertile Eggs

One of the most exciting and stimulating activities to engage in as part of the nature program in camp is the incubation and hatching of fertile eggs. The miracle of life from a small egg is observed in its stages and reinforces the wonder of nature and its ways. An incubator may be made from a styrofoam picnic chest (send for booklet "How to Build a Still-Air Incubator," L-8-1a, Cornell Cooperative Extension) or one may be bought from scientific or farm supply companies (see Appendix). Make sure it has a clear cover for viewing. You may hatch several kinds of eggs—chicken, quail, duck, goose or fancy fowl (lovely blue/green eggs hatch into black Aracauna chicks). Chicken eggs are the most reliable and chickens are easier to raise and handle (and ultimately, to dispose of). Order between 12 and 24 eggs.

Release frog exactly where you found it.

To be successful:

1. Order eggs from a reliable source.

2. Set up the incubator and adjust the temperature to 100° F (99°F-101°F). Set humidity to 50% by placing water directly onto bottom. Do this well before hand so you don't have to play with the thermostat while eggs are inside. (They are very sensitive to high temperature and a 2 degree deviation can kill them.)

3. Pick up (or have delivered) the eggs as close to camp opening day as possible.

4. Keep them cool (but do not refrigerate) until you are ready to "set" them (put them in incubator).

5. Put them into the already warm incubator immediately upon your arrival. (Have someone plug in the day before if you're not around.)

6. Turn the eggs three times a day. First have them with numbers up; then alternate, with numbers down. Note: After the 18th day, stop rotating, increase humidity and put something soft over mesh.

In just 21 days, you will be able to offer the campers a marvelous sight—the chicks will begin to hatch and the nature shack will be the most popular spot in camp.

Even before the 21 days, you as nature specialist can engage in a variety of activities that will insure that the experience is a vital learning one.

1. Show the campers the eggs at the various stages. Use a filmstrip projector to direct a beam of bright light through the egg. By the 4th or 5th day, you will see the developing embryo vividly. Every camper should have the opportunity to observe this marvel.
2. The eggs should be numbered for identification purposes and also as a means of indicating which one(s) have been turned. Older campers may do this for or with you. The process gives you the chance to explain why (to keep the membrane from sticking to the shell) and how the hen knows this. (She doesn't, but acts on instinct or because her bottom gets hot and wants a cooler surface.) Campers may also weigh some and predict (or discover) weight gain or loss. Older campers can study the anatomy and physiology of the eggs, learning the details of the parts and their functions. They may wish to open and examine eggs either while developing (naturally, this kills the chick, so few are willing to do this) or those that never hatch. Send for the booklet L-8-2A *From the Egg to the Chick* by A. Romanoff from Cornell Extension (see Section V) for explanatory materials.
3. Younger children enjoy hearing you read aloud the books *A Chick Hatches* by Cole and Wexler and *From Egg to Chick* by Millicent Selsam. After reading or listening to the books and viewing the eggs, they will have many questions. The children also enjoy making little chicks from fluffy pompoms and felt. These are nice little mementos of the hatch; and, when the campers overhandle the real chicks because they feel so soft and look so cute, you can suggest they touch their make-believe chicks instead.

Baby chicks hatching.

4. There is an experiment in which a fertile egg is carefully opened into a Ziploc baggie and suspended in the incubator. The embryo develops within a transparent skin/shell. Naturally, it cannot survive, as its real shell is the best possible container for it—permitting exchange of molecules of gases through its minute pores, yet too small to permit bacteria to pass through! Another similar experiment is described in *In Vitro Observations of Chick Embryos* by E. Shano (Cornell Extension Publication L-8-2). A 2-inch section of PVC pipe is cut, Saran placed over the opening, and the egg carefully opened into it. The development is then viewed through the plastic. Sometimes wild bird eggs are found; you might try incubating them, but this is rarely successful.

After the Hatch

If you are planning to hatch chicks, then you must also provide a suitable brooder for them (see Appendix). The chicks need food, water and warmth (90 degrees F.) for about 10-14 days before they can be placed outdoors. Therefore, you will need to make, have made, or buy a brooder. Chicks should be left in the incubator until they fluff out, then, be placed in the brooder.

The major reason duck egg hatching is not recommended

is that (although they are incredibly cute after they hatch) they are wet birds and will immediately start splashing the water they're drinking from. They eat and drink simultaneously, getting the brooder all wet and dirty. You'll be constantly changing their paper, unless you set them up separately from the chicks. They just cause too much work when kept indoors. If you buy slightly older (8-10 days) ducklings, you can put them outdoors at once and their splashing will just water the ground.

Children (and you) will spend hours watching the baby chicks. Some interesting observations may be made while so engaged. For example, a primitive pecking order begins to emerge very rapidly as the larger, stronger chicks become bossy. Weaker chicks are pecked at and may die. You can try isolating those in trouble, but they are also quite sociable and will peep when all alone. They also show an amazing hostility to any newcomer, especially if it is a stranger species and a different-looking chick. Once a black chick hatched from a blue-green egg and he could never remain with the others. He had to be kept totally away from the yellow (later, white) chicks and lived with the older poultry, not too successfully even then. Astute campers may want to carry out simple behavior or other experiments. Use your discretion.

Sometimes chicks can't survive and their suffering is slow and upsetting for children. The best way of terminating the chicks is to partially fill a bucket with water. Place the chick in the water and immediately cover it with another water-filled bucket holding the chick down. Death occurs within one minute. Be sure to carry out this unpleasant deed when kids are not around, since it will disturb them. You may explain that, in nature, not all offspring survive and grow into adults, and that nature provides for this by enabling each species to produce enough offspring so that at least some will make it to maturity. It is necessary to teach this principle in another context; that is, when considering animals as predators and not being judgmental about this fact of life. Youngsters must come to view organisms as neither good nor bad, but carrying out their lives in accordance with their innate biology. Even the pecking and ostracism observed as part of chick behavior must also be viewed in this context—that it is the nature of this animal to act in this particular fashion. We cannot apply human standards to this behavior.

After the fluffiness is gone, the chicks seem to lose their appeal for the children. They'll also be flying out of the brooder. When it is time for them to go outdoors, choose a pleasant, sunny day to introduce them to their new quarters. A pen for chickens also needs a mesh roof, if possible, so that they do not become prey for hawks. Also, be alert to sudden chill in the weather; listen to weather reports and, if an evening requires a winter jacket for you, catch your young chickens and bring them indoors for the night. When the brooder is built, be certain it has a screen cover top for occasions such as this.

Raising Butterflies and Moths

Some moth and butterfly species may be ordered from biological supply companies; check the catalogs. A more satis-

fying and camper-involving activity is a search for Monarch (and other species') eggs and/or caterpillars. Locate an area where milkweed, the preferred food of the Monarch, grows in profusion. Search alone first, to make sure you'll find at least one egg. You may have to try many times before being successful. Later, with a group of campers, carefully and methodically turn over the milkweed leaves and look for the tiny (1 mm.), pearly, oval egg or the black, white and yellow-striped caterpillar. Cut the plant carrying your prize and carefully place it in a carrying box. Try not to disturb the caterpillar as it will curl up and drop off. If that happens, just put the caterpillar back on the leaf; it will relax, uncurl and re-attach itself to the leaf.

When you return to the nature hut with the group, place the stem of the plant through a hole in a piece of cardboard (see *Insect Cage* section in Appendix) and then into a paper cup with water in it. The egg will hatch in a day or two, and the caterpillar will amaze all with its voracious appetite as it consumes the milkweed leaves. Be alert to replenish the milkweed as it is consumed. The caterpillar will grow rapidly; after 7-10 days, it will be about 3-5 cm. long and will no longer be actively feeding. Make certain there is a cover on the insect cage well before this time is reached so that you will not misplace your next stage.

The caterpillar will be climbing to an overhanging ledge (branch in nature, lid of cage in this case) to prepare itself for the next phase of its life cycle. It will attach itself to the lid, and hang there in a J-shape, while its body undergoes rapid and remarkable change. As many children as possible should be witness to this phenomenon. You can put the entire cage (very carefully) on a table on the porch (but not on a windy day) for all to view. At the precise moment, it will begin to shake off its old caterpillar skin to reveal the exquisite blue-green chrysallis within. Thus it will remain for the next 14 days while it undergoes the next change in its metamorphosis, to an adult Monarch. If egg-laying and finding take place early in the summer, the entire four stages may be witnessed. If not, you will need to release the insect in whatever stage it is at camp's end, or tape it securely in its correct position in a way that will allow it to fly away after emerging. Find a fence near flowering plants for this. Other alternatives are to take it home yourself or give it to a responsible camper.

If you take it or send it home as a *caterpillar*, be sure you have a source of fresh milkweed. The Monarch is migratory and will fly South for the winter. (See section on *Participatory Activities* in *Mixed Bag*.)

This type of activity may be done with other species of butterflies and moths; you must be certain to locate its food source.

Raising butterflies

ANIMAL CARE CHARTS

FARM MAMMALS	HOUSING NEEDS	FOOD NEEDS	HANDLING/SPECIAL NOTES
GOATS	Roofed shed, with raised wooden floor, straw for bedding. Chain-link fencing.	Commerical feed, supplemented by *selected* kitchen scraps, and frequent browsing excursions. Make a salt lick available or add salt to water.	Be sure to order *young* goats. Request that supplier get them used to people *before* camp begins. Buy a large dog collar so you may leash them when allowing them to browse. If possible, keep two together as they like company and will bleat if alone.
LAMBS	Roofed shed, with raised floor, straw for bedding. Chain-link fencing.	Commercial feed. Need to graze. Some kitchen vegetable scraps.	Must be *young*—request lambs born late in spring, if possible.
CALVES	Roofed shed, with raised floor, straw for bedding.	Commercial feed. Grazers, need large, grassy area.	Should be handled young by supplier to acclimate to humans.
PIGLETS	Roofed shed.	Up to eight weeks old, feed commercially prepared food. After that age, they can eat anything—scraps from kitchen.	When older, very messy. Friendly and intelligent when young.

SMALL MAMMALS	HOUSING NEEDS	FOOD NEEDS	HANDLING/SPECIAL NOTES
RABBITS	Outdoor house (wooden). Note: Rabbits will dig out of pens. Precautions should be taken.	Pellets; supplement with carrots, dark green outer leaves of lettuce, other greens.	Buy only from reliable source, where animals are from *docile* breed. Children tend to overhandle; limit this. *Caution:* If rabbits escape into wild and are missing for a few days and then return, they will have to be *destroyed*. Rabbits are carriers of *tularemia*, a dangerous contagious disease.
GUINEA PIGS	A cage, with water bottle, litter, newspaper lined.	Pellets; supplement with carrots, outer lettuce leaves, apples.	Very boring animal. Also dirty.
HAMSTERS	Small cage or Habitrail with exercise wheel and tunnels.	Pellets; need wood shavings to gnaw on.	Nocturnal, thus may sleep all day and be active at night (when no one's around to watch). They have interesting nesting and other behaviors and are used extensively in animal behavior studies.
GERBILS	Small cage or Habitrail with exercise wheel and tunnels.	Pellets; need wood shavings to gnaw on.	May bite when cornered. Pairs will reproduce.
MICE	Small cage—a good two-story round, plastic hat-box with mesh floor is available (check catalog). Plenty of *shavings and newspaper*. An inverted plastic bowl with a hole in it gives them a hiding place.	Pellets; supplemented by various treats, bird seed, nuts, mouse mixture. Do *not* feed lettuce.	They will produce offspring and the lucky campers may witness the birth process and baby nursing. *Caution:* Overcrowding may result in cannibalism, etc.

ANIMAL CARE CHARTS

FOWL	HOUSING NEEDS	FOOD NEEDS	HANDLING/SPECIAL NOTES
DUCKS Wild (Mallard) Domestic (Peking, other)	House (wooden dog house). Must have swimming pool.	Commercial poultry feed. Supplement by kitchen vegetable scraps (cucumber peels, beet tops, etc.)	Pool needs to be drained/washed periodically. Get as 10-14 day old ducklings.
GEESE	House—keep with ducks.	Commercial poultry feed. Plant scraps.	Get as goslings (10 days old).
CHICKENS	See section on *Hatching from Eggs.* House with roost (perch). Fencing on roof of pen.	Commercial poultry feed. Supplement with occasional mealworms.	May need barriers to prevent their squeezing through chicken wire when they are little.
FANCY POULTRY	Same as ducks, geese. Keep with them.	Commerical poultry feed.	
WILD BIRDS	Build or have built bluebird or other houses. Must be put up in spring.	Feed daily by putting wildbird seed on feeder a short distance away from shack, near edge of woods.	Use binoculars to view what wild birds come to the feeder. Have them and a field guide available.

REPTILES AND AMPHIBIANS	HOUSING NEEDS	FOOD NEEDS	HANDLING/SPECIAL NOTES
SNAKES	Wooden, screened cage. Keep warm. Put in branch for climbing.	Check guide books for food suitable to species. May eat earthworms, mealworms, insects, etc.	May be caught or purchased from pet stores. Caught snakes may be very timid and refuse to eat. Avoid quick movement when handling. Do not handle when shedding skin. Be sure to provide water. Keep for a few days, then release.
TURTLES Land	Box with leaves.	Earthworms, snails, slugs, insects, apple, banana, lettuce.	Painted or box turtles are attractive land turtles. Snapping turtles are dangerous and should be avoided.
Aquatic	Pool, if swimming species.	Bits of meat, eggs, fish, plant scraps, mealworms, canned fish (tuna).	Clean tank after feeding aquatic turtles so odors are not offensive.
FROGS	Plastic or glass tank. Water on bottom. Keep cool.	Mealworms, other insects. *Live* food. Try lean beef, small fish (for larger).	Skin must be kept moist at all times.
TOADS	Plastic or glass tank. Grass, leaves on bottom. Water for drinking.	Mealworms, flies, other insects, earthworms, lean beef (on a toothpick). Keep water in a dish.	Do not do well in captivity. Release after a few days.
SALAMANDERS	Plastic or glass tank or bowl. Lots of leaf litter. Terrarium, moist environment.	Try commercial fish flakes. Chopped lean beef. Try mealworms. Offer on end of a toothpick.	Handle only with moist hands. Best place is a habitat terrarium. Remove to separate area to feed, so as not to contaminate terrarium with leftover food. Aquatic salamanders will drown in still water; a bubbler is necessary.

ANIMAL CARE CHARTS

FISH AND OTHER AQUATIC ANIMALS	HOUSING NEEDS	FOOD NEEDS	HANDLING/SPECIAL NOTES
TADPOLES	A tank. Provide a bubbler for oxygen. Use pond or lake (not tap) water only.	Commercial tropical fish food (flakes) and sometimes vegetation—spinach (cooked), cooked oatmeal, lean meat.	*Do not overfeed.* Food rots and causes illness. Watch for signs of maturity—development of legs, shortening of tail. This signals change from aquatic to terrestrial stage. Lungs now used for breathing; thus, some rocks must be provided so that frog can stick head above water to breathe.
CATFISH AND OTHER FISH	Aquarium tank, bubbler; lake water only.	Aquatic plants; commercial fish food.	Easy to catch, near edge of lake. Simulate their natural habitat by re-creating a lake habitat aquarium, putting in a variety of plants and other aquatic animals.
CRAYFISH	Aquarium tank, bubbler; stream or lake water only.	Little bits of meat, kitchen scraps.	Stream or lake dweller. Pincers may may hurt children. Handle by picking up behind head.
POND INSECT LARVAE	Aquarium tank or bowl. Mud from pond bottom. Pond water only.	You will probably not need to add any food.	Keep for several days. View through lens. Use a pipette or straw to examine individual specimens in small jar or through microscope. Hours may be spent examining and identifying the many species found in ponds.
WATER SNAILS	Aquarium tank.	Algae, scavenger.	Will keep your tank clean by eating algae on side.
HERMIT CRAB (Land)	From pet stores. Aquarium tanks.	Get instructions from pet store.	Shy, but interesting. Not indigenous to country.
LAND SNAILS	Moist, woodland terrarium.	Lettuce, celery tops, spinach leaves.	Interesting to observe.

INVERTEBRATES	HOUSING NEEDS	FOOD NEEDS	HANDLING/SPECIAL NOTES
BUTTERFLIES AND MOTHS (as caterpillars)	Homemade cage. See Appendix.	Be certain to collect whatever plant it was feeding on. Identify the plant so you can replenish.	Identify the species. Release at hatch if not harmful. See special notes on locating Monarch eggs or larvae.
EARTHWORMS	Homemade (see Appendix) or large, glass jar filled with soil, dead leaves.	Feed on dead, decaying leaf litter, or other vegetation. Keep moist.	Whatever container you use must be kept covered with dark paper since earthworms shun light. Point out the tunnels and castings made as the earthworms eat. Campers should appreciate the importance of the role played by the worms in aerating soil. Agriculture would not be possible without them.
CRICKETS/ GRASSHOPPERS	Little wooden cages, bought in Oriental stores.	Various plant materials, seeds.	Interesting to observe their (sometimes successful) attempts to get out of the cage, as they search for minute openings.

ANIMAL CARE CHARTS

INVERTEBRATES (continued)	HOUSING NEEDS	FOOD NEEDS	HANDLING/SPECIAL NOTES
ANTS	Commercial or homemade glass cases or large jars.	Plants, bread crumbs, sugar, water. Try different material.	Interesting to observe. Keep covered and moist. See Section III, page 34 for suggested experiments.
MEALWORMS	Any container—plastic shoebox, aquarium.	Bran or oatmeal flakes. Slices of potato or apple for moisture.	Very easy to care for. Use to demonstrate metamorphosis as all (except egg) will be readily visible. They also serve as a food source for frogs, toads, snakes and chickens love them.
SPIDERS	Insect cage or large jar with holes in top. Put plants or twigs in.	Provide caught flies or insects.	Crab spiders make interesting specimens. They will catch and eat flies you serve them. Be alert for poisonous species (see guide books).

WILD BIRD FEEDING TABLE

INSECT-EATERS	SEED-EATERS	FLESH-EATERS	FREQUENCY
NESTLINGS (unfeathered) Chopped egg yolk, lean, red meat (liver, kidney or lean hamburg), milk and pablum, cottage cheese, mashed insects	Chopped egg yolk, lean, red meat (liver, kidney or lean hamburg), milk and pablum, cottage cheese, mashed insects	Small bits of lean, red meat (liver, kidney or chicken), worms, cottage cheese, chopped egg yolk	Important to begin day's feeding not later than 6:00 a.m. and continue till 7:00 p.m. every half hour.
FLEDGINGS (out of nest) Same as above plus whole insects	Same as above	Same as above	Every hour
ADULTS (able to pick up food) Whole insects, worms, starter mash, (procured at grain stores), bone meal, cottage cheese	Wild bird seed mixture, fruit, cottage cheese, starter mash, bone meal	Mice, frogs, worms, crustaceans, chicken or duck heads from butcher shop, sliced liver, kidney, lean stew beef	Food placed where they can get it. *Water* given adult birds *only*.
Warblers Vireos Robins Orioles Bluebirds Meadowlarks Kinglets Red-wings Killdeer Blue Jays	Sparrows Cardinals Goldfinches Bobolinks	Hawks Eagles Owls	

Finding Animal Remains

Sometimes, in the course of a hike, alone or with campers, you may find the remains of a dead animal. What you make of this depends on your own squeamishness and that of the campers. Death is a phase of life; in fact, one of the characteristics of a living organism is that it eventually dies. So you can use the occasion to discuss it, and the decomposition that will be all too apparent. Naturally, older children will be more interested than younger. While camp is not the place for morbid discussions, use your judgment.

If you wish, however, to go further and utilize the dead animal as a specimen, there are two ways to do this:

1. A recent death (such as a road kill or dead bird), if it's in good shape, can be skinned and stuffed as a study skin. A study skin may be prepared by very carefully removing the skin by slitting it from the flesh (the way a butcher would do it, only try to keep the skin intact). Replace with cotton and mount. (See books on taxidermy for complete details.)

2. A decomposed animal may be stripped of its remaining soft tissue and its skeleton retained. To remove the flesh and skin from partially decomposed remains, try mealworm beetles. (Museums use dermested beetles, but they are voracious and hard to control.) Then, soak in solution (diluted halfway) of laundry bleach which will dissolve the remains and also disinfect them. This may take many days; but it is best to check on the remains regularly because bleach will even dissolve bones. The skeleton may then be reassembled using wire and glue. Older campers would enjoy doing this with you or even doing it on their own.

Note: In either case, do *not* handle the animal. Wear gloves (rubber or other). Pick up with a spade or shovel. Bacteria grow rapidly on a dead animal. Be aware that there are several species of animals that are "endangered species." These animals should not be stuffed.

SECTION III. Activities

The Discovery Walk

Nature in the summer, in the country, is omnipresent. It's everywhere all the time; you should be prepared to seize any opportunity as it arises (see chapter on the Teachable Moment in Mixed Bag).

One excellent technique that combines structure with spontaneity is the Discovery Walk. The *structure* exists because the walk takes place at a prescribed time and at a specific place, such as a trail through the forest, the edge of a meadow where the field and the forest meet, the pond's edge, the dirt roadside. The *spontaneity* derives from not knowing exactly what will be discovered, or who will do the discovering. The challenge of the unknown, of the exploration, is part of the enjoyment.

You should prepare for the walk by scouting the area for suitable places where you would take kids, so that you have an idea of what might be found. You can even be more directive, knowing what things are available for them to discover, while allowing *them* to make the discovery and experience the thrill that comes with it. Example: Early in the summer, spittle bugs will emerge from eggs and eject their protective frothy bubbles onto plants. Thus, you may start the discovery process by picking a plant stem that has the froth on it and passing it around, wondering aloud, "What could this be?" Have them look inside, (they may not want to touch it, so you'll have to) and discover the tiny leaf-hopper nymph creating the froth. Use guide books to locate its picture; read its explanation aloud. Look closely at it with a lens or in a bug box. How and why does the insect do this?

The purpose of the Discovery Walk is multi-leveled: it develops awareness and appreciation, and it instructs. You want the children to observe things closely. Show them how to really see an area: stop and turn leaves over, bend down, pick up something and examine it, look behind the bark of a tree, use a lens, a magnifying mirror under things, move a rock or twig aside, crush and smell something, use a flashlight to look into something dark, ask questions, consult the guide books. *The closer you look, the more you see.* A discovery walk can effectively be done in a very small area—even sitting on the grass and discovering what's immediately around you (see Micro-Hikes). Be sure to put things back the way they were and try to limit the damage to the natural items.

You, too, will be a learner because, after a while, the children will sharpen their powers of observation and point out things to you. They'll see things you've missed.

Emphasize the *learning together* aspect. Do not feel that you have to be the repository of all nature knowledge—very few people possess this knowledge. Rather, point the way and lead children to the realization that there is much to discover and marvel at in the natural world, and that a receptive mind and eye (and ear and nose) will reveal those wonders. Books may help us to know and understand more; curious people never outgrow their desire to find out more.

At some point, without becoming too philosophical or schoolish, sit back and have the campers reflect on the total picture. Let them be aware that an insect eating a leaf is part of the ecological whole (and so are we).

All sorts of follow-up activities may stem from the discovery walk—flowers to be identified, insects you may wish to cage and keep for a while, or aquatic specimens. Other activities may suggest themselves at the time; just be alert to the possibilities and maintain the excitement.

Carry lenses, bug boxes, baggies, insect nets, a pen-knife, field guides in your box or backpack. Let kids hold the equipment but keep track of who has what. Be sure you can identify poison ivy. Point it out to the campers and teach them to identify it. Most of all, enjoy and discover!

The Theme Field Walk

Nature walks can be the discovery type or they can be more structured with a particular goal or theme in mind. That does not mean that you turn your back on interesting discoveries; but a theme walk will allow you to focus on one aspect of the natural world.

Begin all such walks with background information on the object of your walk. Example: Mushroom Search. What are mushrooms? How and where do they grow? What is their role in the food chain? What kinds are there? etc. The follow-up can also be tied into the theme. If the theme is mushrooms, you could make Spore Prints; if it's caterpillars, you can cage one, or make an egg-carton caterpillar.

Suggested topics for theme walks:

1. A Dead Tree Is Home to Many Living Things
2. A Rotting Log Is Home to Many Living Things
3. A Tree Is Home to Many Living Things
4. Animal Homes
5. Ants and Aphids
6. Berry Picking—blueberries, raspberries, strawberries
7. Caterpillars
8. Finding Evidence of Animals
9. Galls
10. Insect Homes
11. Lichen and Mosses
12. Mushroom Search
13. Spiders and Their Webs
14. Spittle Bug Search
15. Tastes and Odors—Sensory Search
16. Touch-Me-Nots, Jewelweed

Nature Craft Activities

Nature crafts may or may not be suitable for your program. This is a matter that should be discussed with the camp director and/or head counselor before camp begins and before any materials are ordered. One of the problems that may arise is the overlap of the nature and other arts and crafts programs in camp. You do not want to usurp project(s) from the crafts person. Another problem is that children may then see nature as just an extension or subdivision of the crafts program. Yet, crafts and nature can be brought together effectively, and many projects are worthwhile. After all, nature serves as the inspiration for many art forms; and, a crafted article can serve as a memento of a lesson and reinforce a concept. A drawing made of a twig or pine cone or acorn or leaf forces the person to concentrate on the natural object and really see it—its shapes, textures, nuances.

Thus, nature craft should not be viewed as an end in itself, but as one means of teaching about the natural world. In addition, younger children especially need to express themselves in art media; they will obtain pleasure from the expression and associate this pleasure with nature.

Be sure to try all projects by yourself before doing them with campers.

Nature Study for Children 3-5 Years Old

Having a camp nature program for very young children (3-5 years) presents an unique opportunity to teach a conservation ethic at a stage where attitudes and values are beginning to take shape. Their curiosity about the world around them, coupled with few preconceived ideas about nature, make these children ideal learners. Since most resident camps do not accept such young children, you are most likely to encounter these little ones in a day camp or nursery school setting.

Some activities, such as Tree Bingo, can be adapted for younger children; others are their exclusive domain. Your aims should be multiple: to show the children that nature is beautiful and not to be feared; that nature is to be marveled at and appreciated; that they must demonstrate respect and not abuse the natural world. Little children are less inhibited than older ones, and this can be turned into an asset. Try dramatic play. Have the children pretend they're animals. How would the animal act? What would it eat? What kind of noise would it make?

Scale down the arts and crafts activities so that little fingers can handle them. Some parts of the activities may need to be pre-done. For example, using a cut branch, pre-cut bird shapes and punch holes in top of them. The kids can color them, learn their names, put yarn through the holes and hang

Pre-cut bird shapes for little fingers

them on the twigs. Show pictures of cardinals, blue jays, goldfinches, robins, so that they realize birds come in the colors they find in their crayon boxes.

You can also pre-cut oak tag or construction paper in the shape of an organism for "My _____ (Frog, Butterfly, Flower, etc.) Book." Then, each page within the book is devoted to a different aspect of the organism's life—what it eats, where it lives, etc.

Utilize the pictures from *Ranger Rick* and other magazines. Cut and mount on cardboard and use these to tell about the animal depicted. Put a few of these together into a theme for the day. Combine with available specimens (nests, feathers, eggs, skins) to bring in more reality. National Wildlife Federation's *Your Big Backyard* is specifically designed for the younger child and should be one of your subscriptions. Another good device is the flannel board. For instructions on how to make and use one, see Flannel Board Habitats in this section.

An important aspect of the nature specialist's role in dealing with younger children is to attempt to dispel myths about the natural world that the child may have already been exposed to from television and stories. There is nothing inherently wrong with fantasy regarding nature, providing the child is made to realize that it is make-believe. Generations of children have been raised with the big, bad wolf or other ideas. Children need to be gently reminded that those are just stories and we enjoy them for the fun of the story. Having real animals on hand reinforces the reality, which, in many ways, has just as many fascinating stories as the fantasies.

Popular active games, like "Squirrel in the Tree," can be adapted so that it reinforces what you may have discussed about why animals need shelter (or cover) and that sometimes they vie for housing or feeding sites. "Simon Sez" is a game that can be made into a nature game by giving instructions of animal movements or sounds such as: jump like a kangaroo, slither like a snake, caw like a crow, wriggle like a mosquito larva. Play "Musical Chairs," using bird call recordings.

Little children could pretend they are birds hatching from eggs and being fed by the parent. How would they open their mouths? What would happen to the amount of room in the nest as they grew bigger? The children could enact the flying away from the nest, especially if they've had the chance to observe the real thing. This game gives you the opportunity to talk about what birds eat, what they make their nests of, how they fly, etc. Sensory experiences are also very good with younger children (see Sensory Activities in this section).

Incorporate children's songs and finger play into lessons. The "Eentsy Weentsy Spider" is more than just a song to the nature specialist; it is a way to teach about spiders. Look, then, at all the songs and stories in the collection and see how they fit into the nature program. Change the words around, if necessary. "A Little White Duck" is another good choice. "Old MacDonald Had a Farm" is good as is; and it can also be done as "Old MacDonald Had a Woods," using forest animals. Add the sound made by the animal and the movement. Naturally, each one adds on to the one before it.

Read and have the children enact Shel Silverstein's wonderful book, *The Giving Tree*. Or do likewise with *The Lorax*. Modify the Scavenger Hunt by using pictures instead of, or in addition to, words. If you're talking about beavers, have the children try to duplicate the beaver's gnawing style using a raw whole carrot. Substitute pictures for words in activities that call for written material. Since the size of the groups for younger children will usually be smaller, the group's counselor and the specialist together can give individual attention to help these little ones in whatever is required.

Young children should be encouraged by your example not to demonstrate aversion to living creatures. They are so malleable at this age that it can be accomplished. Thus, it's "Oooh! A spider! How wonderful!" not "Ugh," "Yech," or whatever.

Be alert to the nature lesson in every pre-school activity and you will be rewarded with the most responsive age.

Nature and Older Campers

Summer camps are no longer the exclusive domain of children; many adults and even those over 65 are attending camp. A nature program with mature people and senior adults can be productive and rewarding, since nature can be enjoyed at every stage of life and learning is really a lifelong process. The advantages of conducting a camp nature program with adults are numerous. Their attitude towards you and what you are offering may be more positive. They appreciate nature. Their life experiences provide you with material to draw on in explaining or describing things. They may possess greater intellectualism than their juvenile counterparts. They will have a greater ability to concentrate, a longer attention span and they will be less easily distracted. Consequently, you could try activities that require time and patience. As with younger campers, adults will come to camp with varying backgrounds and abilities which you must consider when planning your activities, but that is no different from the task for the nature specialist for a camp of youngsters.

Realistically, in a camp for older adults (65 plus), any physical limitations must be taken into consideration. Prior to camp, discussion regarding this aspect must be held with the camp director so that the nature specialist has a true picture of the abilities and disabilities of the camper population. Some older people may be hard of hearing or have arthritis or other conditions which will limit their participation and your program must be adapted to meet these limitations. A note of advice for those dealing with older people: Avoid the condescending attitude which sometimes occurs when younger people speak to elders. Older folks might also need the same kind of encouragement youngsters need to try something new or different.

The activities deemed suitable for mature persons have been marked with [M] in the Special Notes column. Some may require minor modification. See the sample program at end of the Activities section. In addition to the activities listed in this section, adults would also enjoy: collecting, identifying, and classifying all kinds of specimens, doing research, carrying out simple experiments, craftwork, all the more thorough, time-consuming activities that younger people would find restrictive.

Day Camps

Day camps, too, offer the opportunity to conduct a successful nature program. Many day camps utilize former resident camp sites and are located in country areas. Others may be in buildings such as churches, community centers or schools. Depending on the site, modifications of the program described in these pages would have to be made. Read through the activities to select those that apply. Despite the short camp day, day camps can also offer their campers a full nature program. These OBIS Modules are recommended:

> 014 Large Groups
> 017 Human Impact
> 022 Pavement and Parks
> 001 Schoolyard

Other specialized camps for retarded children or adults or physically or emotionally handicapped can also utilize most of the activities. The specialist for these situations must select those activities which are suitable, and/or modify any to meet the needs of the campers.

Programs can appeal to all ages.

Activities Guide Chart

All the activities are listed in alphabetical order with a description which includes aims, materials, and procedures to be followed. The Key to the Activities Guide classifies each activity according to several criteria which will enable a naturalist to select the activity most appropriate for a particular group. The first criteria specifies whether the activity is Indoor, Outdoor/Quiet, or Outdoor/Active. The second indicates the age level; the third shows whether there is a related craft activity. The fourth criteria shows the amount of preparation required: none, some, or extensive. The Special Notes section contains additional short information on the activity. An M in the Special Notes column indicates that the activity is appropriate for adults.

ACTIVITY	Indoor	Outdoor/Quiet	Outdoor/Active	Age Level	Craft Activity?	None	Some	Extensive	SPECIAL NOTES	
Adjective Game		X		9 +		X			Good for all day hikes	M
Adopt-A-Tree		X		7 +			X		On going; start at beginning of summer	
Animal Dissection	X			10 +			X		Not for everyone	M
Animal Homes/Insect Homes			X	7 +		X			Theme Walk	M
Ants and Aphids			X	8 +		X			Theme Walk	M
Bark Rubbings		X		6 +		X			See Adopt-A-Tree	M
Bingo	X			5 +			X		Many varieties	
Bird-in-Egg	X			7-8			X		Do in conjunction with hatching	
Bird Snatch	X			8 +		X				
Bones and Straws	X			11 +				X	Requires some sophistication	M
Box Concentration	X			All Ages		X				
Color Cards		X		7-8			X			
Corn Husk Dolls	X			9 +	X		X		Can prepare with campers	M
Counting Populations	X			9 +		X			Count beans	M
Creating An Ecology Web			X	9 +		X				
Dot Adaptations	X			10 +			X		Punch dots	M

ACTIVITY	Indoor	Outdoor/Quiet	Outdoor/Active	Age Level	Craft Activity?	None	Some	Extensive	SPECIAL NOTES
Dried Flowers A. Rings	X			9	X	X			These activities are more enjoyed by girls, although boys might also enjoy. The campers do all the preparation. M
B. Shakes	X			10	X	X			
C. Bowls	X			11	X	X			
Egg Carton Caterpillars	X			4-5	X	X			
Envirolopes (OBIS)			X	9 +			X		Makes envelopes
Finding the Evidence			X	10 +			X		See Discovery Walks M
Find the Tree			X	9 +			X		
Find Your Mate			X	7-9		X			Noisy, short duration Make index cards
Flannel Board Habitats		X		3-8				X	
Flower Dissection		X		9-10			X		Pick the flowers M
Grocery Store		X		9-10			X		Collect and accumulate food containers
Hay Infusion		X		11 +		X			Children do the preparing M
Hootie, the Owl	X			4-8	X		X		
Leaf and Plant Prints		X		8 +	X		X		See Achievements M
Leaf Skeletons		X		10 +	X	X			
Leaf Soup Relay			X	9 +			X		
Litmus Making and Testing	X			10 +			X		
Lorax, The		X		All Ages		X			Read to yourself a number of times—suitable for dramatization
Micro-Hikes			X	9 +			X		Many variations M
Million-Year-Old Picnic		X		9-10			X		Short, may be combined with another activity
My _____ Book	X			3-8	X		X		

ACTIVITY	Indoor	Outdoor/Quiet	Outdoor/Active	Age Level	Craft Activity?	None	Some	Extensive	SPECIAL NOTES	
								PREPARATION		
Natural Dyes	X			10+	X			X	Complex, long, but good	M
Natural Weaving		X		9+	X		X		Cut cardboards to size	M
Owl Pellet Study	X			10+			X			
Peanuts		X		7+		X			Can be a craft activity, too	M
Photo Quiz			X	10+				X		M
Picturing Adaptations			X	7+			X		Can be age level adjusted	M
Pond (or Lake) Study			X	9+			X		See "Sealed World" or Water Habitat Aquaria	M
Populations Game (OBIS)			X	10+			X		Great!	M
Potpourri	X			11+	X		X			
Pressing (and Drying) Flowers		X		10+		X			Children should gather them, too. Can be used in crafts.	M
Predator and Prey			X	7+		X				
Rock Creatures	X			7+	X		X			
Rotting Log Investigation		X		10+		X				
Saran Aquarium	X			5+	X			X	Young children will need helping hands	
Scavenger Hunt			X	9+			X		Pre-printed sheet. Last or late activity.	
Sealed World		X		9+			X		Should follow Pond Study	M
Sensory Experience			X	3-11	X					M
Skull Keying	X			12+			X		See Owl Pellets, Skullduggery Among Mammals	M
Soil Investigation			X	9+					Make a Berlese Funnel. Needs 2 periods.	M
Spatter Prints		X		9+	X		X		See instructions for boxes	M
Spore Prints	X			8+	X	X			Good follow up to Mushroom Hunt	M

		PREPARATION							
ACTIVITY	Indoor	Outdoor/Quiet	Outdoor/Active	Age Level	Craft Activity?	None	Some	Extensive	SPECIAL NOTES
Spraying Spider Webs			X	8+		X			
Sunprints		X		8+	X	X			Make the "developer" jar or box. Pick a clear, bright day. M
Task Cards			X	9+			X		Like Envirolopes M
Terraria		X		8+	X	X			Children do the preparing. Kept for display. M
Territorial Tag			X	9+			X		Write out the tags M
Theme Discussions	X			All Ages		X			M
Toothpick Hunt			X	9+			X		Dye toothpicks M
Touch-Me-Nots/Jewelweed			X			X			M
Track Casting			X	10+			X		Scout the area M
Tree Bingo		X		All Ages				X	See Appendix for details on how to make cards. M
Water Habitat (Aquaria)		X		7-9			X		Kept for display. Can follow Pond Study. M
What Is It?		X		3-9		X			Good introduction M
Who Am I?		X		3-7			X		

For additional activities, consult the OBIS series (see Appendix J for source). Include also gardening, animal care, plantings, games and puzzles, discovery walks, and others when planning your weekly or daily program (see the sections on Sample Program Schedules, pages 70-72.

Adjective Game

Materials:

Use whatever is around at the time, such as a rock, twig, bark, plant, moss, leaf, etc. Try to select an object that has some interest about it.

Procedure:

Sit in a circle. Pick up the object and use an adjective to describe it. Pass it to the next person, who must repeat the last adjective and then provide another. The adjectives should all be different and should not be restricted to the visual—try smell, texture, etc.

When you've gone around the entire circle, try another object. If the children are very responsive, or if some one child is so inclined, the group or just one person could incorporate the adjectives into a poem which could be printed.

Adopt-A-Tree

Adopt-A-Tree is an on-going activity that would start the first week of camp and continue throughout the summer (and perhaps be picked up again the summer after). Write up an adoption certificate for each child's tree.

The camper can learn as much about the tree as possible. What kind is it? How tall is it? How big around? About how old? Who lives in it or on it or near it? What does it give us (clean air, shade, coolness, moisture, oxygen, wind break, etc.)? What kind of seeds does it make?

Make rubbings of its bark and leaves. Draw its picture. Write a poem about it. Hug it. Listen to its inner stirrings. Love it. Make a booklet about it. Protect it from harm.

Animal Dissection

Aim:

To show children the inner organs of animals.

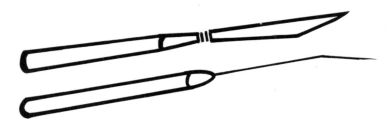

Materials:

Dissecting kit (probe, pins, scalpel, scissors), wax pan. Possible specimens: frog, fish, grasshopper.

Procedure:

Follow instructions for dissections that are specific to the animal you are dissecting. These instructions are available from the biological supply companies (see address in Appendix).

Boys seems to enjoy this activity more than girls; make certain that there is interest on the part of the children before you start this. Excuse any children who do not wish to take part. Try to point out the interesting things they will see, but don't force it on anyone. Campers may draw and label what they see. After dissection, the remains may be preserved in formalin or buried.

For aids, request Bioreview Sheets from Carolina Biological Supply; Turtox Key Card (see *References* in Appendix).

Animal Homes/Insect Homes

Begin a discovery activity about animal homes, including those of insects, by talking about some way animals use homes—as shelter or protection from the elements or predators; as nurseries, places where they deposit their eggs or raise young.

Show and look at birds' nests, mud and paper wasps' nests, cocoons, or whatever you have available to show in the nature shack that will spark curiosity and motivate the group to look for homes. Then, either as a whole group, or in smaller teams of 2-4, go out to look for various kinds of homes animals have made or adopted.

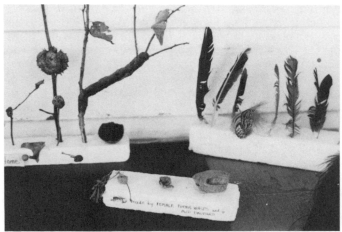

Insect homes

Search for the holes of woodchucks or foxes, beaver lodges, squirrels' nests, woodpecker or owl holes in dead trees. Perhaps one specific locale has been home to many different animals over several seasons—this is very common in nature. Look for the little mini-roadways made by field mice as they ply their way from home to feeding places through the grass.

A careful, slow walk along the edge of a field, stopping and looking at bushes, turning leaves over, using a lens, re-

veals many varieties of insect home-makers— leaf-rollers, leaf-miners, galls, insect egg sacs on leaves, webs. Sometimes a single shrub can yield enough of a variety to occupy all the campers for the entire nature period. Each home or nursery can lead to a fruitful investigation. Perhaps you could create a chart, or take some insects back to the nature shack to set up for watching.

The house-hunting also lends itself to writing of an article for the camp newspaper, or retelling at the campfire, or becoming one of the items for the nature scavenger hunt. The possibilities are as endless as the number of animal homes you'll find on your theme walk.

Ants and Aphids

Ants are very interesting to study and experiment with. One way to investigate ants is to have a theme lesson about them, followed by a theme walk to find some ant colonies.

Ants keep aphids the same way people keep cows; they "herd" them on plants that have sweet juices. The aphids, a fightless species, use their sucking tube-like mouths to pierce plant stems and suck out the juices. The ants then "milk" the aphids by stroking the aphids' abdomens with their feelers. The aphids then release a drop of the sweet liquid which the ants drink. The ants actually move the aphids about on a plant and from plant to plant.

After describing this fascinating behavior, take your group out and look for ants actually conducting this aphid/cow activity. Look for plants that have lots of ants crawling on them. Then, look closer, because the aphids are much smaller and harder to spot—they are somewhat transparent. Lenses, with handles, are convenient for this investigation because most children and adults won't want to get very close to the ants. If you disturb the plant by shaking or moving it, the ants get very excited and may even move the aphids as if to protect them from harm.

This behavior may often be seen on Meadowsweet (spiraea latifolia) and other sweet-smelling flowers. Patience may be needed to witness the milking or herding behavior. It is recommended that you scout the area first to ensure finding examples before leading the campers there. Evening primroses are also known to be aphid "pastures."

You might also locate ant hills or underground colonies. Be careful, however, since there are several species of stinging ants—and the stings are highly irritating. The underground colonies (those that do NOT create ant hills) seem to be less annoying and can provide interesting investigations. Examine the hole; observe the bits of soil that have been brought to the surface from under the ground and lie at the entrance. Watch the way the ants come and go from the hole. Do they all take the same path? Experiment by putting some cookie crumbs a short distance from the ant hole. How long does it take an ant to find the crumbs? Does it return to "tell" the other ants? Or, does each ant find the crumbs by itself? If you find the ants following a distinct trail to the food, disrupt it by placing a stone in the way or by washing away an inch or two of the path with detergent. How does this affect the ants' behavior?

You may also find ant colonies under logs or rocks. You'll see their larvae and pupae and, when you disturb their dwelling by lifting the rock or the log, the ants will immediately begin running about, attempting to protect and move their young. If you're creating an ant colony display (see Appendix C, page 119), these ant families make good inhabitants. Carefully scoop up with a trowel and transfer to the prepared ant home.

All of the above activities demand a certain degree of patience and curiosity; undertake them with older campers who have both. Their patience will be rewarded by witnessing complex and fascinating behavior.

Bark Rubbings

This activity is designed to make children aware of the *textures* of tree bark and of their similarities and differences.

Materials:

Newsprint or rexo paper; thick crayons with paper removed; masking tape.

Procedure:

Tape paper to tree bark. Rub with crayon until pattern emerges. Identify the tree, if desired. Mount the rubbing as an art object.

Investigate bark more fully. Prepare a chart comparing the bark of two trees.

1. What is its color?
2. How does it feel?
3. How does it look? Describe.
4. Does it have an odor? Describe.
5. Is the bark thick or thin?
6. Do the cracks in the bark run up, down or sideways?

Tree #1	Tree #2

Think about:

1. How might a tree's bark look during different stages of growth?

2. Does the same tree appear to have a different kind of bark at its top than at its base?
3. What similarities did you observe between barks of different trees?

Display the various rubbings and see if they can be used to identify a tree.

Variation:

Match each other's rubbings with actual trees.

Bingo Games

Commercially created nature rubber stamps are very popular with the younger children. They will use the stamps in different ways; one way is to create a Bingo game with them.

Materials:

Nature Impressions® rubber stamps, paper, stamp pads (re-ink, if necessary). Set of calling cards you've made, one per stamp.

Procedure:

Depending on the number of stamps, have the children fold the paper into boxes. They share the stamps to put a different picture in each of the boxes. Then, play as regular Bingo (or Lotto). Use the stamping or calling time as an opportunity to discuss whatever animals are depicted.

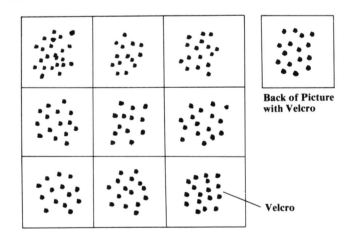

Back of Picture with Velcro

Velcro

(This game is good for an optional period).
Use National Wildlife Federation stamps as prizes.

Variation:

Cut lots of pictures of plants and animals from magazines or use National Wildlife Federation stamps. Mount on cut index cards. Put Velcro on back. Create blank Bingo or Lotto boards with other side of Velcro. The children can create their own boards, pressing the picture onto the Velcro. Use 9 or 16 spaces.

Chick in egg

Bird (or Chick) in Egg

A delightful crafts activity for younger children; a good culmination and memento of chick hatch.

Materials:

Eggshell halves (from kitchen), cotton balls, toothpicks, black and orange colored paper, shirt cardboard, yellow chalk or powdered tempera, paper bag, hole punch, glue, scissors, rulers, pencils.

Procedure:

Wash eggshell halves and allow to dry. This presents a good opportunity for you to show the inside of the eggshell, discuss the functions of the membranes, and find the air pocket. While they are drying, crush some yellow chalk (or use the powdered tempera) inside of a paper bag. Drop the cotton balls in and shake the bag to coat the cotton. That's the chick's body. Two circles, punched out of black paper with a hole punch, are glued on for eyes. For the beak, use a piece of toothpick colored or dyed orange, or a small piece of orange construction paper cut and folded in a triangular shape.

Stick the toothpick beak into the cotton or glue the paper beak on. Then, drop glue into the shell and set the chick in it. For greater stability, glue the completed shell with chick onto a cardboard square or circular base.

(Adapted from Estelle Bard's directions from an original idea by Dorothy Hosey, as printed in the ESSA Newsletter. Used by permission.)

Bird Snatch

This activity is designed to reinforce identification of birds (or leaves, or flowers). It is the nature version of the popular game of Snatch the Club or Steal the Bacon.

Materials:

Audubon (or other) Flash Cards of Birds (or flowers, or trees). Or, you may substitute cut-out pictures of these. Select the ones the campers are already familiar with.

Procedure:

Divide the campers into two teams of equal size (and ability). Count off the campers on each team and assign a number which they are to remember. If the teams are uneven, the last camper numbered gets two numbers.

Place the bird cards face up on a long table or grassy area. Briefly hold each one up and review its name. The leader then calls a number and says the name of a bird. The campers whose numbers were called rush up to the table and attempt to cover the correct bird card with their hand, palm down. (By not having the players pick up the cards, you avoid having them torn or damaged.) The person whose hand is first on the card earns a point for that team; the team with the most points wins.

Start with 10 cards. After a round where every camper has had a turn, introduce two or three additional cards, making it more of a challenge. After another round, add more cards to maintain the challenge.

Variation:

Use other flash cards—flower, mammal, trees (or use real leaves.)

(Suggested by Carlton Beil.)

Bones and Straws

Aim:

To have the campers discover a basic principle in physics and biophysics. (Sounds complex, but it's not.)

Materials:

Paper or plastic straws, straight pins. A variety of animal bones, cow, chicken . . . get from the butcher. (Cook them, then cut straight; soak in bleach, if necessary.) Lenses, marker, newsprint paper (to record).

Procedure:

Divide the group in half. Give one half the straws and pins and challenge them to use the straws to build the tallest possible free-standing structure. Give the other half the bones and lenses. Challenge them to try to find out why bones are so strong. Keep the groups separate from each other.

The group building the straws should (hopefully) discover that the structure will collapse without supporting struts in triangular arrangement. (If they are not discovering this, you may have to subtly suggest it.)

After about fifteen minutes, ask the groups to share their responses to the challenge. The bones group should go first. List their responses on the newsprint. Then the straw group should respond and show their structure. The ensuing discussion should bring out the structural anatomy of bones, which, when looked at closely with lens as well as the naked eye will reveal triangular struts which provide strength without adding bulk or weight. This is particularly apparent in bird bones, which must be strong without being heavy, so that the birds can fly.

(An original, uncopyrighted concept. Used by permission of Donald Cook.)

Box Concentration

The purpose of this activity is to give children further exposure to natural items, reinforcing their knowledge.

Box concentration

Materials:

A large empty box, yarn, four to ten objects from the nature shack—such as: rock, nest, twig, acorn, pine cone, ferns, mushrooms, flower, snake skin, leaf, bark, butterfly, feathers, etc. Paper, pencils.

Procedure:

Make sure the children know the names of every item. Review if necessary. Give out paper; have the children fold it in quarters (one box for each round). Place objects on a sheet of paper that has been divided into sections, using yarn.

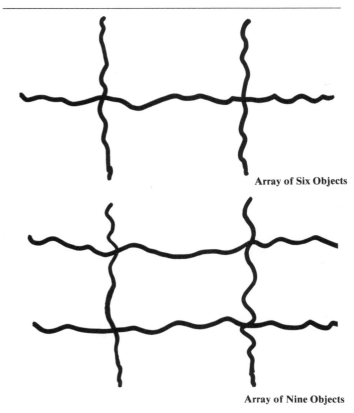

Array of Six Objects

Array of Nine Objects

Example:

Direct the children to concentrate on the objects for one minute (more or less). Then, cover the whole thing with the box. Children try to remember the objects and where they were located. They may either write the name of the object or draw it. Call time after two minutes or so (use your discretion). Correct sheets can earn a wildlife sticker. Or, round one may just be a test run to practice the game. For further rounds, change sections around, change objects or increase number, depending on age level and ability of children.

Outdoor Variation:

(More active; not sedentary.) Create the dividers on grass or other flat area. Place objects in boxes. Dividing groups into two or three teams, the kids go out to find objects and *duplicate* the array.

Color Cards

The purpose of this activity is to have children observe the range of colors in the natural environment.

Materials:

Color cards—index cards painted (and laminated) in various hues and colors or, use mat board, cut up—obtainable in photo supply stores or, visit your local paint store and pick up color sample cards. Mount on sturdy cardboard and cover with clear contact or laminate.

Procedure:

Distribute color cards, one per child (or one card for two in a team). Ask them to find something that matches the color as closely as possible. Share the findings.

Variations:

1. Hide the cards, with half showing. Have the children hunt for the cards.
2. Use only green (or only brown) cards from paint store with variations in hues and shades. This requires a finer ability to distinguish the differences and makes campers

aware of the many different greens (or browns) to be found in nature.

3. Use the paint store color strips to make a large color "wheel." Have the children go out and find objects, return and place them on the color wheel where it matches.

These activities lead to a discussion of such topics as pigmentation, camouflage and protective adaptation.

Corn Husk Dolls

Materials:

Lots of corn husks, corn silk, yarn, wire or twist'ems, marker, styrofoam ball for head, glycerine.

Alert the kitchen to save the husks when they serve corn-on-the-cob. Get corn husks ready (either by yourself—or kids like to join in). Rip them off the bottom core and discard any rotting portions. Keep the silk in a separate pile. Spread the husks and silk in the sun to dry (may take more than one day).

The now dried husks must be re-moistened in hot water to which two teaspoons of glycerine have been added. Soak for five to ten minutes until pliable.

For bendable arms, you'll need florist's wire (the flexible type) or twist'ems. Roll about 6 inches of husk tightly in a bundle (or around wire) and tie ends with strips of corn husk (or yarn.) (See Fig. A)

For sleeves (more attractive, a bit harder), cut a 3-inch by 4-inch piece of husk. Place this over one end of arms and tie at hand. Pull extending husk back over tie forming puffed sleeve. Repeat for other side. All husks should meet in center and be tied with strip of husk or wire. (See Fig. B)

For head, use small styrofoam ball, or make a small ball with husk scraps. Cover with two or three strips of husk and tie at neck, making sure ends are long enough for arm piece to slip under. (See Fig. C)

For bodice, stick arms under head strips (see Fig. D) and secure. You will cover this with two pieces (2-inch) of husk by wrapping them criss-cross over the doll's shoulders and crossing at the waist. Tie at waist. (See Fig. E)

For the skirt, use two or three large husks. Hold doll with head up. Fasten skirt tightly around waist so that the strips of the skirt go above and over the head and arms. (See Fig. F) Now, while holding the tied waist, turn the skirt pieces over so that the tie is not visible. (See Fig. G)

Trim edges of skirt. Wet again, if necessary, and put the doll with its skirt billowed over something so that it dries with its skirt out. Make hair, scarf, apron, broomstick (twig) with straw, face, etc. For a simpler version, see the next page.

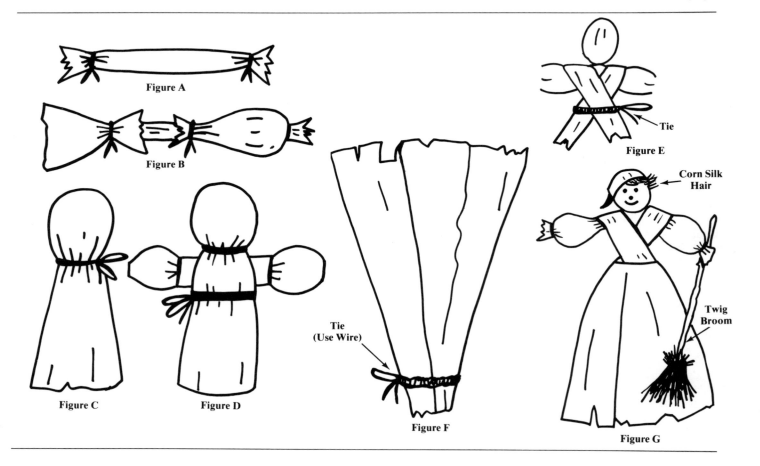

Figure A

Figure B

Figure C

Figure D

Tie (Use Wire)

Figure F

Tie

Figure E

Corn Silk Hair

Twig Broom

Figure G

CORN HUSK DOLL   An Easy (for Little Fingers)

1

Materials: Prepare (dry) corn husks for doll shown on page 38. Select 12 husks of approximately similar widths and trim off the very tips—do not cut husks to the same length.

2

Tie husks tightly as close to the top as you can.

3

Tie all husks together about 1-1½ inches down from first knot.

4

Cut off excess, leave a little hand.

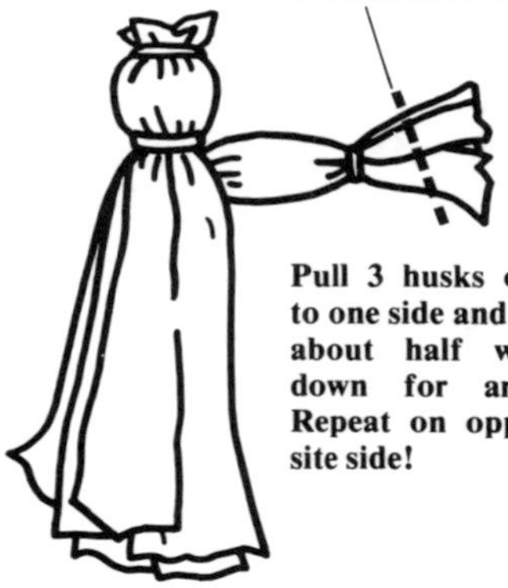

Pull 3 husks out to one side and tie about half way down for arm. Repeat on opposite side!

5

Tie off remaining 6 husks at waist.

6

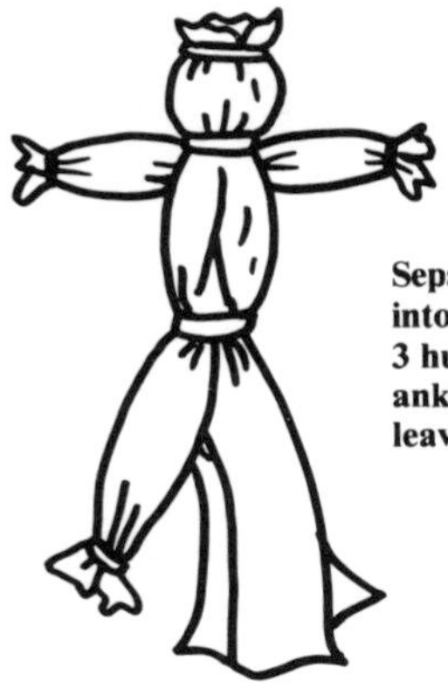

Separate husks into 2 bundles of 3 husks and tie at ankle. Trim to leave foot.

7

If you wish to pose doll, tie into desire pose while wet—it will stay when dried.

8

Finishing: Let doll dry at least 24 hours. Paint face with paint, magic markers, etc. Decorate and outfit doll as an Indian, or be creative and make it any style you choose!

9

(Used by permission of Linda Palter.)

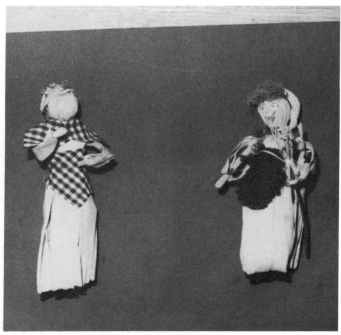

Corn husk dolls

Counting Populations

Field biologists frequently need to count populations of animals in a given area. Since wild animals are captured with difficulty and do not stand still for census taking, the scientists utilize a technique of random or representative sampling. This technique can be readily demonstrated in the nature shack, using simple materials; then, if you wish, it can be transferred to some live population.

Materials:

Macaroni shells or lima beans (whatever is available), colored marker.

Procedure:

Count out 100 beans and put them in a container (only *you* know how many there are). When the children come, ask them to guess how many beans are in the container. Explain that you are going to show them a way to "guesstimate" amounts by taking and making a representative sample.

With the children, remove ten beans and have the children mark the ten with a conspicuous mark (red?). Then, return the beans to the container and mix them up. Have a child reach in, without looking, and pull out ten beans, spreading them in front. Count the number of beans that have a red mark. Write down this number. Do it again with another child. Write down that number. Do it several times. The numbers that prevail should all be quite close, and if averaged, one number will be it.

Using this formula:

$$\frac{\text{total population (unkown)}}{\text{\# marked at first}} = \frac{\text{\#pulled out}}{\text{\#found marked}}$$

Clear the equation and solve for X. (Young children need not do the math. You do it.)

Example:

Out of the ten beans you pulled out, only one should have a mark on it, then:

$$\frac{X}{10} = \frac{10}{1}$$ cross multiply to clear, X = 100.

(Do this by yourself at first, trying different totals, to prove to yourself that the method works!) Then, let the kids count the beans to see that there are indeed 100 total.

Variations:

Try it with a different population, for example, seeds or rice. This time, the total amount should be unknown to anyone, even you. If there are many seeds (or grains), you may have to pull out more than ten to get any marked ones at all (see mathematical formula in its actual form below). You could also try it with a living population, such as mealworms, marking ten with a dot of nail polish, blowing it dry, returning them to the container, pulling out ten and doing the math. Field biologists capture some animals, tag them, return them to the wild, re-capture some randomly and use the formula to extrapolate.

$$\frac{P_1}{S_1} = \frac{P_2}{S_2}$$

P = the population $\quad P_1$ = total population, unknown

$\quad\quad\quad\quad\quad\quad\quad P_2$ = random population you pulled out

$\quad\quad\quad\quad\quad\quad\quad S_1$ = total sample you marked originally

S = marked sample S_2 = sample you found marked when you pulled them out

For another technique used in counting large populations of stationary items (trees, plants, stars), see OBIS Bean Bugs, a Quadrat Census activity.

Creating an Ecology Web

A fun activity, with an important message about interconnections and interdependence.

Materials:

Index cards with name and/or drawing or photographs of some aspect of the environment—enough for one for each child. Include: air, soil, water, sun, trees, other green plants, fungi, bacteria, domestic animals, food crop plants, earthworms, bees, birds, carnivores, herbivores, etc. You may want to have a brief explanation of each one's role in the ecosystem, e.g., "I am the SUN. I provide light so that plants can make food. I also provide heat . . . etc." This can be written on the index card and read by the camper.

Procedure:

Have the children form a circle on a grassy area. Give out a card, or have each child select one. The child holds up the card and either reads aloud or says what he is. When all have finished, they are to put their cards down and take three steps forward into the center of the circle. Each person grasps one hand of someone else in the circle that is in some way related to oneself (really, everything—but they should briefly ask each other how). Then they must grasp the hand of someone else. The goal is to untangle the web without letting go of anyone's hands. They have to crawl up and around each other's arms and legs to open the circle. Try not to break hands.

(Adapted from New Games.)

Dot Adaptation

Concept:

Protective coloration; natural selection.

Materials:

Fabric with all-over print design (florals) or patterned tablecloth. Colored dots made by using a hole-punch on ten different colors of paper. Small paper cups (1-2 oz.). Newsprint and markers.

Procedure:

Give each of ten children a cup containing a single color of dots. Have each one carefully count out ten dots of their color. They then scatter their ten dots all over the cloth. A total of 100 dots is now on the cloth. Explain that five hungry birds have now appeared on the scene and will hunt and eat dot insects. At a given signal, the five campers are to look down and pick up dots until they each have fifteen (total of seventy-five). These campers are to be like birds and must look away each time they pick up a dot, and they must pick up the first dot they see when their gaze returns to the cloth. When this phase is completed, gather the edges of the cloth together, shaking it so that the remaining twenty-five dots fall into the center. Five other campers now separate the remaining dots into their colors and count them. The

number of each color is recorded on a chart and the dots return to the cloth.

Example: (Total twenty-five left)

Red	Orange	Blue	Yellow	Light Green	Dark Green	White	Black	Purple	Pink
2	1	4	2	2	5	0	5	4	0

Round two (really, the next generation) now begins. Since the dots that were left were not eaten, they have "survived," reproduced and for next year or generation, their numbers have tripled. Therefore, the campers who have the dot cups are to triple the numbers on the chart and count out that number of dots.

Example:

Using above results, Red (is now)-6, Orange-3, Blue-12, etc. Add these seventy five to the twenty five left and you once again should have 100 dots. These should be scattered on the fabric. Five other campers are designated as birds and repeat the procedure, picking up dots, looking away, etc., until fifteen for each (total seventy-five) are collected. Once again, the remaining dots are counted and tabulated on the chart. A lively discussion on the implication of this activity should ensure. Be sure to include all the children as counters, birds, etc.

You should discuss selective pressure, evolution, adaptation, camouflage, depending on the group's ability and intelligence.

(Modified by the Audubon-Greenwich Center staff; developed from an idea by Dr. J. Stebbins. Used by permission.)

Dried Flower Preparation

General Tips:

Always place a strip of paper with the date and collector's name with the drying plants. Dried flowers can be stored indefinitely in an air-tight container. Keep a record of which flowers dry best with which techniques. In rainy or humid weather, allow extra drying time.

METHODS

Air Drying:

Preparing dried flowers

Hang cut flowers upside down by the stems in a dry, airy place. Air drying takes about two to three weeks. Flowers such as pearly everlasting and strawflowers dry very well this way, retaining both color and shape. Flowers and leaves for natural dye materials or potpourri can also be prepared this way.

Drying Media:

Drying flowers

Combine one part borax, one part cornmeal, and one-half part salt (or one part borax to five parts cornmeal), or buy a prepared silica gel made specifically for flower drying. Place a shallow layer of the drying medium in a pan. Place upside-down blossoms on top and then carefully add more medium until the flowers are covered. After four to twelve days (depending on the size of the flowers), take the flowers out and brush off any remaining mix with a soft paintbrush. Many flowers can be successfully dried this way; but, be careful because it is possible to *over*-dry using a drying medium.

Pressing:

Pressing flowers

An easy and reliable method that produces two dimensional flowers. Place several sheets of newspaper on a hard surface. Arrange flowers the way you want them to look when dried, and carefully cover with two sheets of news-

paper. Keep adding layers of flowers and newspapers. When you have all your flowers sandwiched, the whole pile is placed under several phonebooks, or encyclopedias, or any other convenient weight. Drying time is one to two weeks. Some flowers may lose their color (blue seems especially prone to fade), but this is foolproof with foliage.

Glycerin:

Woody stemmed branches with attractive foliage can be preserved with a solution of one part glycerin to two parts water. Split or crush the bottom of the branch and stand it in a glass of glycerin solution for one to three weeks. As the solution is soaked up, the color of the leaves will deepen, and you can remove the branch when you have achieved a pleasing tone. This works best with firm, thick foliage.

Using glycerin method

Uses:

Arrange dried flowers in a shadow box, or weave into a yarn wall hanging. Make weed pots from clay or tree bark. Use pressed flowers to decorate boxes, bottles, stationery, etc. (Arrange the pressed plants and then paint over entire surface with Modge Podge or any clear finish. Or, cover with clear contact paper.) Mount and label pressed plants for a botanical collection.

Uses of dried flowers
(by Linda Palter—used with permission.)

Dried Flower Activities

A. Rings

Materials:

Drapery rings, felt, cardboard, white glue (dries clear) mixed with water. Assorted dried flowers and ferns, bark, tweezers.

Procedure:

Trace the ring on cardboard; cut out circles. Cut two felt circles of the same size. Glue the cardboard circle between the two felt circles. Arrange the dried flowers (whose stems have been cut to about one inch) decoratively. Glue them to

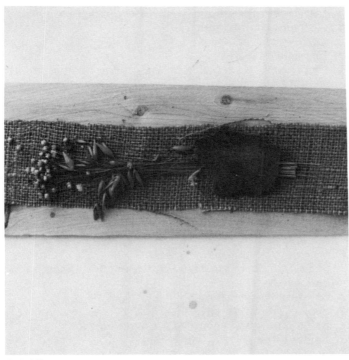

Dried flowers

felt by dipping stem into watery glue and placing on felt. Glue stains felt, so glue a cut piece of bark over the stems so that it looks as if the flowers are in a pot or basket. If needed, a ring or hook may be attached to the drapery ring as a hanger.

B. Shingles or Cedar Shake

Materials:

Dried flowers, glue, bark, cedar shakes or other wooden shingle, ribbon.

Procedure:

Arrange dried flowers on shingle. Glue and staple onto shingle. Cover with bark and glue bark with strong glue. (May be necessary to weight down until glue dries). Decorate with bow.

C. Bowl

Materials:

Rose bowl, florist's foam, glue, colored gravel, tweezers, scissors, spoon.

Procedure:

Wash and dry bowls thoroughly. Carefully arrange and place dried flowers in florist's foam which has been cut into one-inch cube, flat on the bottom. Fill it in well, and artistically; try to achieve different heights and angles. The foam will hold it. Squeeze white glue onto the bottom of the bowl; using tweezers or your fingers, carefully lower the flower filled foam onto the glue. Allow to dry for several hours, or overnight. Use a teaspoon to carefully place colored gravel in bowl up to edge of foam so that the gravel is level or slightly higher than the foam and covers it.

Arranging dried flowers in a bowl

Egg Carton Caterpillars

This is a crafts activity for younger children. It should be done in conjunction with an examination of a live caterpillar that the children have observed and discussed.

Materials:

Sections of pressed paper egg cartons, cut apart; tempera paint and brushes; colored pipe cleaners; felt or paper scraps; glue, optional—moveable eyes.

Egg carton caterpillar

Procedure:

Cut apart the egg cartons so that six egg holders are in one section. Since camps usually order eggs by the case, ask the kitchen to save the cardboard dividers that separate the layers of eggs. Invert one section of six. One end piece becomes the head and the other cups are the body. Paint as desired, with fanciful colors, dots, patterns. Poke holes at the bottom of the body sections for legs which are bent pipe cleaners inserted into the holes. Felt scraps or moveable eyes can be glued on the head. Pipe cleaner antennae may be added.

It is not necessary to be scientifically correct. The activity is just for fun and fantasy. The leader can direct the conversation during the activity so that campers also understand real caterpillars and their role in nature.

Envirolopes (OBIS)

OBIS (Outdoor Biology Instructional Strategies) has an excellent activity where children have to find specific items. This idea can be used as is or adapted to be more interesting or to last longer.

Instead of large white envelopes, try empty shoe or cigar boxes. Send the children out in teams of two or three to locate the items listed on the box or on task cards.

Examples:

1. Collect six different leaves
2. Select six weeds of different sizes
3. Pine or other evergreen cones (three or four)
4. Five different seeds
5. Seed pods
6. Rocks
7. Acorns or other nuts
8. Different colored soils
9. Rotted or charred wood
10. Ferns
11. Mosses
12. Bark from ground

Customize your list to the area and time of season and kids' knowledge.

(This material has been adapted from OBIS, Outdoor Biological Instructional Strategies published by Delta Education, Inc., in Nashua, NH. The OBIS program consists of ninety-seven activities similar to Envirolopes Game. These activities may be obtained from the publisher at Delta Education, Inc., Box M, Nashua, NH 03051.)

Finding the Evidence

Most animals shy away from people, but the sharp observer can find their traces if one knows where to look and what to look for. Children love to play detective and search for the clues animals leave behind. Capitalize on this; create an excitement about the search.

Materials:

Variety of field guides, including track guide. Lenses, paper and pencil. Optional: clipboards.

Procedure:

Discuss what kinds of things you'll be looking for. Animals make their presence known by: actual sightings, dropped feathers, food remains, droppings, holes in trees or ground, tracks, tree markings, ground markings. Campers are to find as many animal traces as possible. They may list them, or check them off on a prepared list—or you may hold a master list and check each off as you come to it.

Things to look for:

1. Bark tracings—made by bark beetles
2. Bird egg shells
3. Boring beetles—listen with your ears against a tree trunk
4. Cicada castings, empty nymph cases, emergence holes.
5. Cocoons, empty or full
6. Earthworm tracks in mud
7. Eggs laid on leaves
8. Empty insect exoskeletons—left when mature insect emerges
9. Galls
10. Holes in tree trunks, made by different woodpeckers
11. Leaf miners' trails on leaves
12. Leaves on weedy plants which have been eaten—by whom?
13. Leaves rolled by insects
14. Mouse trails (look in the grass for tiny paths)
15. Mushrooms nibbled on
16. Old birds' nests—who made them?
17. Recycled homes—mice using wasps' nests, bees, using mouse nests, etc.
18. Remnants of mud wasps' nests
19. Sandy mounds—ant hills (Watch out for stinging red ants.)
20. Sawdust—carpenter ants
21. Snail or slug track (silvery line)
22. Soil removed and deposited for tunnel home
23. Spider's web
24. Spittle bug's foamy home (early in summer)
25. Squirrels' nests—big cluster of leaves, high in trees
26. Tracks

27. Tree leaves partially eaten—by whom?
28. Tunnels
29. Worm castings

A good camera with a close-up lens may be able to capture some of these for display or for a scrapbook.

Caution: Before starting the walk, the campers should be cautioned not to stick anything into a hole in the ground or in a tree. It may injure the occupant or the person on the other end. Bees, for instance, make nests underground and will sting when disturbed. Just look.

Find the Tree

This activity directs the participants to examine a tree carefully without the sense of sight.

Materials:

Blindfolds, or old masks with eyes taped. Or, kids can just close their eyes and promise not to look.

Procedure:

Select a fairly level, partly wooded area. Have the campers work in teams of two. One of the pair agrees to be blindfolded (or close his eyes). The sighted person selects a tree and leads the blindfolded person to that tree. The unsighted camper then examines the tree in as many ways and places as possible—feeling, smelling, hugging, etc. When finished, the person is led back to the start, perhaps by a different route. The blindfold is then removed and the person tries to find his/her tree. The roles are then reversed, and the activity repeated.

This experience helps a camper focus on the individuality of each tree. Just as each person, although sharing similar characteristics with other humans, has a distinctiveness, so do trees.

Find Your Mate

A noisy, active activity for twenty or more participants. The idea of the game is to have children role-play animals by using animal calls as their clues in locating members of their own species.

Materials:

Prepare double sets of index cards, each set having the name of an animal on it. Example: frog, cow, snake, bee, turkey, lion, owl, etc. A blindfold for each participant.

Procedure:

Explain to the children that one reason animals make sounds is to locate others of their own species. Give out the mixed-up pairs of index cards, telling them they are not to reveal the animal written on it. Then, they are to put on the blindfolds; you collect the index cards. At a signal, the participants are to make the noise of the animal and locate their own mate by sound or call.

This game can be fun and instructive, though noisy and silly. It is rather short (ten minutes) and can be used when just a few minutes need to be filled, or you can expand by prefacing or concluding with discussion of how animals find their mates. What other ways, besides calls, do they use? (Scent, lights, display.) Follow up by taking a walk away from man-made noise and listening carefully for animal sounds. The activity can be a prelude to a night hike. Also see OBIS *Sound Off*, where a variety of noisemakers are used.

(Adapted from New Games)

Flannel Board Habitats

The flannel board has many uses; one excellent one is to depict *habitats*. You can buy a board, or it is just as easy to make one.

Materials:

A piece of heavy cardboard at least 30 inches by 24 inches or larger. Cut two pieces of cardboard to make holders so the board will stand up by itself, or lean or hang it. Cover with colored felt or flannel, the color of the background of the habitat you're depicting—pale blue for sky, green for grass, medium blue for water. Cut out from magazines or trace and draw pictures of various animals and plants. Mount on oak tag or cardboard. Glue flannel or felt on the back so that it will stick to the board.

You can also cut the felt itself into shapes of trees, birds, plants, animals. Then, at each session, do a different habitat—forest, field, pond, stream. This becomes an activity called *"Who lives here?"* Have the children put the proper plants and animals in the habitat as you discuss with them why a specific organism can live in a certain place and not in others. Why can't an elephant live on the tundra, or a fish in the desert? After several of these sessions, it would be hoped that youngsters will begin to realize that habitat is a place where animals (and other living things) get the things they need to live from the place they live in.

Note: Audubon Aids, available from Richardson Bay Audubon Center (see Appendix), have pre-printed flannel board stories with outlines you can trace and use. These are no longer in print but can be purchased until supplies run out. Also available from: Kryger Science Center, 211-45 46th Road, Bayside, NY 11361 ($1.50).

Flower Dissection

Aim:

To have the participants understand the role played by flowers, that they produce the seeds for the next generation of plants.

Materials:

Large, simple flower, scissors or knives, lenses, flower chart showing parts of flower, microscope and slides.

Procedures:

Select a large, showy, simple flower, such as a Day Lily, one that grows in profusion so that you may give one to each child (or one for two campers). Discuss why some flowers are showy and odorous. Show some which are not showy or fragrant (like grass flowers). Why aren't they? Identify and compare parts of the flower with charts. Cut into the ovary to see the developing ovules. Follow up by examining a variety of flowers and trying to locate the parts (perhaps evening primrose, musk mallow, hawkweed, or marigolds). Some may already show seeds—pull the dried petals off and look. Try to get a few grains of pollen under the microscope for campers to view.

Grocery Store

This activity examines where the food we eat comes from and also demonstrates in a subtle way the mathematics involved in food pyramids and energy transfer.

Materials:

A variety of empty food cans, cartons, frozen food packages, all with labels intact. You can accumulate some at home, or get them from the camp kitchen. Pasta boxes, tuna cans, vegetables, fruit, bread labels, meat, fish, cereals, cheeses, eggs. Yarn, cut into lengths and tied into four large circles (six feet each). A large shopping bag, four index cards which you've labeled green plants, plant eaters (or herbivores), animal eaters (or carnivores), decomposers.

Procedures:

All the empty food packages should be in one or two shopping bags. Have each child take an item from the bag without looking. They should look at the label of foods made from combined mixtures (e.g.. breads, cookies, prepared foods).

Lay out the four circles of yarn on the grass, overlapping them slightly, and put an index card in each circle (see diagram).

Each participant should try to figure out which circle to put the food container in, and then do so. If a food contains more than one type, it should go where the circles overlap. When all have taken their turn, you may want to repeat until all items are used.

Then lead a discussion as to why there are more foods in the Green Plant circle than any other and fewest in the Animal Eaters' circle. People do get most of their food directly from plants. Even most of the animals we eat are plant eaters, so the direct link to the green plants as producers becomes obvious. More sophisticated youngsters could discuss transfer of energy and biomass, and all might think about the desirability of eating lower on the food chain.

Sample food items:

Carnivores: Tuna
Herbivores: Eggs, salami, honey, cottage cheese, hot dogs, beef bouillon, hamburgers.

Green Plants: All fruits and vegetables
Decomposers: Mushrooms
Overlap: Herbivores and Green Plants—Chicken noodle soup, ice cream
Omnivores: Herbivores and Carnivores—Bacon, clams
Beer bread (made by fermentation) overlap Green Plants and Decomposers. Yogurt (made of milk with bacterial cultures) overlaps Herbivores and Decomposers.

Children should help each other to decide where to put each item and the group may be called upon to agree or challenge the placement. The point of the game is to make children aware of the important role of green plants in our survival as the first link in the food chain. It is also designed to raise their level of awareness of the interdependence of all living things on each other.

(Adapted from High Rock, Exploring Environments, Ruth Yarrow.)

Hay Infusion

Making a hay infusion results in a very fascinating effect. If you have a good microscope, then this is most worthwhile. This activity must be done in two sessions; getting started may be short or more complex. Get some dried grasses and place them in a container. Add water and cover with lid that has one or two holes punched in it. Set it aside in a dimly lit corner. For greater interest, set up several different containers.

1. Dried grass with cold tap water
2. Dried grass with tap water that had been standing for a day or so (to let chlorine out)
3. Dried grass with pond water
4. Dried grass with lake water
5. Other plants with any of the above

The next time this group comes to you (two to four days later), have them examine their hay infusions. Check for color, cloudiness, odor, etc. Examine with a hand lens. Then, get a few drops on a slide (with a well), and look at it under the scope. Try all powers.

Hootie, the Owl

A good follow-up for theme discussions on birds, or nocturnal animals, or just for artistic pleasure, is an oak-tag owl with wings that pop up.

Materials:

Oak tag, scissors, crayons or markers, round-head paper fasteners, string.

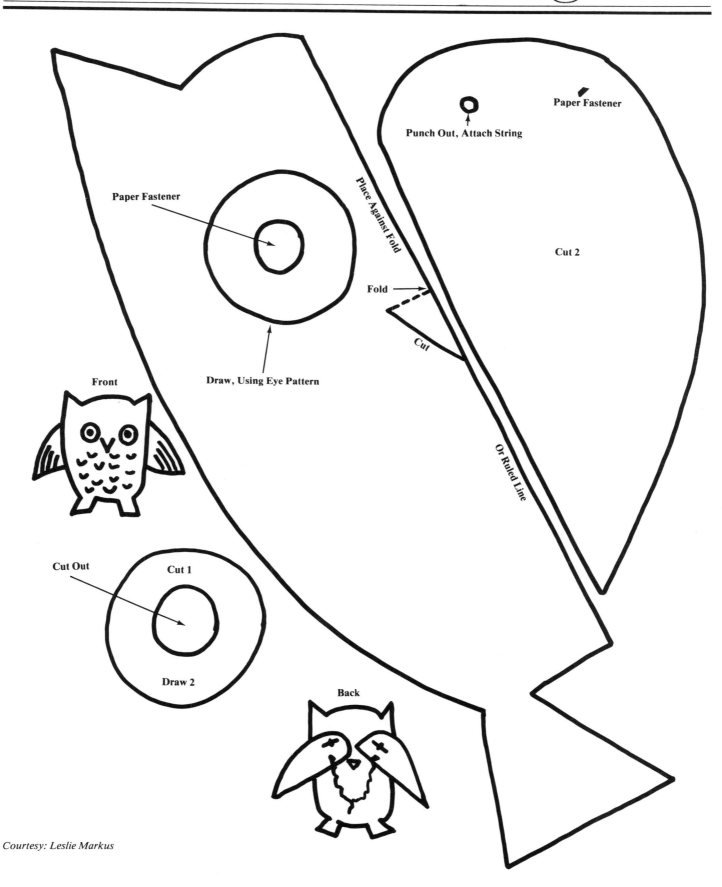

Paper Fastener

Punch Out, Attach String

Place Against Fold

Cut 2

Fold

Cut

Or Ruled Line

Paper Fastener

Draw, Using Eye Pattern

Front

Cut Out

Cut 1

Draw 2

Back

Courtesy: Leslie Markus

Procedure:

Use the patterns for the owl and carbon paper to trace onto oak tag. For the body part, you can fold the oak tag and place the flat edge against the fold. Cut and open out to have a full body. Or, draw a ruled line down the middle and hold the flat edge of the pattern against the line. Reverse to get a whole body. Just be sure the master pattern you give the children to trace has a full body. Also trace and cut the wing and eye patterns. The campers then use the patterns to trace a body and two wings. Cut these out. Use the eye pattern to draw two eyes on the face of the owl. Have them look at a photograph of an owl to confirm that an owl's eyes are located on the front of its face—to give it excellent vision. Cut the beak and fold it up. Decorate the owl with wing and body feathers. Use two round headed paper fasteners going through the center of the eyes to attach the wings behind the body, with the straight side facing down. Knot each end of a piece of string in each of the other holes in the wings. When you pull the string down, the wings will pop up.

While cutting, coloring, and assembling, discuss the habits of owls, where they live (in barns, dead trees), what they eat (mice, voles, shrews), and their importance to us (they help to control the rodent population).

Leaf Skeletons

A very beautiful finished product that also displays the fine network of veins that transport food and raw materials throughout the leaf.

Materials:

A discarded hairbrush or toothbrush that is made of animal bristles, piece of board, piece of old carpet.

Procedure:

Tack the carpet piece to the board. This will be the pounding board. Place a fresh green leaf, top side up, on the board. Hold it firmly in place with one hand, while tapping it gently with the brush until the fleshy part is worn away, leaving only the skeleton. Turn the leaf over now and then, as needed. They may be pressed and dried, or you may try to dye the pressed skeleton for another effect. Mount on contrasting paper.

Another way to create leaf skeletons is to boil the leaf in water that contains washing soda (Na_2CO_3). When the flesh of the leaf feels slimy, remove. Then, gently brush the soft flesh from the stiffer veins.

(Try these processes yourself before trying it with children.)

Leaf and Plant Printing

These are three separate activities, but the techniques used are applicable to all three.

Rubbings:

Put the leaf or plant down on a flat surface. The veins of the leaf should be up for the best effect. Place a sheet of white or colored paper on top. Using a flat crayon from which the paper has been removed, and holding it down flat, rub back and forth over the paper. The outline of the leaf will emerge.

Leaf print

Printing:

Use lots of newspaper; spread out. Use inexpensive paper. Use washable, water-based printer's inks that come in tubes, and rollers (brayers). Set up three to six glass sheets and squeeze a different color ink on each; use a separate brayer for each color also. Use the brayer to spread the ink out on the glass sheets and then onto the plant. Turn the plant face down on a clean sheet. Take a flat wad of newspapers and press down on the plant. Lift up the newspapers and the wet plant. It should have left its imprint on the paper. With practice, and depending on the person's artistic sophistication, the finished product may turn out to be very beautiful. You could frame or mount them after they dry.

Bleach Prints:

Use Clorox bleach, half diluted with water (be careful not to splash your clothes). Dip leaf in solution. Let excess drip. Press, vein side down, on colored tissue paper, using a folded paper presser. Allow to dry. Interesting effect as bleach removes color from tissue paper in leafy pattern.

Leaf Soup Relay

A lively game that will help children see the differences in leaves, and aid in identification.

Materials:

Gather five to six leaves from twelve or more different trees. Mix the leaves well in a basket or box. This is the "soup."

Procedure:

Divide into two (or more) teams. Ten children on each team is a good number. Line the teams up, either facing each other or facing you, but at a distance, twenty feet or so. Spread the soup on a table or the ground. At your signal, the first person runs up and takes one leaf, any leaf from the "soup." He runs back and hands it to the next player, who runs to the "soup" and must select a leaf from a different tree. He runs back, gives the two leaves to the next player who then must select a third *different* leaf from the soup. Each person must select a different species. The team which selects the ten (or eight or however many children are on a team) different leaves first is the winner. For subsequent rounds, have the children switch positions so that the more difficult selections do not always fall to the same players.

Variation:

Prepare a list of the tree leaves that are in the "soup," and write them in numbered order on a large index card. Person #1 has to get Leaf #1 (and only that one). Person #2 has to get Leaf #2 (and so on). This variation requires more knowledge. You could also accompany the name list with a picture so the children can more readily identify it.

(From the New Jersey School of Conservation.)

Litmus Paper

Materials:

Red cabbage, paper toweling, vinegar, baking soda.

Preparation:

Chop up and boil a few of the most purple leaves of a red cabbage. Boil for about twenty minutes in a small amount of water, but do not let the water boil off. Allow to cool.

Procedure:

Bottle some red cabbage liquid for future use. Dip some paper towels in the solution and hang up to dry. You now have an indicator that will show acids (turn it from purple to red) and bases (turn it from purple to blue). (You could do this alone or with children.)

Children can use this just as regular litmus paper. Let them each have one sheet of towelling they can use for testing. First, let them use vinegar, then baking soda mixed with water. Tell them that these are test substances: the vinegar is an acid, the soda is a base, the cabbage juice was neutral. They can then test a variety of substances: water, milk, rainfall, lake, pond, stream, soda, chocolate milk, apples, bananas, oranges, lemons, onions, laundry water, whatever is around.

Discuss acid rain with them.

(Adapted from the book, More Research Ideas for Young Scientists, by George Barr. Used by permission.)

The Lorax

The Lorax by Dr. Seuss is an *exceptional* book; it carries a vital message, and Dr. Seuss tells it in his own special way that intrigues, entertains and provokes its young listeners.

Familiarize yourself with the book. Then, depending on time constraints, either read it aloud (with as much dramatic expression as you can muster); or, preferably, devote more time to it and think about running it as a special program. It could be used at an evening campfire—where the campers play the roles, memorize the parts, create and wear costumes, make props, etc. The impact of the story will be greater if more of a fuss is made. Perhaps you could persuade the dramatics specialist to make *The Lorax* a fully staged production.

If not, reading it will have to suffice. Devote a period to it, if possible, involving kids in discussions or in providing movements and/or sound effects. For example: divide the group into parts. Each time the reader mentions a certain role, like the swami swans, that group provides the sound of the swami-swans—maybe a "humma-humma-humma." Do the same with the other creatures, giving each particular sound effects or motions.

Jazz it up—expand on it—create a mural or collage—its message should be brought home to every child.

Micro Hikes

Materials:

Strings for each camper, or each two campers (about ten feet, depending on area), hand lenses, pop sticks.

Procedure:

Talk about the smallness of many organisms. Have the children gain an ant's eye view of the world by crawling slowly along the string with the lens close to the ground. Start from a central place and work outward. The kids can mark any interesting discoveries with a pop stick and, after a few minutes, share their discoveries. They must be very thorough, slow and methodical.

Variations:

1. Have them make the string into a circle. Then, with and without the lens, have them discover the wide variety of plants (and animals) to be found within the circle. The string may be of a specified (one square foot?) size.
2. Same procedure as (1), but have them *count* the number of each type of plant or animals.
3. Use twigs to mark off a specified area (one or two feet).
4. Bent coat hangers can also be used.
5. They can classify things observed. Determine the classification by age level of kids or their degree of sophistication.

Example: 1) Living vs. Non-Living
2) Plant, Animal, Mineral
3) Living vs. Dead
4) Natural vs. Man-Made

6. If children like to write, someone could write it up as a little story, e.g., ''An Ant's View of the World'' . . . for publication in camp newsletter.

Million-Year-Old Picnic

Aim:

To demonstrate that many materials are non-biodegradable and will persist in the environment for many, many years.

Materials:

Assemble and keep in shopping bag any or all of the following: aluminum can, glass jar or bottle, aluminum foil tray, paper bag, waxed paper, plastic baggie, plastic fork and spoon, styrofoam cup, paper cup, waxed paper cup, empty plastic potato chip bag, empty can.

Procedure:

Tell the campers you are going to go on a Million-Year-Old Picnic, and carry your shopping bag to a grassy spot. Explain that any food left over from a picnic would either be eaten by an animal or would decay within a short period of time. Then, one by one, pull out the items and have the kids guess how long they think each container will take to decay and return to the soil. Be sure they know what the material is. After all of the items are spread out, challenge them to arrange each item on the grass, in some order that indicates how long it would take to decay.

When complete, try to re-arrange correctly and lead a discussion of littering, waste disposal, over-packaging, etc. Let them choose between alternatives, e.g., should we have our take-out hot drinks in paper or styrofoam cups? Should we wrap our lunches in foil, plastic or waxed paper? What about bottle laws?

Guesstimates of rates of decomposition:

1. paper plate—5 years
2. plastic cup—250 years
3. aluminum can—500 years
4. glass bottle—1 million plus years

You might want to think about three stages people go through in enjoying and using the outdoors.

1. Leave something of yours—debris, graffiti.
2. Souvenir/take it with you.
3. Leave it alone stage.

Perhaps you may want to inscribe and post the motto:

Leave nothing but footprints—
Take nothing but pictures.

(Used by permission of Eileen F. Doocey.)

My _____ Book

A good follow-up activity for theme discussions or achievement sessions. Most suitable for younger children.

Materials:

Oak tag or large construction paper, long white rexo paper, crayons, scissors.

Procedure:

After a theme discussion, the children depict the ideas learned by drawing them and putting the drawings in a booklet. You could create an oak tag pattern for the cover, or all the pages could be cut to that shape, colored and the facts shown. Example: My Butterfly Book.

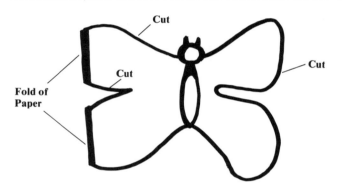

My butterfly book

Page 1 might show a butterfly egg and say that the butterfly lays eggs. Page 2 might show a caterpillar and say that the egg hatched into a caterpillar. Page 3 might show a caterpillar (bigger than on page 2) eating leaves and Page 4 would show a chrysallis. You could do a book for birds, turtles, frogs, trees, flowers, spiders. Be sure that each booklet has facts about the food and shelter needs of that animal so that the children begin to grasp the larger message. These books can be stretched into more than one session, or they can be started in a nature period and finished during rest hour. They can be displayed, or sent home.

Natural Dyeing

This is something that the specialist should experiment with first, because it takes a lot of trial and error and most children want to have quicker success in a camp setting. Perhaps, if there is an optional nature period, work on this with campers as a three or four-step project. It is suitable, too, for older or adult campers. The activity could be split into two to four separate sessions: first, for identifying plants to be used; second, for gathering plant material; third, for mordanting; and last, for dyeing itself. It time doesn't permit a lengthy project, eliminate step one; if need be, gather plants yourself (really not too satisfying); combine steps three and four, and don't dry the mordanted fibers.

Materials:

Hot plate (or other source of heat), rubber gloves, enamel pots, wooden spoon or stirrer, pot holders, sieve, scissors, tongs. Material to be dyed must be 100 percent unbleached cotton or wool. (Mordants are chemicals that are added that allow the fiber to take up the dye. They also change the effect of the dye in various ways.) Wear old clothes.

PLANT MATERIALS TO TRY

Berries/Fruits
Black raspberries
Blueberries
Cherries
Elderberries
Grapes
Pokewood berries
Strawberries

Leaves
Beets
Burdock
Carrots
Lily of the Valley
Plantain
Ragweed
Sumac
Tulip tree
Willow

Flowers
Chrysanthemums
Dahlias
Goldenrod
Hollyhocks
Lilies
Marigolds
Queen Anne's Lace
Zinnias

Roots
Beets
Bloodroot
Cherry
Dandelions
Osage orange
Sassafras
Sorrel

Mordants
Alum
Ammonia
Chrome
Copper Sulfate
Cream of Tartar
Tin
Vinegar

Procedure:

Chop all plant material and place in a pot. Boil for thirty minutes; then strain out the plants. Dissolve the mordant (about one-fourth to one-half teaspoon for every two cups of liquid) in hot water before adding to the solution. Add the mordant and stir well. Or, mordant the skeins first and then dye. Wet the cotton or wool skein first with water as warm as the dye bath. Then, dip it into the dye bath and push it down. Simmer in dye for thirty to sixty minutes; remove, rinse with cold water and hang to dry. Be sure to label each sample with the plant material and mordant used so you can keep track of which plant/mordant creates which color and hue. If the attempts are successful, some older campers might want to try tie-dying shirts or other cloth items.

Two excellent handbooks are available from Brooklyn Botanical Garden (see Appendix):

1. *Dye Plants and Dyeing,* Volume 20, Number 3.
2. *Natural Plant Dyeing,* Volume 29, Number 2

Nature Weaving

Materials:

Corrugated cardboards, cut from cartons with knife, about 8 inches by 8 inches, or larger. Yarn or cord, ruler, scissors. Natural plant material such as grasses, flowers (ones that will dry well, like goldenrod), reeds, twigs, etc.

Procedure:

Measure and mark off one-half inch on top and bottom of cardboard. Using scissors, make slits at the marks. String the up and down columns, catching the string (or yarn) in the slits. Then, weave in and out, first with yarn and then incorporating plants. When completed, tie and remove from cardboard. Use twigs to suspend the weaving as a wall hanging. It is attractive.

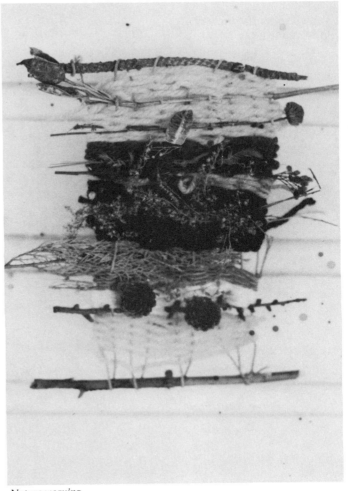

Nature weaving

(Used by permission of Carol Padalino.)

Owl Pellet Study

Owl pellets are fascinating natural objects. If you have a source of them, guard it, because they will be terrific teaching subjects. Use them in your "Guess What's in the Box" lesson, because they are unusual and difficult to discern. Even after handling them and feeling their furriness, unless one knows what the pellets are, observation and touch will not reveal their origin.

When owls eat rodents, they swallow them whole. After their digestive juices digest the flesh of the rodent, the owl's body cannot digest the bones and fur, so these things form a solid mass in the owl's stomach. They are regurgitated by the owl in the form of the pellets. If you have enough for each camper (or have two or three campers share one), owl pellet dissection is a great activity. Using tweezers or a probe, tease the pellet apart. Try to separate the fur and bones—the pellets are perfectly dry and not the least bit smelly or unpleasant. The skulls and bones should be intact and can be reconstructed or laid out in such a way that the rodent it came from is identifiable. Using the skull key or guide, try to figure out:

1. Which rodent(s) the owl ate
2. How many were eaten

All will be surprised to see what is included in this tight little package. Then, children will perhaps understand why the owl is an important friend to the farmer, keeping the farm crops from rodent damage. This is also why it is important not to destroy the places where an owl might have its nest, such as an old, dead tree. Even the *dead* tree is part of the total ecological picture.

If you do not have pellets for kids to take apart, have at least two—one whole and one taken apart, so that children can see for themselves what's inside the pellet.

To enhance this activity, send for the poster *Owl Food*, available from: NSTA, Special Publications, 1742 Connecticut Avenue N.W., Washington, D.C. 20009. Publication #504650. Cost: $1.00.

Sources of owl pellets: Creative Dimensions, Box 1393, Bellingham, WA 98225; Hawks, Owls, and Wildlife, Russell Road, Montgomery, MA 01085, (413) 862-3273.

**Key to Mammals Most Commonly
Found in Barn Owl Pellets**

1. At least nine teeth on each side of upper jaw. (Order Insectivora) 2
1. No more than three teeth on each side of upper jaw; large incisors; canines absent 3

2. Length of skull less than 23 mm; teeth often pigmented a chestnut brown . . . . Shrew
2. Length of skull more than 23 mm; skull has forty-four teeth . . . . . . Mole

3. Two incisors in upper jaw. (order Rodentia) 4
3. Four incisors in upper jaw; two small incisors behind large front incisors. (Order Lagomorpha) . . . . Rabbit

4. Palate extends beyond last molar 5
4. Palate does not extend beyond last molar 6

5. Length of skull more than 22 mm . . . . Rat
5. Length of skull less than 22 mm . . . . House Mouse

6. Molars with flat grinding surfaces . . . . Meadow Vole
6. Molars with rounded cusps; skull length less than 25 mm . . . Deer Mouse

Shrew

Mole

Rat

House Mouse

Meadow Vole

Deer Mouse

(From Addison-Wesley Life Science by Bonnie B. Barr and consulting author Michael B. Leyden. Copyright ©1984 by Addison-Wesley Publishing Company, Inc., Reprinted by permission.)

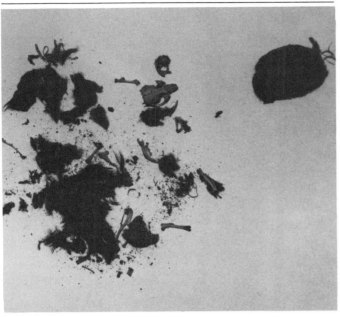

Owl pellets

Peanuts

Peanuts make good subjects for nature study. They're cheap, easily obtained and can be eaten at the conclusion of the activity.

Variation within a species:

Give each camper a peanut. Tell him that this is his peanut and give the group three to five minutes to study their peanuts very thoroughly. Collect all peanuts and mix them up. Ask each person to pick out his own peanut (not too difficult). Discuss variations in configurations that allowed them to identify their own peanuts.

Additional Activity:

This is suitable for a larger group, twelve or more kids. Have the campers measure their peanuts to the nearest one-half cm. On a large sheet of blank newsprint create a histogram, recording with checks or Xs the sizes called out. (See sample diagram below.)

3 cm (largest)	XX
2½ cm	XXX
2 cm (medium)	XXXXXXX
1½ cm	XXXX
1 cm (smallest)	XX

Measuring peanut sizes

OR

½ cm	1 cm	1½ cm	2	2½	3 cm
			X		
		X	X	X	
		X	X	X	
	X	X	X	X	
X	X	X	X	X	X

Note the distribution curve (bell) that may result.

Measuring peanut sizes

Variation:

After the activity, turn the peanuts into peanut people. Decorate with felt, fluff feathers, feet, moveable eyes, paper, etc. Do it around a theme—e.g., "Circus Peanut People" and display the entire set. Or each kid could make and keep his own. Hopefully, for some, looking at their peanut person will recall the lesson on variation within a species.

(Adapted from Exploring Environments by Ruth Yarrow, High Rock Park Conservation Center, Staten, Island, NY.)

Photo Quiz

The purpose of this activity is to make children sharp observers of their environment.

Materials:

Roll of film, camera, large index cards, laminating machine (if available).

Advance Preparation: Walk around camp and take an entire roll of pictures of natural features and areas. Try, as much as possible, to avoid photography of man-made features. Photograph trees, stumps, rocks, views of the lake, the woods, meadows, etc. Get long views and close-ups. Do not photograph transient features, such as flowers. When pictures are developed, mount on large index cards. Number each card on the back and laminate the cards.

Procedure:

Hand out the cards and have kids identify either the place photographed or the place where the photographer stood to get the picture. This may either be done with words (Example: "The path to the lake"), or by actually going to the place depicted. Or the leader may hold up one picture at a time and kids try to identify the place.

Or, another variation would be as a contest, with numbered papers (corresponding to the numbered pictures). You could even become more elaborate and mark each place you stood in with a small, colored paperflag marker and have the kids identify by color each place. This would require much advance preparation, but would be a long, special event, perhaps lasting an entire morning.

Note: If you try to use the same photos year after year, be sure to check that the landscape has not changed too drastically. Trees grow and also die. Actually, this is also a good way to show that the natural world is always changing. Children grow and change; so do other living things.

Picturing Adaptations

This game invites participants to examine ways animals and plants adapt to their environments.

Materials:

Pictures of living things with obvious adaptations, at least one for every pair of participants. *(Ranger Rick* and other nature magazines are good sources.) Index cards, 2 colored marking pens.

Preparation:

For each pictured organism, write a phrase that describes the adaptation on an index card. In another color on a second index card, write how that adaptation enables the organism to survive. When both index cards are matched, they should form a complete sentence.

Examples:

Picture	Adaptation	How it helps organism to survive
Squirrel	A long tail	Helps it keep its balance when jumping through the air
Frog	Bulging eyes on side of its head	Helps it see predators, or prey all around it
Hawk	A hooked beak	Helps it tear up the meat it catches

For the pictures to last, they should be pasted on index cards and laminated or covered with clear contact paper. They may also be color-coded as to easy/hard with colored stick dots. (For the specialist's benefit, to adjust to group ability/age levels).

Procedure:

Spread out the pictures so all can see. Give out the index cards and ask the children to place the card next to the picture it best describes. Continue until all the cards are placed. Then, have the cards read while the pictures are shown. Group discussion should follow, with corrections made as needed.

Suggestion:

Try to keep the pace snappy so that interest doesn't flag. Gear the difficulty of the sets to the age group.

(Adapted from: Exploring Environments by Ruth Yarrow, High Rock Conservation Center, Staten Island, NY.)

Pond or Lake Study

Aim:

To expose children to the diversity of aquatic life; to introduce them to the water as an important habitat. To point up the difference between a lake and a pond—and the reflected difference in the kind of life that lives in each.

Materials:

Dip nets, insect nets, white plastic or enamel pans, strainers, spoons, lenses, small paint brush, small portable microscope, pond or water life guide—plant as well as animal. Optional: plankton net, water scopes [homemade].

Background:

A pond or a lake, if it is healthy, teems with life. The kinds of organisms that live in a water habitat will differ depending on many variables—depth of water, clarity, pH, pollutants, temperature, source of the water, etc. For children, it's just plain *fun* to see what lives in the water. More interested or advanced campers could delve into other aspects of water organisms.

Procedure:

Choose a warm day for this activity. With materials in a carrying basket (allow each camper to hold something!), go to the lake or a pond. On the way, talk about water, clear water, water conservation, breathing through gills, how some insects and all amphibians spend the early stages of their lives in water, aquatic food chains and webs, etc. When you get to the water's edge, have the campers spread out and

Insect life

with dip nets, strainers, etc., carefully search the plants and the detritus (mushy bottom) for organisms. They will be able to see them better, if they observe them against a white background. (Hence, the enamel pan.) Use bug boxes or lenses to get close-up looks. Save a pair of beat-up sneakers so you can wade without stepping in muck. Use the guide books to identify plants and animals discovered. (See Appendix.) Many organisms are microscopic; if you do not bring a good field microscope with you, then be sure to bring a jar full of pond water back with you so that you may place samples under the scope. (Use well slides for live, moving animals.)

Additional Studies: (See Appendix.)

1. Biotic index—you can guage the health of the water by which organisms are present.
2. Make a hay infusion using pond water.
3. Prepare a tank for aquarium and bring back specimens.
4. Send some to the Smithsonian Insect Zoo.

Note: Use insect nets with caution and discretion at water's edge, since kids are careless and will get them wet and/or tear them, thus ruining them for other times. A soft, small paint brush is very useful when removing insect specimens from screens or strainers.

See also "OBIS"—Ponds and Lakes Module 023

Animal Movement in Water
Attract a Fish
Habitats of the Pond
Too Many Mosquitoes
Water Breathers
Water Holes to Mini-Ponds
What Lives Here?

Population Game

Using poker chips to represent available food in the area, youngsters pretend they are deer and go through several generations to discover what happens to their numbers in relation to the given food supply.

Materials:

Plastic baggies and poker chips—enough for ten for each participant. Box or container, long string (30 m), pop sticks (for stakes) marker and newsprint (for writing records).

Procedure:

Count out ten poker chips for each participant and place in a container. Explain to the campers that they will be deer

and their goal is to survive the year by obtaining enough food. The poker chips represent the food, and each deer must obtain at least five chips in order to survive. Set up a string circle (about 10m in diameter) around pop stick stakes (adjust according to size of group) on the grass. Scatter the poker chips within the circle (the deers' feeding grounds); and, at a signal, the deer are to get the food and put it in the baggie. Most or all will get more than the needed five for this round (since there are ten for each player). Now, gather the deer and determine the number of survivors. Record on chart. Put all chips back in container.

You are now ready for Year 2. Since surviving animals reproduce, for each surviving deer, give each another baggie (representing an offspring, another mouth to feed). Do *NOT* increase the number of poker chips (the amount of food). Scatter the food, send the "deer" out to feed; each must still get five chips to survive. Bring the deer back together and count the survivors. Record on the chart. Collect the baggies of all who "died" (did not get enough to survive). Put all chips back in box.

You are now ready for Year 3. Once again, surviving animals reproduce, so those who had two surviving baggies, now get four (always double the number of baggies, one for the surviving adult, one for a single offspring). Those whose deer did not survive should be onlookers. If only one survived, that deer gets two baggies, etc. Repeat the food consumption, tallying and recording.

Go to at least the fourth round (year), and if interest is not flagging, try a fifth. At this point (fourth or fifth), have the campers look at the chart and discuss its implications for food supply vs. population.

	Year 1	Year 2	Year 3	Year 4	Year 5
# Started	10	20	36	38	34
# Survived	10	18	19	17	?
Population game					

The concept to be understood is one of *carrying capacity* of the land; a given area of land can only provide a given amount of food, which is sufficient for only a given number of feeding animals. If more than that maximum capacity survive, there will be insufficient food to sustain the entire population; thus, some will die of starvation.

Note: Children become quite fiercely competitive while doing this activity. You must enforce rules about fighting over food; yet, the idea that fighting over food in short supply *does* break out, becomes an important learning adjunct. Children do not realize what it would mean to be so hungry you'd have to fight for or steal food to stay alive.

(This material has been adapted from OBIS, Outdoor Biological Instructional Strategies, published by Delta Education, Inc., in Nashua, NH. The OBIS program consists of ninety-seven activities similar to the Populations Game. These activities may be obtained from the publisher at Delta Education, Inc., Box M, Nashua, NH 03061.)

Potpourri

Making potpourri is a pleasant activity for girls, primarily. It is an old craft, one that has regained popularity in recent years.

Materials:

Assorted dried leaves and flowers (see list below), essential oils, powdered calamus or orris root (to hold the scent), squares of cloth cut with pinking shears, ribbon cut to size, small plastic spoon(s).

Procedure:

Since the actual making of Potpourri will only take ten to fifteen minutes, it would be wise to talk about the properties of plants and how they have been used over the millenia by people.

1. *As food*—people eat leaves, fruit, stems, flowers, roots, etc., of a variety of plants. Plants are also fed to animals.
2. *As building material*—wood, grass thatch, cork, bamboo
3. *As fuel*—wood, coal
4. *For cloth*—cotton, linen, hemp, rayon
5. *Chemical products*—plastics, paints, rubber
6. *Paper*—from reeds (papyrus), wood
7. *Drugs*—aspirin from willow bark, quinine, penicillin, etc.
8. *Scents, perfumes*—essences and oils are made from flowers and are the ingredients of all commercial perfumes.

Herbs and spices are used to add flavorings to food and have been used for centuries; they were also used to preserve food before refrigeration. It was the search for precious spices that was, in fact, responsible for the discovery of the New World. Use the displayed Smell Jars. Herbal remedies of the past (and now coming back into use) include:

—Oil of *pennyroyal* is an effective repellent of fleas and ticks. Rub into pet fur.
—Oil of *citronella* is a mosquito repellent.
—*Rosemary* or *hyssop*, steeped like tea and cooled in the refrigerator, is good for insect bites and stings.
—*Bay leaves* steeped and strained into a hot tub relax muscles .

(Don't pooh-pooh these old remedies. Remember, penicillin comes from mold and old wives put moldy bread on infections!)

For a moth proofer/insect repellent sachet, you'll need to buy the following:

1. Calendula flowers, ½ lb.
2. French lavender, ½ lb.
3. Uva Ursi petals, ½ lb.
4. Calamus root, 4 oz.
5. French lavender oil, 1 bottle

For each sachet, measure one-fourth teaspoon of first three items, one-eighth teaspoon calamus root and two drops oil. Mix in a paper cup. Place in a six-inch square cloth, and tie with an attractive ribbon.

Pressing and Drying Flowers

Flower pressing serves several purposes; it is decorative, educational, and enjoyable. The flowers must be gathered and this gives the gatherers a mission with a specific goal. Only flowers without thick central parts can be pressed. Pressed flowers may then be used scientifically—labeling, identifying, mounting, like a catalog or herbarium collection. Or, pressed flowers can be used in a decorative way. They may be arranged as pictures, or in a mold for plastic or plaster of Paris. Or kids could use them on note paper or put them between pieces of clear contact paper. There is a botany press made for this purpose, but heavy magazines or books will serve as well. The plants or flowers must be placed between sheets of blank newsprint paper so the moisture is absorbed.

If you will be working with girls, you may wish to try more elaborate dried flower projects and you may want to press flowers in the spring in preparation for summer projects. Pansies will press well and make attractive framed pictures. Don't forget also to press leaves and stems, not just flowers, if you wish to use them in decorative pictures.

Flower drying is a related technique which is used for either scientific or artistic purposes. See the books on this subject for details. Some plants may be dried by hanging upside down; just tie in bunches and suspend from a nail or line in a dry place. Others need silica gel, or a mixture of borax and corn meal. Experiment. Some flowers may be dried in a slow (150°F.) oven. Practice on floral decorations you get at home to see what kinds of flowers may be preserved this way. The dried flowers may be stuck into florist's foam, and put in bowls, or made into pictures using felt circles in drapery rings or on cedar shakes. Or they may be molded with liquid plastic. Check crafts catalogues for suggestions. Goldenrod, Yarrow and Pearly Everlasting are good plants for drying. They are abundant, and look nice when dry. (See page 41, this section.)

Predator and Prey

In this activity, the participants take the roles of predators and prey. Predators must learn to move silently to catch the prey. The prey must rely totally on their sense of hearing to detect and stop the approaching predators.

Preparation:

Choose a fairly open, level site such as a lawn, field, forest clearing or vacant lot. Dry leaves and other plant litter make the best stalking surfaces but most anywhere will work. Get the group into a large circle.

Action:

Introduce the game by defining predator and prey, if these terms are new to the group. A *predator* is an animal that catches and eats other animals. A *prey* is an animal that is captured and eaten by another animal. Ask the group for examples of predators that stalk their prey, such as wolves, owls, foxes, etc.

Outline the game rules to the participants:

1. One member of the group is the prey; the others are predators.
2. The prey stands in the center of the circle with a blindfold on and ears uncovered.
3. Now, one member of the circle is silently chosen by the leader as the predator. As the predator silently stalks the prey, he should pause between each step to see if the prey has pinpointed him. This is the prey's protection—listening for the approaching predator and pinpointing him with his finger. Point out that since in this game the prey cannot run away, the pause between steps takes the place of an escape response by the prey.

Variations:

Before playing any variation of the game, ask the group to predict the outcome.

1. Simulate a hearing loss due to injury or age by placing cotton in the prey's ear or ears.
2. Play the game on different types of walking surfaces, up or downhill, quiet or noisy.
3. Have them get down on their hands and feet to simulate four-legged animals.

Reflect with your group on how difficult it may be for a predator to get a meal that day—that he may, in fact, go hungry for many days; or that the chances of survival of the prey are usually slim. Ask the participants how they would change their bodies to be more effective as predators or as prey.

Follow-Up:

Challenge the group to see how close they can get to various animals. Encourage the kids to watch animals stalking their prey—cats and birds, birds and worms or insects, etc.

(Game by J. Yaitch, Jamestown Audubon Society. Use by permission.)

Rock Creatures

Interesting or smooth rocks are lovely objects in themselves. If rocks are plentiful, you may want to use them in crafts activities. Rock creatures—rocks may be glued together using rubber or silicone sealer. Or, mix white glue with powdered cement to hold them together. Add bits of fabric, felt and moveable eyes for features. Make the creatures realistic or imaginary. An excellent variation of this idea uses the pits of peaches or apricots for creatures. Or, you could recycle styrofoam and create creatures this way. (See OBIS "Invent-An-Animal.")

Rotting Log Investigation

On a hike in the woods, often the decaying stump or log is dismissed too readily when it really offers a rich source of nature activities. Thus, rather than make this example of visible decomposition a side investigation, make it the focus of the day's activities, challenging campers to discover all the things that live in, on or under it and how these organisms interact to break down the once-living tree into re-usable components.

Materials:

Hand lenses (one per camper), bug boxes, field guides (especially non-flowering plants), small penlight, hand mirrors, penknife, clipboard with sheet and pencils. Optional: pre-printed sheet for recording observations.

Investigating a rotting log

Procedure:

Scout the area beforehand and locate either one large fallen and decaying log, or a few smaller ones near each other. (Stumps will also be good.) This way the group can split into smaller teams for careful investigation. Direct the campers *beforehand* to look for both plant and animal life. Have them look on, under and inside the spaces (use flashlight and mirror for this) of the log. Each team of three or four can have a sheet and clipboard on which to record their observations. They should look for fungi, lichens, sawdust, borings, mosses, seedlings, tooth marks, exoskeletons, seed cases, nut shells, holes, webs, pupa cases. Lift the log gently and look underneath to see who lives there, and why. Be sure to put the log down gently so as not to disturb the dwellers. The entire focus of this investigation should be *discovery*.

Summarize the activity by calling the groups together and having them share their lists. Point out how the combination of actions by plants (especially fungi) and animals and weather factors, ultimately causes the total breakdown of the tree into rich soil that supports other life while it decays and afterward.

Sample Chart:

PLANTS		ANIMALS	
What?	Where found?	What?	Where found?
GREEN		LIVING THERE	
NON-GREEN		EVIDENCE OF	

What's in the rotting log

Saran Aquaria

Aim:

To use a crafts activity to depict underwater life.

Materials:

Fish and other marine creature cut-out silhouettes for tracing, scissors, holepunch, markers or crayons, pre-cut colored paper strips, stapler, string, colored construction paper.

Procedure:

Have the children use the cut-outs to trace fish, crayfish, water snakes, tadpoles, snails, etc., onto colored construc-

Saran aquaria

tion paper. Draw scales, eyes and other highlights. Cut colored circles, using the hole punch, for air bubbles. Cut green squiggles for underwater plants.

Assemble the picture on the bottom half of a cut piece of plastic wrap. Fold the top half down over the cut-outs and press so that it clings. Use the cut paper strips to create a frame. Suspend the aquaria with string to display, or put near a window so that light passes through.

Scavenger Hunt

A Scavenger Hunt is best done at the end of the summer since the campers need to know *what* every item is and also *where* it is likely to be found. Here is a sample. Rules and lists must be adjusted to your exact situation. Only items actually *taught* should be on the list. Provide the necessary equipment. For pre-school children, you can add pictures to help them know what they're looking for.

Rules:

Each group must be accompanied by a counselor. Campers will have a certain amount of time to collect as many of the objects on the list as possible. All are to return to the nature shack at the time agreed upon. The winning team will be determined by the nature specialist. All animals are to be *alive*. The nature shack is off-limits. Nothing is to be damaged.

1. Apple (from a tree)
2. Bird feather
3. Bird's nest, empty
4. Blueberries—one dozen
5. Clam shell
6. Grasshopper
7. Earthworm
8. Evergreen cone
9. Ferns—2 kinds
10. Flowers—Bouncing Bet, Queen Anne's Lace, Daisy
11. Lichen
12. Milkweed pod
13. Moss—2 different kinds
14. Moth cocoon
15. Moth, *or* butterfly
16. Mushroom
17. Red elf salamander
18. Seeds from three different plants
19. Spider
20. Tree leaves—red maple, silver maple, sycamore

Additional items:
Something smooth, something bumpy (or rough).

Sealed World

The Sealed World is both a display and an activity. It should be put together as an activity with a group early in the summer and then left as a display for the remainder.

Children should be encouraged to observe it periodically, to see if the plant(s) and animal(s) appear healthy. The Sealed World is what others call a balanced aquarium—where all the elements—plants as producers, fish as consumers, and a snail as scavenger—carry out their life processes in the presence of sunlight for photosynthesis. Gases are exchanged and food produced within the miniature world. Nothing comes in or goes out—just as on the Earth. Thus, the Sealed World serves as a model of the balances of life on Earth.

Materials:

A one-gallon, wide-mouth glass jar with lid, small amount of sandy soil or 1½-inch aquarium gravel, pond water, four or five water plants such as eel grass or elodea, one snail, two minnows (not more than one-inch long), paraffin.

Sealed world

Procedure:

Put sandy soil or aquarium gravel in bottom of jar. Push plant roots into it. Fill with pond water to within two inches of top. Allow one week for soil, water and plants to settle. Then, add snail and minnows. Be sure to screw lid on jar, then pour melted paraffin all around lid to seal it. Use a cardboard collar to keep paraffin above the water level so that light can get through and children can observe. Put the jar in good light but *not* in direct sunlight.

Sensory experiences

Variations:

Do a similar set-up but vary the number of plants, fish and snails. Each different group could do one, and they could be arranged side by side for comparison.

Example:

1 minnow — 5 plants — 1 snail
3 minnows — 2 plants — 1 snail
4 minnows — 2 plants — 2 snails
2 minnows — 1 plant — 1 snail

Be sure to label each and make weekly observations. If and when death occurs, discuss why and what the implications are for our own really Sealed World. (Nothing comes from outside, everything remains.)

(From a Manual for Leadership Training in Outdoor Education, 1970, High Rock Park, Staten Island, New York, and Olivia Hansen. Used by permission.)

Sensory Experiences

Children should be encouraged to use all of their senses in their nature contacts. In addition to feely boxes, a session (or several) can be devoted to feeling various objects, both in and out of doors. Out of doors, feel bark, plant stems, leaves, rocks, animals. Have the children use their cheeks, the back of their hands, even their toes at the lake.

For indoors or grassy lawn sessions, try these. Sew little cloth bags, or use small paper bags. Put a few objects in each bag, and give each child one of his own. Try a bird feather, an acorn, or a peanut, etc. Without looking into the bag, feel one object. Can it be identified just by touch? A similar activity involves using all of the senses to identify a specific individual of a group, i.e., *your* peanut, *your* pebble or rock, *your* feather or leaf. Give each child one. Have him examine it carefully, feel it, smell it, turn it over on all sides, rub it on his cheek. Then, collect and pool them and see if kids can pick out their own. The message of this lesson is although there are distinguishing characteristics of a species (like peanuts, or even people), there are also *variations* within a population that makes one different from another. This is true of rocks and robins and is readily observed in humans.

Another variation is: the smells and/or the tastes of nature. Flowers, leaves, mushrooms, soil. (Note: tasting should be limited to *known* plants.)

Sensing and Sorting

Concept or Skill: Classifying is a way of understanding nature.

Materials:

Yarn for circles.

Procedure:

Each person is to collect three different objects (natural and man-made). Then they are to join in groups of six campers to decide on how to divide the eighteen objects. They may decide to divide by color, texture, function, origin, etc. They may use circles of yarn to help them classify their objects.

Variation:

Have kids group *themselves* and have others guess what the grouping characteristic is, e.g., hair color, size, clothing items.

Skull Keying

In this activity, campers closely examine animal skulls to figure out what animal it was. If they are especially interested, they can also create their own skull keys, using their own observations and research material.

Materials:

Animal skulls that were found and carefully preserved, and/or prepared skulls purchased commercially. (See Scientific supply houses in Appendix.) Each skull should be numbered.

Preparation:

If you buy the skulls, you will know what they are beforehand; but you should not reveal the identity to the campers. If you use found skulls, you will have to determine their identity. Found skulls may also be very fragile and should be sprayed with clear shellac or plastic to protect them.

Procedure:

Depending on number of skulls available in ratio to campers, have campers carefully look at skulls. (No more than three to a skull.) They should note and discuss the location of the eye-sockets, which are different in various species. Let the campers use photographs of the animals to compare the eyes on live animals with the skulls. Have them measure the length and width, though this can be misleading because a young specimen may be smaller than an adult. Note the ear holes, and nose openings. Note any seams on the top of the skull where the bone fused. The dentition (teeth) of the skull is the definitive way in which the identify of the animal is determined, since tooth structure is a reflection of eating habits (see ''Skulldugger Among the Mammals,'' p. 111).

Using whatever specimens you have, allow the campers to create a key, taking into account such factors as overall size, position and size of eye sockets, number and kind of teeth and whatever other distinguishing features can be discovered.

Suggested Skulls to Use:

Mouse or rat—herbivore/rodent; mole or shrew—insectivore; rabbit, squirrel—herbivores; cat or fox—carnivores; raccoon or skunk—omnivores.

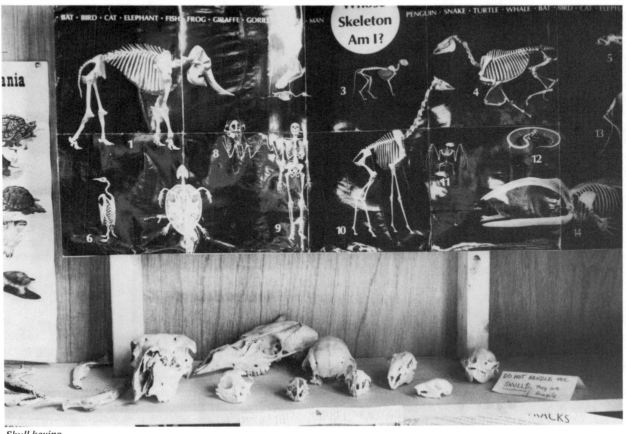

Skull keying

Soil Investigation

Aim:

To show children that soil is an important natural resource which must not be taken for granted and should be protected and conserved.

Materials:

Trowels, screens or strainers, jars, white enamel or other white pan, lenses, baggies, tweezers.

Procedure:

Discuss the role of soil in our lives; its importance in food. Ask them, "What is soil?" They'll say, "dirt" and so ask, "What is dirt?" Take the children to an area where the leaf litter is plentiful. With children looking on, move the top layer of leaf litter aside. Point out that the layer underneath still resembles leaves, but less so. Be sure to mention that the top layer is last summer's leaves, and the next layer is the summer before's and so on. Keep moving leaf layers away and note that each layer resembles leaves less and less. You'll reach a level where the litter is no longer leaf but now is soil. Place some of the litter in enamel pans so children can observe against a white background. If they don't raise the crucial question, "How did the leaves *become* soil?", then you have to pose it. Using lenses, screens, trowels and tweezers, tease some of the litter at each level apart (in the pans). Try to locate and identify any animals you will find. Children will notice and ask about the white thread-like "things" on the leaves (the mycelia of fungi). They may also comment on the wetness and dark color. Have them smell it and describe the smell.

From this experience, the campers should understand that soil is created from leaf and plant litter by animals who physically break down the material and by the action of bacteria and fungi decomposing the material physically and chemically. They should also see that rain and snow aid this process. Children could try to duplicate the making of soil by chopping, crumbling leaves, and rubbing stones. But even through the pieces may become smaller (physical change), the chemical change requires the action of those special agents.

You may wish to take a vertical profile by digging straight down with a flat spade and cutting out a sample, placing the specimen in a large jar or fish tank, so that the layers may be *viewed* through the glass sides. Another activity is to set up a Berlese funnel (see Appendix) to see what creatures live in soil. You will need a microscope to see many of the minute ones that have emerged.

Spatter Prints

Materials:

Empty cigar boxes, or wooden boxes of cigar box dimensions (may also be larger to accommodate an 8½ inch by 11

inch piece of paper), metal screening, nails or upholstery tacks, masking tape (½ inch), tempera paint, toothbrushes.

Procedure:

Cut the screening one-half inch larger than box opening (both dimensions). That will allow a one-fourth inch overlap. Cover raw edges with masking tape so that they are safe. Fold down over edge of box and secure with tacks. The boxes should be open at one end to permit paper and leaves to be slipped in and out.

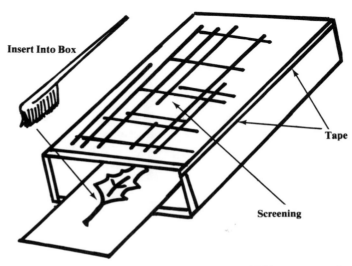

Making a spatter print

To make the spatter prints, place leaf or leaves on paper. Weight with pebbles or rocks that do not overlap edge of leaf. Pass the paper with leaf through opening of box. Dip toothbrush in tempera, allow excess to drip off and scrub back and fourth over screen to get the desired effect.

Variations:

Without the box, experiment by putting leaf and paper on newspaper on floor or grass and allowing paint to drop off a brush; or, scrape a dull knife along toothbrush bristles. Try dipping a sponge in tempera and going around edge of leaf. This outlines the leaf in an interesting pattern.

Spore Prints

A good follow up to a mushroom hunt. Cut the cap off the mushroom. Put it down on a piece of paper. Cover the mushroom and paper with an inverted jar. The next day, you'll have a spore print. To preserve it, carefully (from a distance, and tilting down) spray it with clear, acrylic spray. Some mushrooms have light-colored spores, some dark, so do two of the same mushroom, one on a dark background, one on a light background.

Spore prints

Drying Mushrooms with Silica Gel

Put Silica gel in a plastic container. Bury the stem of the mushroom in it. Pour more silica gel on top, until the mushroom is buried. Cover the container and allow to stand for several days. The mushroom will lose some of its shape and texture, but may be used for display or identification purposes.

Note: Silica gel may be re-used many times. First, pour it through a fine sieve or strainer. Then, heat it in oven at 350° for about an hour. Put it into a container that can be tightly closed as soon as it is removed from the oven.

Spraying Spider Webs

There are two ways to spray spider webs.

A. One is to use a watering mister spray, which can be adjusted to produce a fine spray. This makes a spider's web visible and causes no damage to the web. This method is used to examine and study the structure and location of webs, after spiders have been discussed. Aversion to spiders should be overcome, as they play an important role as predators of insect pests.
B. Webs may also be sprayed with spray paint, but this destroys them. Chase the spider away so as not to kill it with the paint. After you have sprayed the web and while it's still wet, place a piece of contrasting colored construction paper under and behind it and bring the paper gently toward you. Catch the supporting struts first and then the rest. You may have to repeat this several times in various locations before you are successful since it is difficult to do.

Method A is suitable as an activity to do with youngsters, leading a walk devoted to discovering about spiders—where they live, how they earn their living and catch their prey, etc.

Method B is suitable for preparing a display of a real spider's web and should only be done by the specialist and for that purpose. Be careful also, not to spray surrounding structures with unwanted colors. For example, many webs may be found under buildings. If the building is *white,* be sure to use white spray paint so any paint that gets on the building matches. Many spiders also construct their webs on the lakeside docks just above the water. The orb weavers make the most interesting and beautiful webs. Night time may reveal the nocturnal arthropod weaving its engineering trap. Caught against a light, the construction can provide a fascinating study in intricacy. (See reference booklet *Spiders,* Cornell Study Leaflet.) Caution: Some spiders do have poisonous stings.

Sunprints

A great activity, lots of fun, and fascinating to watch. Pick a bright, sunshiny day for best results.

Materials:

Light-sensitive paper—either blueprint paper or ozalid paper. (Photographic print paper may also be used, but it's more expensive and not as dramatic.) Clear glass sheet, such as a picture frame or window pane.

Developer—water with a drop of hydrogen peroxide for blueprint paper; household ammonia, not the sudsy kind, for ozalid. Put it in a plastic gallon jar made light-tight by painting with flat-black paint. Small rocks on the bottom of the jar and a piece of screening on top of the rocks keep the developing paper out of the liquid ammonia. Also a collection of cardboard animal shapes and silhouettes, traced and cut out. (Keep track of these, in a box, because they have multiple uses.) Piece of cardboard or plywood (to act as a tray or holder).

Making a sunprint

Procedure:

The children recreate a habitat, using animal cut-outs (taking turns, if necessary) and real plants. Have them select plants that cast a distinct shadow. Keep the paper covered until ready to use. You may wish to cut the paper in half, as it is quite expensive. Have the children create an interesting (and as far as possible, correct) picture of plants and animals

Sunprints

Sunprints

in a habitat (flying birds in air, etc.). One at a time, place the paper with its picture on the piece of wood. Cover with the clean glass and expose to sunlight. The yellow ozalid paper will turn white—except where the silhouettes are—in five to fifteen seconds. Take the entire package inside (or into the shade), shake off the plants and cut-outs and put the paper in the developer. After a few minutes (seconds for blueprint), remove. Hang them to dry—use clothespin and string. The finished product may be mounted and/or framed.

Task Cards

Concept:

To sharpen observation skills; awareness of differences in plant structures.

Materials:

Index cards with clues written on it.

Examples:

Find a plant with a square ☐ stem.
Find a plant with a triangular △ stem.
Find a plant with a round O stem.
Find a plant with a fuzzy stem.
Find a plant with fuzzy leaves.
Find a plant with thorns.

Find a seed with prickles.
Find a seed that's fuzzy.
Find a seed with wings.
Find a twig with something growing on it.

Procedure:

Give out cards to campers in teams of two. Have them try to locate the items. When they have, they may select a second card (if there are any left). Be sure to leave enough time for sharing the plants found. Allow each camper to handle and examine each specimen to make sure all see each sample.

Terraria

Terraria should be miniature versions of a particular habitat. They may be done in a variety of ways:

1. Individual terraria, made in rose bowls. Each camper makes his own and can keep it (eight years and up).
2. One large one may be made, using a fish tank. (You can use a leaking or even cracked tank, since it will not be filled with water.) This is a group activity.

Put pebbles or rocks for drainage in the bottom. Cover this with a layer of (activated) charcoal, which will keep it from becoming moldy. Briquets will do if activated charcoal

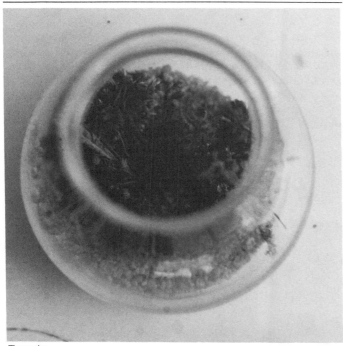

Terraria

is not available. Cover this with a layer of soil. Include rocks to look like boulders and to provide an interesting landscape. If making a large terrarium, build up some parts, slope others. You may wish to sink a small dish for a pool, especially if you are putting in frogs or other amphibians.

Place bits of moss, with soil, lichen and other small plants which have been dug up with their roots intact. Include ferns, if possible. If you want to put in a salamander, add damp sphagnum moss. Arrange artistically and with variety. Fill in spaces with rocks, pieces of wood or bark. Any gathered material that is not used should be returned to wherever it came from.

When you are satisfied with its appearance, spray the landscape with a mister and cover. For individual bowls, cover with clean plastic wrap, held in place with rubber bands; elastic circles that are used to hold braids make good holders. For larger terraria, you may cover with glass; or, if you leave it open, you will have to spray periodically to replenish the moisture that will evaporate. Covered terraria collect moisture and demonstrate the water-cycle in nature, but the moisture that collects obscures the view and they become less attractive. Choose whichever suits your purpose. *Note:* DO NOT overwater. Prune or remove overgrown plants.

Place it in indirect light, north or northwest window. Some suitable plants for terraria are: small ferns, mosses, lichens, club mosses, seedling trees, wintergreen, wild straw-

Terraria

berries, hepatica, violets, partridge berry. Suitable animals include: small frogs and toads, salamanders, earthworms, crickets and grasshoppers. Feed the toads and frogs only two to three times a week. Crickets and grasshoppers will eat bits of apple, lettuce, moist bread. If you keep animals, you must be alert to the removal of accumulated wastes that may rot or dirty the dish-pool; this is especially true if the terrarium is covered. Experiment on your own to see what will be attractive, interesting and not too hard to maintain.

Territorial Tag

Materials:

Three or four sets of trunk-type tags, with wires, preferably in colors; with a description of places written on them.

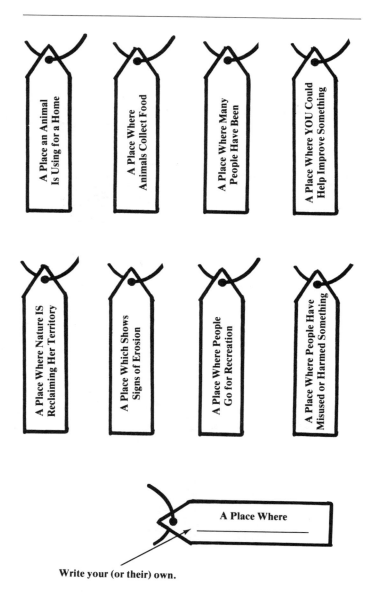

A Place an Animal Is Using for a Home

A Place Where Animals Collect Food

A Place Where Many People Have Been

A Place Where YOU Could Help Improve Something

A Place Where Nature IS Reclaiming Her Territory

A Place Which Shows Signs of Erosion

A Place Where People Go for Recreation

A Place Where People Have Misused or Harmed Something

A Place Where _____

Write your (or their) own.

Procedures:

Divide group into three or four players. Give each team a complete set of all the tags. Set a time and area limit and give general rules. Each group is to find and tag as many things as possible. A team may not tag something already tagged. When all tags have been used or time limit has passed, re-group. Walk around the area as each group shares and defends its discovery and placement. Collect all the tags as you go, so they may be re-used (and so as not to litter).

(From Girl Scout Leader, October 1977. Copyright Girl Scouts of U.S.A.; reprinted as adapted by permission.)

Theme Discussions

Aim:

To have the children focus in on a particular natural family; to demonstrate the order that exists in nature.

Procedure:

Assemble, close at hand, all the materials, displays, specimens, that pertain to the topic you've chosen.

Example: Birds

Nests, feathers, bird call records, bird picture displays, stuffed specimens. Devote the entire activity period to a discussion of birds, pass around the nests, talk about how birds build nests, what they use, where they locate them. Look at bird feathers; show how they are different, get one under the microscope; talk about birds' flight, their bones, their metabolism. Talk about their food needs. Discuss migration. Play some bird calls. Point out the distinguishing features. Show how some birds may be identified by how they walk or perch, or how they fly. Follow up the discussion by some art work (see "My _____ Book" earlier in this section).

Other suggested topics for themes:

Flowers
Frogs and toads
Insects—ants, bees, butterflies, moths, wasps
Lichen
Metamorphosis
Mosses
Mushrooms and Fungi
Reptiles
Spiders
Trees

This could also be two parts: one period for discussion, one for a theme field walk.

Theme discussion: birds

Toothpick Camouflage Hunt

The purpose of this activity is to demonstrate how protective coloration (camouflage) acts to protect organisms from predation.

Materials:

Fifty flat or round wooden toothpicks painted with tempera or food coloring (beforehand) in five different colors—green, brown, yellow, red, blue. (When preparing, paint more than fifty, especially of the brown and green because they'll never be found.) Rope about thirty to thirty-five meters. Newsprint and markers for a chart. (Optional supplementary material—Poster set "How Animals Hide").

Procedure:

Count out the fifty toothpicks with the campers looking on—ten of each color. Make a large circle, about ten meters in diameter, with the rope, on a grassy place, or other flat area. Scatter the fifty toothpicks within the circle in a random fashion. The children stand around the perimeter. At a signal, they pick up as many toothpicks as possible in a two-minute time period. (Shorten the time if necessary.) Count each color retrieved and record on chart.

Example:

Red	Blue	Green	Yellow	Brown
9	8	5	10	4

A complete chart might look like the above. Lead a discussion on why this should be. Talk about the most common colors prey animals come in—and how this allows them to blend into and disappear in the background they live in. Follow up by trying to locate the animals hidden in the posters depicting various habitats.

Variations:

1. Colored pipe cleaners or yarn, cut into short lengths, may be substituted for toothpicks.
2. Discuss survival value of just the opposite kind of protective coloration as seen in skunks, monarchs and other brightly colored animals. They *announce* their presence because they have other means of protection.

3. Discuss mimicry as demonstrated by the Viceroy and other insects which gain protection by imitating the appearance of other species.
4. See *OBIS*—"Invent an Animal."
5. Try the same activity on a packed dirt area (ballfield, parking lot) with same group immediately after. Observe the differences.

Touch-Me-Nots/Jewelweed

Jewelweed (Impatiens capensis, Impatiens pallida) also known as Touch-Me-Nots, members of the Balsaminaceae family, grow in profusion in wet places. They present an excellent means of teaching seed dispersal adaptation because they propel their seeds explosively when the mature seed capsule is touched. Campers of all ages love to look for and find the plant so they can feel the pop and see the seeds ejected as they are touched.

Look for this lovely flower on the campus or on a hike. Explain beforehand that many plants have interesting mechanisms to disperse their seeds. Why this is a desirable adaptation that has evolved for plant survival can also be discussed. The effectiveness of a particular mechanism can account for the success of the plant. The slightest touch will trigger the propulsion in the case of the Jewelweed. The fat seed capsules will be present on the same plants as the flowers at the same time so they are easy to find. Direct the campers to touch the seed pod; it will pop and throw out its tiny, pale turquoise seeds. After everyone gets a turn, encourage them to use hand lenses or bug boxes to investigate the spring-like mechanism that is responsible for the propelling action. The spring will rapidly uncurl and these curls will remain in your hand, together with the seeds if you enclose the whole seed in your hand before allowing the seeds to pop.

Track Casting

Aim:

To identify the wildlife that lives in the area by their footprints.

Materials:

Plaster of Paris (the fast-setting kind) in empty coffee cans with lid, spoons, pop sticks, marking pen, plastic container (gallon or one-half gallon) or large jar with water, trowel.

Preparations:

The area where animal tracks may be found must be scouted in advance. Look on the side (shoulder) of dirt roads, especially near a water source, like a pond or stream. Look for bird tracks, deer prints, raccoons, etc. After a rainfall is a good time to look for the tracks when the ground may be muddy or spongy. If no tracks are found, try creating a track area by making a smooth mud-covered place so that when animals do go by (on their way to drink, for example), they

will leave their tracks. You may have to leave the immediate camp area to find evidence of animals because many animals will not approach places where humans live.

Track casting

Procedure:

Carrying all of the materials, set out with the campers to find the tracks. Although you should lead them to the area where the tracks will be found, let the campers do the finding. You may need to encourage them by talking about Indian's tracking animals or by calling attention to the first track. Once you show them what to look for, the rest must be theirs. When each camper finds a suitable track, have each mark it by sticking a pop stick, with his name on it, next to the track.

Next, mix the plaster by pouring some (one to two tablespoons) into a paper cup and gradually adding water and stirring until it is the consistency of heavy sour cream. Pour the plaster into a track. Do one or two at a time. Depending on weather conditions, the plaster should harden with the track acting as a mold. When it has hardened, dig up track with dirt around it. If and when plaster track is fully hardened, brush off dirt; you may use a toothbrush to remove remainder of dirt.

Note: Do not do this activity in damp weather, or in wet mud. Unmixed plaster of Paris cannot freeze over the winter since it loses its ability to set.

Tree Bingo

Great way to learn the trees and have fun.

Materials:

Play as regular bingo with some modifications. Two versions: easy and hard. The easy version would consist of leaves and fruit of tree that the campers are *familiar* with. Examples: apple, white pine cone, acorn, pine needles, spruce leaves, etc. (Different for every locale.) The hard version would include the ones on the easy card plus all of the others. (See Appendix for instructions.)

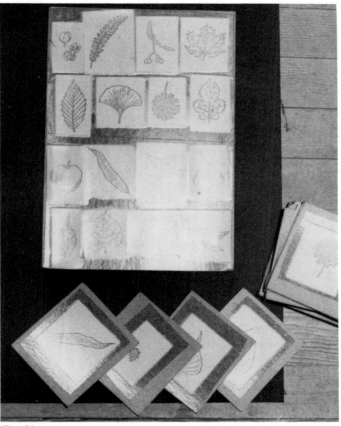

Tree bingo

Another modification is to gradually make the calls more challenging. Example: for the first few rounds, say the name of the tree and its part (leaf or fruit) and show the calling card. Children just have to match up the pictures. The next level of difficulty is to say the name of the tree and its part and display the real thing (the acorn, apple, leaves, pods), only showing the card if kids need to see it. The third level of difficulty (a goal you're reaching for), would be just say the name of the tree and its part, and have the children be able to locate its picture from only its name. Some campers are capable of this, but this skill must be built over a period of

years. Prizes for each round can be the National Wildlife Federation stickers.

(This game was developed by Catherine Pessino and Barbara Neal of the Alexander N. White Nature Center of the American Museum of Natural History.)

Water Habitat Aquarium

Prepare a five, ten, or twenty gallon tank by washing it out with clean water. (If you use soap, be sure to rinse it completely, as traces of it may kill the organisms.) *Note:* If the water is too heavily chlorinated, be sure to allow the chlorine to dissipate by drying the tank in the sun. Put washed gravel on the bottom of the tank; bring buckets or gallon jars of pond or lake water and place in tank. Set up an air pump with bubble-stone aerator, and put in the specimens you've caught. Include aquatic plants in reconstructing the habitat. A light should illuminate the water for viewing, and also provide the light needed by the plants for photosynthesis; however, these are not tropical fish and do not need heated water. Feed commerical fish food, available in pet stores. A few grains of yeast every day will provide food for tiny organisms. If the fish are not active, release them. Be aware that some animals will prey on others in the tank.

Alternative:

If the landscape allows, an interesting project may be undertaken by a group with the specialist's supervision. A portion of the lake or pond, such as a small cove, may be caged to create an observation habitat area.

An activity for younger children would be to use little plastic Dynamint boxes. Peel or soak off the labels. Try WD-40 if the label sticks. The boxes become micro-miniaquaria, to be used with a lens to see what lives in it.

What Is It?

A good first lesson to interest children and to introduce them to the specimens in the nature shack.

Materials:

A cardboard box in which a variety of natural objects have been placed. Select some items that are obvious—a bird's feather, an acorn, a rock, others that are esoteric—an owl pellet; cicada exoskeleton. Try to pick things that can be handled and passed around.

Procedure:

Have the children sit in a circle. Pass around the objects, one at a time. Give each child a chance to examine it, without calling out or saying what it is. When all have had the chance to look, have them tell what it is; or, if they don't know, turn it into a "20 Questions" game. Is it living, once

living or never living? Is it plant or animal? Try to intrigue or pique curiosity. Use the opportunity to point out the oddities and interesting facts. Example: notice the hair lining the bird's nest. What kind of hair do you suppose it is? Where did the bird get it? Why did she put it in the nest?

Suggested items:

Cocoon	Paper wasp nest
Empty insect exoskeleton	Preying mantis egg case
Nest	Snake skin
Large gall	Unusual mushroom
Owl pellet	

Who Am I?

An enjoyable activity for younger children.

Materials:

Animal cards with holes punched and string, long enough to fit over camper's head, attached. You may purchase the cards, or cut and mount pictures from magazines. (Yard sales often have the cards.)

Procedure:

This is a good game to play out of doors, with the chilren sitting in a large circle on the grass. Explain to the children that you will be placing animal cards on their backs, and they are not to peek to see what animal it is. Place the string over their heads so that the picture of the animal hangs down and is visible on the child's back. When all the cards have been distributed, ask for a volunteer to be first. The child walks around the inside of the circle so that all the others can see what animal is depicted. Then, the questioning begins. This phase may be done in several ways.

1. If the children are older, and knowledgeable about animals, then the one who is "It" may ask the questions, e.g., "Am I a mammal?" "Do I live in the water?" Do I have six legs?" Like "20 Questions," with only yes or no answers possible.
2. For younger children, children in the circle can provide clues, one at a time until the one who is "It" realizes what animal is depicted. Example: "You have a big trunk." "You spin a web." The problem with this way of playing is that the participants make the clues too obvious and the person gets it too quickly, and the game loses its excitement. You may have to direct the clue-giving by providing the first few, less obvious clues. Example: For an elephant, rather than saying "You have a long trunk," a less obvious, more subtle clue might be "You are the largest land mammal." After you've given a few, let the campers take over so the game isn't too hard.

Both ways may be scored by counting the number of clues needed to guess "Who Am I" and the one who needed the

fewest clues would be the winner. Collect and carefully count all the cards.

Variation:

Hang the cards so that they are visible in front of the campers. The naturalist asks questions about the animals in a "who is it?" format. For example: Who has tusks? Who swims the fastest?

Sample Programs

On the following pages are sample programs, divided by age level. This schedule assumes two periods of nature a week through age eleven, and one period a week for ages twelve and older. The schedules are merely suggestions; to plan your program effectively, the specialist must custom-design it to fit the interests of the campers and the camp's facilities and philosophy. Note that each schedule, except for preschool age, plans for Nature Achievement Stripe and includes gardening. It is not intended to be complete. Please refer to OBIS modules for additional activities. By keeping certain activities exclusive to a particular age level, you avoid the "Oh-we-did-that-last-year" syndrome. If your camp has a Visitor's Day, you may also want to present an especially exciting activity. The chickens may be hatching at that time, so that's quite exciting. Or, "Tree Bingo" engrosses the children and is especially good for a hot day because it can be played out of doors under a tree.

Knowing in advance what you will be doing at each given time is vital to a successful program. Many activities require materials, setting up and other preparation. Waiting for kids to come in and then saying, "Well, what shall we do today?" is a waste of precious time and leads to disorganization. That is not to say that kids must have a highly structured activity every time they come to nature. The shack, as well as the program, should be flexible and allow for variances while, at the same time, be prepared for a specific activity.

Some time should be set aside for every group and every camper to look at displays, handle and examine things, ask questions, leaf through books, play with puzzles and games, etc. If the shack is open during free play time, this would be an opportune time for those campers who are most interested and excited by the nature program to satisfy their curiosity. They may wish to cuddle or care for animals, find out answers to questions, or try some of the challenges you've set forth.

Sample Program Schedule

Three to Five Year Olds

1. Introduction to nature—rules, *Ranger Rick* pledge, feely box, specimens.
2. Seed planting—each child to have his own plant to care for and keep at summer's end. Discuss needs of plants, what plants are used for. Plant marigolds, grass seed, bird seed, alfalfa seeds, etc. Look at seeds in an apple, an orange, etc.

Week 2
3. Viewing chicken eggs. Read aloud *A Chick Hatches*.
4. Decorating the Bird Tree. Bird day. Nests, eggs.

Week 3
5. Gardening—pulling weeds.
6. Spiders—looking for webs, using a mister, songs, like Eentsy-Weentsy Spider.

Week 4
7. Sensory experiences, activities.
8. Active Games—Simon Sez, Squirrel in a Tree

Week 5
9. Flannel Board Habitat—The Forest
10. Caterpillar Day—search, make from egg cartons.

Week 6
11. Butterfly Day—My Butterfly Book, or tissue paper butterflies.
12. Flannel Board Habitat—The Pond.

Week 7
13. Bark Rubbings; Adopt-A-Tree or Leaf Rubbings, Leaf Scrapbook.
14. Dramatic play—The Giving Tree

Week 8
15. Gardening—harvesting.
16. Picture Scavenger Hunt.

Sample Program Schedule

Ages Five, Six, Seven

Week 1
1. Introduction; go over and explain rules, recite *Ranger Rick* Pledge, show specimens, play "What Is It?"
2. Egg candling, feely boxes, Adopt-A-Tree.

Week 2
3. Read *A Chick Hatches*, candle eggs again. Talk about other kinds of birds. Make My Bird Book or My Chicken Book.
4. Begin Stripe Achievement—Leaves of trees (by walking around camp). Follow-up with leaf rubbings. Make My Tree Book.

Week 3
5. Continue Stripe Achievement—Wildflowers (by walking around camp).
6. Weeding in garden

Week 4
7. Who Am I?
8. Stripe Achievement—Birds

Week 5
9. Saran Aquaria or Hootie, the Owl.
10. Stripe achievement—conclusion—pledge.

Week 6
11. Box Concentration.
12. Bingo—National Wildlife Federation Stamps or Nature Impressions.

Week 7
13. Discovery Walk
14. Harvesting in Garden

Week 8
15. Half- (or all-) day hike, with picnic.
16. Scavenger Hunt

Sample Program Schedule

Ages Eight to Nine

Week 1
1. Learn *Ranger Rick* Pledge—introduction—specimens. What Is It?
2. Discovery Walk, spittlebugs.

Week 2
3. Egg-candling. Adopt-A-Tree, Bark and Leaf Rubbings.
4. Picturing Adaptations (easy version).

Week 3
5. Tree Bingo.
6. Weeding in garden.

Week 4
7. Bird-in-Egg (coincide with chick hatching).
8. Strip—begin. Trees.

Week 5
9. Stripe—flowers.
10. Stripe—birds and pledge (conclude).

Week 6
11. Find Your Mate. Find Your Tree.
12. The Lorax

Week 7
13. Peanut People/Peanut Study
14. Harvest in garden.

Week 8
15. All-day hike. Try Adjective Game.
16. Scavenger Hunt

OR any of the following

Planting seeds (Week 1)
Color Cards
Theme talks—Frogs, Tadpoles
Flowers make seeds—seed search
Ant hunt—making an ant house
Aphid/ant search
Mystery Marauders (OBIS)
Plant printing
Spider search, web search

Ages Ten to Eleven

This is usually an age group with many campers and just about the most receptive to nature activity. They have the intellectual skills and ability needed to carry out the activities and they have the interest and curiosity. The group, therefore, can be divided in half (or even thirds) and the activitiy groups can be split into ten-year-olds and eleven-year-olds. Add the following activities for the older half so that next year, campers will not be jaded and activities will be new.

A Better Fly Trap, *OBIS*
Aquaria construction
Bird feeder building
Corn Husk Dolls
Counting Populations
Dot Adaptations
Creating an Ecology Web
"Envirolopes", *OBIS*
Gall search ("Swell Homes", *OBIS*)
Grocery Store
"Hopper Circus", *OBIS*
Insect hunt and mount
Lichen looking
Litmus Making and Testing
Picturing Adaptations (harder)
Metamorphosis (mealworms)
"Moisture Makers", *OBIS*
Mushroom hunt
"Populations Game", *OBIS*
Sealed World
Touch-Me-Nots/Jewelweed
Spatter Prints
Spraying Spider Webs
Sunprints (clear day)
Terraria
Tree Bingo (harder)

Sample Program Schedule

Ages Ten to Eleven

Week 1
1. Toothpick Hunt, egg candling.
2. Animal tracking.

Week 2
3. Stripe Achievement—flowers, trees.
4. Stripe Achievement—birds, pledge.

Week 3
5. Weeding in garden.
6. Task Cards or Envirolopes.

Week 4
7. Flower Discussion, followed by seed search.
8. Leaf Soup Relay.

Week 5
9. Theme walk—Gall Search ("Swell Homes," *OBIS*).
10. Territorial Tag.

Week 6
11. Photo Quiz.
12. Harvest in garden.

Week 7
13. Natural Weaving.
14. Million-Year-Old Picnic.

Week 8
15. Predator-Prey.
16. Scavenger Hunt.

Sample Program Schedule

Ages Twelve to Thirteen

1. Stripe Achievement (all in one session).
2. Egg candling. Hay infusion set up or flower pressing.
3. Hay infusion examination (microscopic).
4. Weeding in garden.
5. Animal dissection (or owl pellet dissection or potpourri).
6. Quadrat census ("Bean Bugs", *OBIS*)
7. Soil investigation or all day hike.
8. Garden harvest or berry picking.

OR

Discovery walk
Dried flower bowls
"Follow the Scent", *OBIS*
Insect hunting and mounting
"Moisture Makers", *OBIS*
Photo quiz
"Population Game", *OBIS*
Theme walk—lichens, mosses, and other non-flowering plants
Tree Bingo

Sample Program Schedule

Ages Fourteen to Fifteen

1. Stripe Achievement—all parts in one session. Egg candling.
2. Flower picking and pressing or animal dissection.
3. Weeding in garden.
4. Bones and Straws.
5. Owl Pellet Study/Skull Keying.
6. Natural Dyeing.
7. Garden harvest, or berry picking.
8. Flower Pictures (using pressed plants) or all-day hike.

Sample Program Schedule

Mature Adults

The following schedule is based on a two-week session, with Nature programmed every other day and lasting between one and two hours.

1. Discovery Walk—with or without a theme.
2. Concept Games—Dot Adaptation; Picturing Adaptations; "Envirolopes" (OBIS).
3. Natural Dyeing or Weaving (Crafts).
4. Bones and Straws, Population Game, Toothpick Camouflage (Concepts).
5. Nature Crafts—Leaf Prints, Leafy Skeletons, Spatter Prints.
6. Tree Bingo (harder version) or Pond Study.
7. All-day (or half-day) Hike.

Adapt according to weather, physical ability level of campers, need or desire for sedentary vs. active, craft vs. intellectual pursuit. Tailor to meet needs and desires of particular group.

SECTION IV. Mixed Bag

Participatory Activities

One of the best ways to promote a conservation ethic is by setting and living the example. If campers can see their own role in the larger picture, then they will come to understand that each person is one link in the ecological chain. Naturally, you must show that insects are not to be stepped on, unless they pose a threat. Likewise, flowers that are the only specimens of their kind in a given area should not be picked. Birds and squirrels are not targets for rocks, nor should other animals be teased or manhandled. Tree trunks are not for carving nor are the branches for swinging. Respect for living and non-living things in the environment must permeate all you do and teach (without preaching).

Another way to promote a healthy attitude toward the environment is by direct participation in a variety of activities. Many scientists need the cooperation of persons to assist in their acquisition of knowledge. For example, the Laboratory of Ornithology at Cornell University has an on-going nesting bird study. With the cooperation of people all over the country, who keep records of which birds are nesting where, they then feed the data collected into computers and determine answers to questions of habitat, range, endangerment, etc. The items (see sample card on following page) are not very technical, and an older child is capable of handling the information requested. If birds are nesting at a place in camp where these observations may be readily made, this could be a great activity for interested campers (perhaps best done as an optional activity for one or two campers).

Knowledge gained from such studies has been responsible for rescuing such species as peregrine falcons from near-extinction. To participate, write to: Laboratory of Ornithology, Cornell University, 159 Sapsucker Woods Road, Ithaca, New York 14853. Request information and cards for their North American Nest Record Card Program.

Another on-going scientific research project that depends on data input from diverse areas of the country that children can also participate in is the Insect Migration Research study being conducted by the University of Toronto. Using evidence gathered, entomologists were able to trace the migration patterns of the Monarch butterflies. Campers can participate by either catching or raising, then releasing, tagged butterflies. The miniature tags are numbered and are on sticky paper. The butterfly (or moth) is gently held, a tiny area of scales scraped, and the tag stuck on. The time and place of release is recorded and the insect is then released. If and when a numbered specimen is found, the minute writing instructs the finder to notify the University of Toronto where and when it was seen. Thus, migratory patterns are tracked. This activity may even be carried out after the camp season is over, since some butterflies may not have hatched by then. Send pupae, tags and instructions (and a postcard addressed to you, with spaces for the data—number, sex, date and place released) home with *responsible* campers. See the section on Animals in Chapter II for instructions on how to find and raise Monarch butterflies. Write to: Professor F. Urquhart, Scarborough College, University of Toronto, West Hill, Ontario, Canada, MIC 1A4. Request a membership form as a research associate in the insect migration study. They will ask for a small donation and will mail the tags and instructions. It is an exciting and rewarding activity for campers and for you.

Bird nesting study

No. Col. 1-12 (Col. 2-14, side 1)	13	If used for colonial nesting check here ☐ and see instructions

	DATE		Eggs	Young	Edit	Build-ing	Adult On	COMMENTS
	Month	Day						Stage of building, if eggs warm, age of young, if banded, etc.

OUTCOME INCLUDING CASES WHERE OUTCOME UNKNOWN (circle where appropriate)

01 Unknown because not revisited
02 Young seen leaving nest
03 Parent(s) excited near nest
04 Parent(s) with young near nest
05 Nest empty, intact
06 Nest empty, damaged

07 Nest deserted
08 Failure due to weather
09 Failure due to predation
10 Failure due to invertebrate parasites
11 Failure due to cowbirds

12 Failure due to competition with other species
13 Failure due to human activities
14 Failure due to pesticides (give details separately)
15 Other (describe above)

	76	77

Please complete both sides and return at end of season to your Regional Center or to Laboratory of Ornithology, Cornell University, Ithaca, New York 14850. We thank you for contributing your time and efforts to this program.

	78	79	80
			2

Bird nesting study

Another participatory program that is exciting for campers is the Insect Zoo program at the Smithsonian Institution in Washington, D.C. They maintain a fascinating zoo collection of live insects and are continuously in need of fresh specimens. Write to: The National Museum of Natural History, Smithsonian Institution, NHB Stop 101—The Insect Zoo, Washington, D.C. 20560. Request a list of the specimens that they want; they will send mailing instructions and mailing labels. Then, take a group of campers on a "bring 'em back alive!" safari to collect specimens. The campers can participate in packing and mailing, too. Ask the zoo to send an acknowledgement so the campers will get the positive feed-back on their role.

Become members of Audubon Adventures, a service for youngsters, conducted by National Audubon Society from their center in Greenwich, CT. Though designed primarily for classroom use, the ten monthly issues could be accumulated and sent in bulk to a participating camp. Use one per week. Members receive a packet of individual newsletters written for ages eight to twelve, a teacher's guide, decals, and memberships cards. The advantage of camper participation in such a program is that it fosters a sense of belonging to a collective group who appreciate and love nature and who seek others of a similar outlook to enhance their enjoyment and to encourage the protection of the natural environment. For further information, write to: National Audubon Society, 613 Riversville Rd., Greenwich, CT 06830.

The Sigma Chemical Company utilizes fireflies in producing luciferin and luciferase for scientific research. The chemicals are derived from the luminous tails of the fireflies and serve as indicators for the presence of living tissue. It is used in diverse experiments such as cancer cell growth studies, polluted water, and to detect life in space. In the past, they were paying one cent apiece for the fireflies. Contact them for information and instructions: Sigma Firefly Scientists Club, 3500 De Kalb Street, St. Louis, Missouri 63118.

Contact a nearby university or college. Perhaps someone in the biology department could utilize the campers in their reserch. By taking part in scientific and environmental experiments as active participants, young people are gaining their first experiences as activists—those who do. Hopefully, this attitude will carry over to their adult lives, when their activism will serve to protect the environment. Be alert to other opportunities to participate with children in experiences they will remember.

Working with Others in Camp

The necessity for maintaining any relationship in camp is based on cooperation and interdependency. In addition to the day-to-day relationships that exist in a camp setting (always more intense than a regular working relationship because you eat three meals a day together and live closely with your co-workers), there are special relationships with other members of the camp staff whose cooperation is essential to the success of the nature program.

Naturally, the camp director or administrator must be responsive to the nature specialist and the needs of the program. They must be supportive of your efforts and allow you the freedom to try new projects or be flexible within the limitations of camp policy. They must see to it that counselors and campers display the proper attitude toward you and your program. (*You* are ultimately responsible for the attitude developed—but administration helps to set the tone and establish beginnings). On the other hand, you must be responsive to the needs of camp directors and administrators. If it rains, and they need to send campers to you instead of to swimming or tennis, and you're doubled up in time or number, you must understand and be flexible. Or, if you are asked to do an evening program, don't examine the fine print in your contract to see if it's required of you. Camp is a cooperative effort; and, as long as you're not being taken advantage of, be flexible.

Try to include the counselors and unit heads in your programs and activities. Their help may be needed for supervision; and, by interesting them in what you do, you will gain important assistance. Be sure you have the chance to address the staff at orientation sessions held prior to camp opening, so you can establish what is expected in the way of cooperation. Nature learning may occur when they are at other activities (e.g., insects, birds, or other animals and plants may be observed during a sports activity). Show the counselor how to act when kids excitedly point out something. Discuss with them the need not to demonstrate aversion to snakes, bats, spiders, insects, etc. Encourage them to come to you with questions and to actively participate in the nature program.

Another very important group of staff is the maintenance and grounds crew. If you plan to do any gardening, you will need to depend on the maintenance or grounds crew to start the garden and take care of it until camp begins. In addition, they may have to do much of the weeding and other chores if you are unable to get around to it. They will have to prepare the pens to receive animals and may have to assist you with animal care. If there is a carpentry shop, you may depend on their know-how to construct animal shelters and other wooden items. The shavings produced in the shop can serve as litter for small mammals—guinea pigs, gerbils, hamsters and mice. (Why buy litter when you can utilize the free shavings?) Thus, you will be working very closely with and be dependent on the maintenance crew. Therefore, try to anticipate your needs so that you do not impose difficult deadlines. Many emergencies arise in camp; and, by being ahead of the game and reasonable in your requests, your needs will also be satisfied. Since many of the people who are employed in that capacity will probably be year-round residents, they may also be a rich source of information for you. They may locate and save paper wasps' nests, cut and saw wood for future projects, clean and put up bird houses in the spring. They will also possess nature knowledge that comes from living close to it. They'll know more about the handling and care of farm animals, and they'll be knowledgeable about many plants. They'll be able to identify many local birds and other animals. Look upon these people as a resource, and you'll be rewarded with decent, friendly relationships that may endure, year after year.

Most specialty counselors never get to see the inside of the camp kitchen. However, the nature specialist must work closely with the kitchen staff. First, you need to get food for the animals—rabbits and guinea pigs like to eat lettuce and other greens and love apples. Goats may also eat fresh vegetables, but you have to try many foods with goats. Thus, you will be in the kitchen every morning to pick up food; a good time to do this is immediately after your own breakfast. In addition, certain projects you may wish to do with the campers may require that the kitchen save things such as melon seeds (for stringing or collage), suet (meat fat) for your bird feeder, corn husks (for corn husk dolls or weaving projects).

And, if you will be gardening, the kitchen may serve what is harvested. They may have to cook some vegetables, too. If you pick blueberries, the cook might bake them into muffins, or make pancakes, syrup, or tarts. Thus, you will need to maintain a good working relationship with the kitchen staff. Keep in mind that their job is to provide the meals for the camp—anything they do for you is a favor. So, as far as possible, do the work yourself (e.g., washing freshly picked lettuce, peeling cucumbers, etc.). Better still, this kind of work should be done with campers in a communal effort, with everyone participating.

You may also need secretarial work done (stencils cut for contests, collating). Be sure to give advance notice, so no one feels pressured. You may need to share materials with the arts and crafts specialist; that is mutually beneficial.

The general rule, then, is to understand all camp staff have their own jobs to perform. Camp is a cooperative venture and being pleasant, willing to share, and not overly demanding will go a long way to allow the camp to function more smoothly and with less hassle. You will benefit by keeping this understanding in mind when dealing with other staff.

Besides other camp staff, you may find that you will have to deal with local residents. They may include the local Audubon person, the game warden (conservation officer), veterinarian, storeowners, camp neighbors, and farmers. Start and keep a file with the names and phone numbers so you will have quick access should the need arise to contact any of them. Remember, in your dealings with any of these people, you are representing a camp.

The Teachable Moment

"In the fields of observation, chance favors only the mind that is prepared."

LOUIS PASTEUR

So much of nature is unpredictable that one needs to be constantly alert to the teaching possibilities that present themselves in the course of the summer. The best preparation for seizing the teachable moment and capitalizing on it is to be observant of the natural happenings and to always ask yourself the question "How can I use this occurrence in my program?" Since these events cannot be predicted, I can only try to alert you to possibilities that may turn up (or ones that did turn up for me), and show you how I utilized them. (Some were potentially or actually disastrous, but were nevertheless, learning experiences.)

1. *Rainbows.* If you are fortunate to witness the exquisite phenomenon of the rainbow, be certain to seize the opportunity to share this experience with the campers. Knowing how and under what circumstances rainbows occur will make the likelihood of your seeing one greater. During, or immediately after a rainstorm, if the sun should start to shine, look for one—you may even be blessed with the spectacular sight of the double rainbow. In 1981, such a rainbow lasted for half an hour, at a convenient time, when the entire camp was headed for the social hall. Even though it was after dinner, I called the headquarters on the intercom phone and had the double rainbow announced on the loudspeaker. This way, everyone at camp, indoors and out, was alerted. Cameras clicked; oohs and aahs were expressed. At that point, silent contemplation of its beauty was sufficient. The next day, during nature time, it was discussed, its causes explained and a prism demonstrated. The younger children (up to age ten) drew pictures of it. For many, the mental image was indelibly printed.

2. *Bee Swarm.* When a beehive gets too crowded, scouts search for another site. Then, about half of the hive (several thousand bees) leave the hive to take up housekeeping at the new site. The swarm may temporarily alight on a tree or fence post to rest and collect its members. One summer, such a swarm collected on a tree outside of the dining room just before lunchtime. The call for the nature specialist went out; seeing the swarm, I seized the moment and ran to get the telescope and all available binoculars. Setting the telescope at a safe distance from the swarm and focusing directly at it enabled every person in camp to peer into this teeming mass and to witness firsthand an unusual behavior by unusual social creatures. (A professional beekeeper was called; he removed the swarm by locating the queen and placing her in a box with a hole. Within an hour, all the rest had followed her into the box, and he carted the load off to his apiary!)

3. *Mud Wasp Nest.* A female mud-wasp started to build her nest on a painted sign on the porch of the nature shack. Instead of swatting her off, I set up barriers and put up a sign with an arrow, describing what was happening. Unfortunately, a few days later, a camper accidentally knocked the nest down. When the now dry and brittle clay nest shattered and its contents were strewn on the porch floor, we used that opportunity to observe firsthand what we had heretofore only read about in books about wasps: that the female paralyzes spiders and other insects, then places them inside the nest so that when she lays her eggs, the hatching larvae have fresh meat to eat. There were live, but paralyzed spiders within, awaiting their fate as food for wasp larvae.

4. *Tadpoles in a Puddle.* On an all-day hike, some distance from camp, we came upon a puddle with hundreds of tiny tadpoles in it. Realizing that the puddle would soon dry out and the tadpoles with it, I returned to the site with a pick-up truck and filled two pails full of water and tadpoles. I released some in a pond, put some in a tank, and since there were so many, put two or so in small bowls and gave each cabin a bowl with food in a small cup plus instructions on how to take care of them and what to look for. What I did not realize and only found out later, to my dismay, was that these particular kinds of tadpoles became frogs within two or three days—just about the time it would have taken the puddle to dry up. As a result of my lack of awareness, many of the new frogs drowned because they passed from gill to lung stage rapidly and had no means of getting air from their bowls. We all learned a valuable lesson: people, even well-intentioned, should not always interfere with nature's plans. Somehow, the adult frogs were able to gauge that the size of the puddle was just right and would dry up at just the right time to enable their offspring to have a solid perch from which to raise their heads to breathe in air above the water.

These four instances are intended to demonstrate how the daily phenomenon of nature may be incorporated into an effective nature program. The nature specialist must be always alert and make the other members of the staff, as well as campers, aware of the natural happenings around them. It may require that you make yourself available at non-program hours to interpret happenings and to exploit an occurrence. If you demonstrate an openness and enthusiasm, children and staff will run to you to report sightings—birds fallen out of nests, fascinating mushrooms growing in odd places, creatures behaving in interesting ways, flowers in bloom—making the constant presence of the natural world felt and perceived.

Pregnancy in Twenty Mammal Species

Here are the number of days in the pregnancies of some mammals.

1.	African elephant	640	11.	Honey Badger	180
2.	Rhinoceros	560	12.	Panther	93
3.	Giraffe	450	13.	Cat	64
4.	Porpoise	360	14.	Dog	64
5.	Horse	337	15.	Fox	54
6.	Cow	280	16.	Kangaroo	40
7.	Orangutan	275	17.	Rabbit	31
8.	Human being	267	18.	House Mouse	19
9.	Reindeer	246	19.	Hamster	16
10.	Polar Bear	240	20.	Opossum	13

This list could be used in a variety of ways:

1. List and post by itself.
2. List and post with pictures of animals obtained from nature magazines, or Safari cards.
3. Paste or draw picture of animal on card, put number on back to turn it into a guessing game.
4. Paste or draw picture of animal with lift-up card for display/game.
5. Write name of animal (or picture) on one index card, numbers on another. Have campers try to match, or arrange in ascending or descending order.
6. Use as a starting point for discussion. How are numbers of days related to such factors as size? Which ones of the mammals are more highly developed at birth? Which ones

are more dependent and/or undeveloped? Compare human's gestation period with the others (#8). A good time to carry out this discussion or play as a game would be if and when one of the small mammals you keep in the nature shack either shows signs of pregnancy or gives birth. (If you keep mice, gerbils or hamsters, this is likely to happen during the camp season.)

Reproduction is a source of endless fascination for all ages and its discussion belongs in the nature shack with the nature specialist, an important interpreter of its biology.

Quotables

Poets and writers are capable of expressing important thoughts with effective words. In turn, their words often have profound effects on those who read or hear them. The nature specialist should share these quotables with campers in a variety of ways. If you are a calligrapher or can persuade someone on camp staff who is to inscribe them, do so. They should be posted in the nature shack or on the bulletin board. Perhaps there could be a quote of the week. It could go in a camp newspaper or in a camper's scrapbook. Or each could be accompanied by an appropriate photograph of nature, taken from the popular magazines such as *Audubon, Wildlife,* or *Natural History* and mounted. Following are a few samples of some for you to ponder, others more suitable for campers.

Sample Quotations To Be Used by Nature Specialists

"If you think ahead one year, plant a seed.
If you think ahead 10 years, plant a tree.
If you think ahead 100 years, educate the people."
KUAN-TSU 3RD CENTURY B.C.

"In the early years we are not to teach nature as a science, we are not to teach it primarily for drill, we are to teach it for loving."
LIBERTY HYDE BAILEY

"Nature Study . . . consists of simple truthful observations that may, like beads on a string, finally be threaded upon the understanding and thus held together as a logical and harmonious whole."
ANNA BOTSFORD COMSTOCK

"It is not enough to take people out of doors. We must also teach them to enjoy it."
ERNEST THOMPSON SETON

For Display for Campers

"Whatever befalls the earth, befalls the sons of the earth. Man did not weave the web of life; he is merely a strand in it. Whatever he does to the web, he does to himself."
CHIEF SEATTLE, 1854

"We travel together, passengers on a little spaceship, dependent on its vulnerable reserves of air and soil; all committed for our safety to its security and peace; preserved from annihilation only by the care, the work and the love we give our fragile craft."
ADLAI STEVENSON

"One touch of nature makes the whole world kin."
WILLIAM SHAKESPEARE

"Hurt not the earth, neither the sea, nor the trees."
REVELATIONS 7:3

"Nature has made neither sun nor air nor waves private property: they are public gifts."
OVID

"Everything is hitched to everything else."
BARRY COMMONER

Sometimes, youngsters (and adults) need to be jarred into examining their own behavior so that they can see the negative consequences. Although a nature specialist will not want to emphasize the negatives, neither should one close one's eyes to the ugliness created by litter or graffiti. To that end, one could post prominently a photograph of "people pollution," with a question, "Is this how *you* leave a picnic site?" This will make a point without lecturing or belaboring. It is complicated for a child to understand that wasting electricity or overconsumption is the indirect cause of acid rain. There's a place (small) for this approach in a camp nature program.

Pledges

The National Wildlife Federation Creed

I pledge myself, as a responsible human, to assume my share of man's stewardship of our natural resources.

I will use my share with gratitude, without greed or waste.

I will respect the rights of others and abide by the law.

I will support the sound management of the resources we use, the restoration of the resources we have despoiled, and the safe-keeping of significant resources for posterity.

I will never forget that life and beauty, wealth and progress, depend on how wisely man uses these gifts . . . the soil, the water, the air, the minerals, the plant life, and the wildlife.

Ranger Rick Pledge

(also known as National Wildlife Federation Junior Pledge)

I pledge to use my eyes to see the beauty of all outdoors.

I pledge to train my mind to learn the importance of nature.

I pledge to use my hands to protect soil, water, woods and wildlife.

And, by my good example, to show others how to respect, properly use and enjoy our natural resources.

I give my pledge as an American to save and faithfully to defend from waste the Natural Resources of my country—its soil and minerals, its forests, waters and wildlife.

Audubon Junior Pledge

As a citizen of my country, I pledge myself to try in every way I can, to conserve its natural resources: its soil, water, plants and wildlife, and to protect them from harm and waste.

MOTTO: (when traveling or hiking through natural areas)

Take nothing but pictures,
Leave nothing but footprints.

Declaration of Interdependence

We the people of the planet Earth
With respect for the dignity of each human life,
With concern for future generations,
With growing appreciation of our relationship to our environment
With recognition of limits to our resources
And with need for adequate food, air, water, shelter, protection, justice and self-fulfillment
Hereby declare our interdependence
And resolve to work together in peace and in harmony with our environment
To enhance the quality of life everywhere.

Dr. Russell W. Peterson, President
National Audubon Society

Animals Come in Odd Bunches

Although not frequently heard in conversation, these terms are the correct way of describing the animals listed, according to the author.

1. a murder of crows
2. a clowder of cats
3. a leap of leopards
4. a sloth of bears
5. a rafter of turkeys
6. a smack of jellyfish
7. a skulk of foxes
8. a labor of moles
9. a peep of chickens
10. a crash of rhinoceroses
11. a paddling of ducks
12. a siege of herons
13. a rag of colts
14. a drift of hogs
15. a charm of finches
16. a trip of goats
17. a knot of toads
18. a shrewdness of apes
19. a parliament of owls
20. a troop of kangaroos
21. a gaggle of geese
22. a pride of lions
23. a watch of nightingales
24. a muster of peacocks
25. an exaltation of larks

(From An Exaltation of Larks by James Lipton. Copyright © 1968, 1977 by James Lipton. Used by permission of Viking Penguin Inc.)

This list can be used in a variety of ways:

1. Print on individual index cards with group name on front and animal name on back.

A skulk of . . .	foxes

2. These cards could be displayed under photographs of the animal, with a "Lift up for the answers" for self-directed learning. Print answer upside down.

3. Or print on two separate index cards and try to match in a game.

4. Or, discuss (with mature campers) how or why these terms might have come about; some are obvious, others more obscure.

5. The list could just be copied and displayed in the nature shack for reading and fun.

Competitions, Achievements, and Contests

Nature Achievements

Is there a place for passing minimum standards for achievements in nature in a camp setting? The answer to this question, first of all, must be guided by camp policy which is set by the camp director and carried out by the staff. My philosophy is that reaching for some goal or standard is a motivational force that causes humans to strive for it. The swimming program, for example, awards Beginner, Intermediate and Advanced swimmers cards for each level achieved, and the camper is required to demonstrate mastery of certain strokes to attain the level.

This is also true in nature study. The nature specialist needs to be careful not to place too much emphasis on this aspect nor act as a taskmaster. It is better to attempt to show how a camper can learn about the order which exists in the natural world and begin to understand it.

A sample achievement might be to demonstrate the ability to identify (from the area's specimens) flowers, trees, and birds. The campers in the nature program may also be required to recite the Ranger Rick pledge. It can be more easily memorized after it has been explained and understood by the campers; the Ranger Rick pledge speaks in a language children can understand. For the youngest campers, every nature session can begin with the recitation of the pledge.

The number of trees, flowers, birds (maybe insects?) to be learned is geared to the age level of the campers.

For:		
	5-7 year olds—	3 of each
	8-9 year olds—	5 of each
	10-11 year olds—	7 of each
	12-13 year olds—	8 of each
	14-15 year olds—	10 of each

This arrangement is totally flexible and can be altered to suit the intelligence and interest of the campers. If you plan to conduct achievements, describe these at the first session. Older campers may want to get it done as soon as possible. They can often complete the entire series in one 45-minute session. It may be wiser to launch achivement at about the third or fourth session, so that campers will view the nature They can often complete the entire series in one 45-minute session. Allow "old" campers to teach new campers. (This is important because it illustrates an excellent teaching technique. Kids are proud to show others what they've learned and to assume the role as teacher. It may be wiser to launch achievement at about the third or fourth session, so that campers will view the nature shack as a place of excitement rather than as a school.

Following are teacher suggestions for the challenge items.

Wild Flowers

Fresh wildflowers should always be on display, in a vase or homemade holder (see Appendix). The common names of the flowers should be displayed along with them. Teach each flower, pointing out the feature that gives that flower its distinctive character and often its name. This will help the child to associate the name of the flower with the way it looks.

Examples:

Daylilies—bloom and remain open only one day, hence their name. Any specimen you pick that has several flowers on it will have some open, some not yet opened, and some already withered and closed.

Yarrow (which is often confused with Queen Anne's lace)

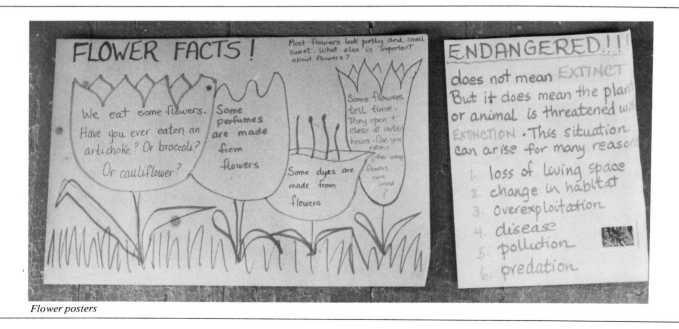

Flower posters

point out the leaves which are distinctively feathery, like the feathers on an arrow and that rhymes with Yarrow.

Buttercup—shiny reflective yellow petal, hold it under your chin . . . you like butter!

Heal-All—The native Americans used it as a healing herb for cuts and wounds.

Refer to the book, *How to Know the Wildflowers,* by Mrs. William Starr Dana. Use it to help you use mnemonic devices.

For the one or two youngest groups, go out and find and pick the flowers with them. Bring them back. Do it that way so they can see the flower in its habitat. This also provides you with the opportunity to discuss when and under what conditions one is permitted to pick wildflowers.

Trees

Use Audubon Tree cards; cut the names off the bottom. A better way is to use the actual leaves, dried and pressed within clear contact paper. Try to choose trees found in the area.

Begin by teaching the major divisions by which trees are identified:

Evergreen vs. deciduous
Simple vs. compound
Alternate vs. opposite

Tree identification

Leaf display

As in flowers, try to grasp the distinctive feature of each and emphasize that feature; use mnemonic devices or stories that assist in memory.

Example:

The *gingko* is the only remaining species of a once prevalent family, now extinct. The gingkos we have in this country were originally brought here from China. The leaf resembles a *Chinese fan*. When the person sees the fan-shaped leaf, they remember the story and the name.

The *mulberry* leaf is asymmetrical and irregular. Trace the edge as you go "All Around the Mulberry Bush."

Once again, for younger groups, go out of doors walking around to the actual trees, showing the leaves, bark, general configuration, anything noteworthy, e.g., peely bark of sycamore, fuzziness of leaf. Take the leaves off wild cherry, and have them rub the leaf gently on their cheeks to note its extremely smooth surface. Crush a twig and have them smell the pungent cyanide gas. This tactile and olfactory experience helps to reinforce the identity of the tree. It may take a bit of research on your part, but it will enhance your own knowledge of the local trees. Whatever method *you* use to remember the tree, pass it on to the youngsters.

The youngest campers enjoy making leaf rubbings (with fat, uncovered crayons) of the leaves they can now identify. This is a good culmination for the leaf challenge; they can put each on a page (newsprint), write its name, fold and put together with staples or punch holes and have a booklet, "My Leaf Book," to keep or send home. Middle-agers may do the same, or use paint (or water-bsed printer's ink), and brayers for leaf prints or spatter prints, made by scraping a paint-dipped toothbrush across screening. (See Spatter Prints in the Activities section.)

Birds

Live specimens are not available; and, unless you've luckily inherited someone's stuffed bird collection, you will have to use pictures, paintings or photographs. Use Audubon cards or charts with names deleted; try to select birds they will see in camp (or at home). Point out distinctive features— a crest, color, beak, size. The bird's name might be related to its physical characteristics. The *red-winged blackbird* is a black bird with red patches on its wings. Some are named for their song as well (e.g. the yellow warbler). Some may be identified by postural or behavioral characteristics. Woodpeckers are often found on the trunks of trees, tapping away. Some may be identified by flight pattern or silhouette. Read the backs of the Audubon cards for information you can translate for associating the name with the bird. Some

Bird display

children (and adults) are word-oriented, others are ear (sound) oriented. The Audible Audubon or other bird song recordings may help, since many birds are heard well before they are seen. Try to learn the songs and calls each bird makes.

The category of Insects can be used for an achievement with a method similar, i.e., using dried or living specimens, if available. If not, pictures would have to be substituted.

A list should be kept of every camper and a record of their successful achievement by means of checks or color-coded dots. Their final task is to be able to recite, from memory, the *Ranger Rick* conservation pledge (or another one). Achievement awards can be announced at campfires, services, or in the dining room—wherever it is customary for such announcements to be made. The point to get across, is that the nature program is as much a part of camp as the sports and other non-athletic activities. It should be considered as an integral and on-going aspect of summer camp. If this attitude is not current camp policy, you can help make it so—in small steps, of course. It may take several summers.

If you are introducing nature achievement for the first time, there may be initial resistance on the part of campers and/or administrators. If so, modify it, or introduce it gradually, perhaps as a contest or challenge, citing the few who have met the challenge. If the camp has an overall competitive policy, then gradually nature can be made competitive, too. A green stripe, to be sewn on a shirt, can serve as the badge that advertises that its wearer has satisfied the achievement.

Other Contests and Competitions

1. *Does your camp have a Color War or Olympic Competition?*

Some camps have neither, some have both. Some may never have had nature as part of the camp-wide competition and may or may not consider it suitable. If you can convince the staff that nature can and should be a part of the competition (as a culmination of all they have been exposed to during the course of the summer), children will know they should sharpen their skills to gain the competitive edge. A good team competition for nature is the nature scavenger hunt. For items for a Scavenger Hunt, see the Activities section. Include only items discussed and described over the course of the summer.

By assigning a point value for each found time—more difficult items earn more points (e.g., a live salamander may be worth five points, an oak leaf, one)—and setting a time limit, the teams vie for the larger number of points. As often happens, counselors get caught up in the activity, too; but that may be viewed in a positive light, since they can also learn. (Kids who've been through the summer nature program usually know much more than counselors or inexperienced adults. They know the *what* and they'll know *where* to locate it.)

2. *Contest (or Question) of the Week*

Such on-going and repetitive contests maintain interest in the nature program and encourage research and the seeking of knowledge. Depending on your budget and camper interest, prizes could be awarded every week, or points can accumulate and the person with the most points wins. The prize serves as a reminder or souvenir that the camper retains, not something fleeting.

Keep paper, pencil and answer box available outside the shack, so that kids can participate even when you're not there. Sample questions:

1. Name three evergreen trees growing in camp.
2. Name three nocturnal animals.
3. Name three crested birds.
4. Name three social insects.
5. What local animal is a marsupial?

Suitable prizes:

1. National Wildlife Federation stamps plus the stamp book to put them in. This costs $2.50 and is a donation to NWF; order a number before the summer so you'll have them on hand.
2. Assorted nature coloring books, available at museum shops, or from Dover Press. (send for their catalog.)
3. T-shirts imprinted with a nature logo or conservationist slogan]"I am WILD about NATURE!"] and a suitable picture.
4. Many artists use natural items in creating their artwork. An older child might appreciate and cherish such a prize—pressed flowers in leaded glass, etc.

One note of caution: you may find that a few kids become nature "stars" and start winning all the contests. That's all right, up to a point; the child may be just the one who needs the opportunity to shine. However, this can also serve to discourage others from trying, so you have to be sensitive to this. Perhaps limit the number of contests a person can win (three?). That person could act as a judge with you for later contests.

3. *Miscellaneous Poster Contests*

Many commercial and educational posters are available from a variety of sources: Audubon, National Wildlife Federation, Scholastic, Weekly Reader, etc. With some alteration, the posters can be adapted to fit a contest format.

Example: NWF's "Life Along a Fencerow" (one of series of four mural-type posters) depicts many plants and animals in a given habitat area. By adding small color stick-on dots and numbering the dots, an identification contest is created. Contest blanks with corresponding numbers are made available (see sample below), pencils, and a box with slit for entries. The person who can identify the most is the winner. Make reference books available.

"Life Along a Fencerow"—National Wildlife Foundation

This artwork portrays the plant and animal life you might see in an eastern meadow along an old wooden fence. How many plants and animals can you identify? Match the number and the name.

1.	17.
2.	18.
3.	19.
4.	20.
5.	21.
6.	22.
7.	23.
8.	24.
9.	25.
10.	26.
11.	27.
12.	28.
13.	29.
14.	30.
15.	31.
16.	32.

Your name_____ Cabin #_____

Be sure to have some contests open only to younger campers, so they can compete only with their age peers.

Example: Skeleton Poster (Weekly Reader)

Whose Skeleton Am I?

Tree posters with names blocked out. Parts of tree posters from *Ranger Rick* or *National Wildlife* may be cut out and mounted; questions about them may be asked. There are myriads of contests that you can create, some narrow in scope, others more general.

1. Name the Rabbit (or goat or duck) contest
2. Guess the number of mouse babies that will be born.
3. Guess the number of mealworms in the container.
4. Be the first to spot a hawk.
5. Catch the first tadpole.
6. Which egg will hatch first?
7. What bird am I? (with Audible Audubon)
8. Wonder Weeder of the Week

The major consideration to keep in mind is the purpose of any contest, achivement or competition. It is not to find and reward the winner but to serve as a motivator and to spark interest in your area. To the degree that the competition fulfills these goals, it is the measure of the success of and the justification for its use.

Rainy Day, Evening, and Special Programs

Rainy days should not present a major problem if you're well-prepared. Understand that normal outdoor camp activities cannot be conducted in inclement weather—no swimming, tennis, softball, etc. Thus, the program director may have to double up on the various indoor activities available. Nature falls into this category—assuming that the nature facility can accommodate children comfortably. Program on rainy days can be a free period, or you could utilize commercial nature games. (See chart in Appendix.) Or, you may wish to conduct a nature arts and crafts lesson. One of the easiest and most worthwhile activities for bad weather is the nature filmstrip; many are currently available. They may be purchased or borrowed from schools or libraries. If you have a VCR, you could tape some of the better NOVA and National Geographic specials. Purchase the National Wildlife Federation slide sets or filmstrips.

In the absence of a screen, a white sheet or tablecloth is a fine substitute. If the filmstrips are captioned, have kids read them. Use a pointer to emphasize significant items. [Some sound filmstrip sets (older ones) come with records wich are bulky and breakable. If you have any of these, transfer the narration to a cassette tape. Many filmstrips come in sets which are in large boxes; these, too, present shipping and storage problems. Suggestions—remove the cassettes and cannisters and guide books from large boxes, and put them all in a smaller box—a shoe box. Be sure that they are labeled for quick identification. Your entire summer rainy day progrms can be carried in one shoe box.]

Be sure to have several electrical adaptors (three-prongs to two-prongs) and multiple outlets and extension cords on hand so that you will not have to start searching for them. Many camps have inadequately wired buildings. Be careful, too, about blowing fuses when utilizing the equipment. Test it out when you first arrive so you do not leave your audience sitting in the dark when you begin your rainy day program.

Filmstrip Listings

Following is a suggested list of available filmstrips.

PRODUCED BY:	SET NAME:
National Geographic	*Life of Animals*
	1. Animals and Their Families
	2. Animal Homes
	3. How Animals Move About
	4. Ways Animals Get Food
	5. Ways Animals Protect Themselves
National Geographic	*Animal Behavior*
	1. Migration
	2. Defense
	3. Obtaining Food
	4. Room to Live
	5. Continuing the Species
National Geographic	*Places Where Plants and Animals Live*
	1. The Woods
	2. The City Park
	3. The Seashore
	4. The Stream
	5. The Meadow

PRODUCED BY:	SET NAME:

National Geographic *Life Cycles*
1. Insects
2. Amphibians and Reptiles
3. Fishes
4. Birds
5. Mammals

National Geographic *Kingdom of the Plants*
1. Trees
2. Green Life
3. Complex Plants
4. Plants Serving Man
5. Simple Plants

Coronet Films *Trees*
1. The Different Kinds
2. Their Structure
3. Flowers, Fruits and Seeds
4. How They Grow
5. Their Products
6. Their Importance

Ecological Communities (more difficult)
1. The Deciduous Forest
2. Ponds and Lakes
3. The Stream
4. The Meadow
5. The Thicket
6. The Northern Coniferous Forest

Learning About Ecology
1. Life Cycles
2. Living Things Depend on One Another
3. What is a Community?
4. What is a Food Chain?
5. Adaptations for Survival
6. How Humans Affect Living Things

Photosynthesis
1. Photosynthesis
2. Chlorophyll
3. Sugar and Starch
4. How Plants Produce Food
5. Synthesis
6. Review

Moreland-Latchford *Ecology: Exploration and Discovery (not so good)*
1. Organisms and Environment
2. Ecosystems
3. Population
4. Food Chains
5. Habitat
6. Plant and Animal Communities

PRODUCED BY:	SET NAME:

Moreland-Latchford *Bird Life of North America*
1. Birds and Their Environment
2. Fowl-like Birds
3. Waterfowl
4. Shorebirds
5. Perching Birds
6. Predators

The World of Plants
1. How Plants Grow
2. Kinds of Plants
3. Where Plants Grow
4. The Parts of a Plant
5. Plants and People

Kingdom of the Animals
1. Africa: Imperiled Paradise
2. Reptiles: Relics of the Past
3. Chimpanzees
4. American Wildlife
5. Insects: Ad Infinitum

Plant Reponses to Environmental Conditions
1. Response to Light
2. Response to Gravity
3. Response to Touch
4. Response to Temperature Changes
5. Review

Dramatic Presentations

1. *The Lorax*—See Activities section and read the book. Adapt the story for dramatic purposes, turning the narration into action, having persons in costume do the dialogue. Be as elaborate as time will allow.
2. Creative dramatics around an environmental theme. Have an environmental or nature dramatics evening. Work in groups of eight to fourteen campers. Give them a theme. Materials for costumes, and sound effects are optional. Allow them time (twenty to thirty minutes) to invent a depiction of that theme, using mime, movement or whatever they're capable of. When each group has completed its preparations, then the groups perform for each other. The audience should be able to discern what the theme or topic was from the action. Some possible topics:

A day in the life of a bird
Evolution (older campers twelve plus)
Food chains or webs
Metamorphosis
Morning in the forest or meadow
Seasons of the year

Or, pick narrower themes, use smaller groups, give less time.

The World is getting smaller.

Example:

Hatching
Spinning a web
Rainbow
Rainstorm
Sunset

Some Action—Socialization Experiences

Lap-sitting and other physical problem-solving experiences are part of Action-Socialization Experiences. Like many of the New Games, some of them may be adapted so that they fit environmental or natural topics.

Examples:

1. *Lap-Sitting.*

Instruct the participants to form a circle, all facing in one direction with left shoulders pointing into the center of the circle. They must move the circle inward so that they are able to touch the shoulders of the person in front of them. When all are in place, the entire group will slowly sit down, each person landing on the lap of the person behind. It may have to be tried a few times before being successful, with the participants moving the circle closer or whatever is needed. This can have a nature theme by likening the close cooperative circle to ecological balance, or global interdependence.

2. *The World Is Getting Smaller*

This activity requires that three wooden circle be cut and painted to look like a map of the world. Dimensions of the circles should be approximately 36 inches, 24 inches, and 18 inches in diameter. (Smaller for smaller groups.) Challenge your group to find a way for all members of the group to stand on the Earth at one time with no feet touching the ground for a count of five. The circle should be large enough so that a group could accomplish this. When they have done this, substitute the next smaller size and explain that although the Earth may not really be getting smaller, certain resources are finite and being used up, and population is rising, thus, in effect, the resources of the Earth are fewer, proportionately. This time, the challenge is more difficult, and kids will have to be ingenius to try to solve it. Repeat once more, emphasizing the shrinking of the Earth's resources, especially energy, before presenting the small circle. It will be practially impossible for the group to accomplish this. They'll have fun trying and you can lead a discussion on how we can slow down the rate of the consumption of natural resources, by conservation, population control, etc.

Nature-Oriented Campfires

Based on Ernest T. Seton's *Woodcraft League of America,* campfires can have a decidedly nature orientation. They may be tied in with Indian lore and Indian legends since the native Americans lived very close to nature and many of their rituals were full of nature symbolism. For example, the months of the year were lunar months and each one is named for a natural characteristic.

January	— The Snow Moon
February	— The Hunger Moon
March	— The Awakening Crow Moon
April	— The Grass Moon
May	— The Planting Moon
June	— The Rose Moon
July	— The Thunder Moon
August	— The Corn (Maize) Moon
September	— The Hunting Moon
October	— The Leaf-Falling Moon
November	— The Mad Moon
December	— The Long-Night Moon

The campfires may be held weekly or every other week. They could be around a theme or involve rituals and contests. Legends could be told, poetry recited, songs sung, dramatic performances presented.

The nature campfire might be a good time to announce achievement awards and contest winners or retell special nature events of the week—let campers do this, but make certain they tell you first. Example: "Cabin _____ found a nest of baby robins in a tree near their porch. We watched the mother feed the babies." Two weeks later, these children might report that the babies were now grown and had flown away.

Younger children might find such a campfire more to their liking. If so, have it with only the lower half of campers. Or, balance it with the kinds of things older children will accept, such as Indian competitions. There is still a place in camp for the old-fashioned Indian ritual; and, if it is handled well, it can still be popular.

The Rainstorm

With *many* participants (whole camp) in a semi-circle or circle, instruct the group that they are to imitate *what* you do and *when* you do it and to *keep doing* it until you indicate otherwise.

Then, move in front of those assembled, doing the following motions/sounds in order, moving gradually around the circle with groups imitating you. Do the entire circle with one step before going on to next.

1. Rub palms together back and forth (wind)
2. Snap fingers slowly, then quickly (first raindrops)
3. Clap hands, not all people in same rhythm (steady rain)
4. Slap thighs
5. Stamp feed rapidly on ground, while sitting. (heavy downpour)
6. Slap thighs
7. Clap hands
8. Snap fingers quickly, then slower and slower
9. Rub palms

Don't tell them what the sound is, they'll realize themselves. Be dramatic. Try it a second time for a better effect.

Good for campfire activity.

Astronomy

Astronomy is best done in camp because you are far away (hopefully) from air pollution and you should also not have the light interference associated with cities. Star and moon gazing are thus unobstructed by these urban problems.

A *good* telescope helps to make the astronomy evening(s) or night(s) better, but it is an expensive item and is not absolutely necessary. If camp has one, familiarize yourself with its operation well before the time you'll use it. Do it in the daytime, so it may be calibrated to landmarks.

The best things to view through a telescope are: the moon; Jupiter, with four of its moons visible; Saturn and its rings; and Venus. Consult star charts for what is visible, when and where to look. One interesting side learning from using the telescope is that the viewer becomes more aware of the rotation of the Earth, i.e., even though the telescope and the image one is viewing are perfectly stationary, the image will not remain in view for more than a few minutes. The telescope (unless it has an Earth motor that moves with the Earth's rotation) will have to be constantly re-adjusted because the Earth's rotation causes the image to move out of the field of vision *while you are looking at it!* This movement is not so apparent to the naked eye gazing up at the stars or moon.

Without a telescope, there are still many astronomical activities. You can locate and identify the constellations (see the H. A. Rey book), map them, talk about navigation by the stars, use a compass to help you. Summertime brings meteor showers and shooting stars, hardly visible near big cities. You may even get to see the Aurora Borealis (Northern Lights). Check the newspapers. Be alert to announcements of eclipses that are due to occur during camp season, or as in 1986, the return of Halley's Comet, or any special sky phenomenon.

A few problems may arise that perhaps can be avoided by discussing them beforehand with the head counselor. Some astronomy activities may occur after younger children's bed-time, or just at lights out. A clear night, however, can be one of the teachable moments and that is why you should be prepared to take advantage of the weather and sky condition. And, of course, it's just wonderful to look up, see the universe's awesome view, marvel at its incredible size and beauty, while lying on your back in a country meadow.

For a set of outstanding astronomy activities, contact: Lawrence Hall of Science, Astronomy Education Program, University of California, Berkeley, CA 94720. Request "Sky Challenger" activities and copies of "Star Gazers' Gazette."

Field Trips

Send away for brochures from the Chamber of Commerce of camp's locale, or look in the telephone book or newspapers to locate special places or events that may take place in the camp area. Contact the national or state park rangers for that area.

Examples:

Fish hatchery—the state may operate a fish hatchery in the area. Try to arrange a tour.

Plant or tree nursery—tours may be possible. State or privately operated.

Wildlife preserve—check with local Audubon or game warden. There may be a nearby Nature Center

County Fair—avoid the honky-tonk and amusement area. Visit the animal exhibits, especially when judging is taking place.

Pick-your-own farm produce—ask around; write to the state agricultural department for its listing; check out the local newspapers. Ask the local general store owners.

Quarries or other fossil areas. Ask local people.

University biological field study areas—get permission for a small group tour.

Many of the aforementioned might be suitable for late in the camp season (last week). Be sure to make vehicle arrangements well in advance.

Early Morning Bird-Walks

If *you* like being up and about in the early morning hours, consider an early morning bird walk with children. There's a special feeling to be out and communing with nature while the majority of humans are still asleep. It's more quiet and the animal world is more active, too.

Arrangements must be made in advance. First, clear the idea with the head counselor and camp director. Second, decide where you will venture. Announce the walk to campers and have them sign up. Depending on how many you'll attract, you'll have to schedule them in advance. The *maximum* number to take with you is ten campers; (a fewer number is better). They are to have their clothes ready and laid out at the foot of their beds. Their counselors must know the night before which campers will be going. If you are to wake the campers, visit the cabin and learn the location of the beds, so you don't awaken the wrong people. Or, have those who are going mark their bunk in some way.

One hour is probably sufficient. So wake the kids up, individually, about one hour and fifteen minutes before regular wake-up time, tell them to dress quietly and meet you outside. Don't be surprised if a cabinmate decides to come along at the last minute. Use your discretion, since the counselors may not be aware that particular child is going. And, it will increase your numbers and may make the walk too large and unwieldy. Don't forget binoculars, guide books and perhaps a cut-up orange for each person.

Watch your time. Walk away for half the allotted time, so that you will return at the right time. If you leave at seven and breakfast is at eight, walk until seven-thirty so that you'll be on time. There is a field sheet in the Appendix you can bring and use.

Birds tend to be most visible at *edges,* where fields and forests meet. But walking through the woods, while dew is still wet and making webs visible, has a special feeling and can be pleasurable without identifying birds. Mist may be coming up from a lake, insects active and a lovely smell more apparent. The campers will usually cooperate with the hush of the morning and not be noisy. If they are, be sure to encourage them to almost silence, because they have volunteered for this activity and should be quiet to gain the most from it. You might want to bring along a tape recorder and record some of the sounds. You can make a fuss over the participants at the end of the series—call them ''Early Birds'' or some other cute name; perhaps inscribe a scroll or plaque; provide a symbolic button or memento, write their names in the camp newspaper, etc. They'll remember the experience.

Night Hikes

Night hikes are taken for fun, adventure, and to conquer fear of the darkness. Although it may be part of a camp's tradition to tell ghost stories or make children afraid at night, this is *not* the role of the nature specialist on a night hike. The nature person interprets the natural world. There is plenty of real excitement without playing on the fears that children already have towards the dark and the unknown. Scary stories may have their place in camp, but leave that to others. You'll want to build trust and confidence and to show campers that night is a time of activity for many animal species. An alert and knowledgeable group can find many things in the woods at night that are not found in the daytime.

First, be certain you know your way well. Walk only on paths you're thoroughly familiar with. Stick to paths and/or roads even though they're unlit; your eyes will gradually become accustomed to the dark as the pupils fully dilate. A road or path is safest and will be visible; moonlight and starlight will illuminate the way. Even in their absence, by looking upward where there is a gap in the trees, you'll see the tops of trees silhouetted against the sky, so that you'll know you're on the road. Wearing light-colored shoes or jackets will make participants more easily seen in the darkness.

Know the landmarks—lakes, streams, etc.—so you will know where you are at all times. Bring a few flashlights and a compass. Have kids carry or wear jackets since the

temperature can drop. They may also wish to bring and use insect repellent. Walk away from all sources of artificial light and encourage the participants not to use the flashlights unless absolutely necessary for safety purposes or when you are doing something that requires illumination. Light causes the pupils to contract again and then it takes time to reaccustom to darkness. If lights become necessary, have the children direct the light downward with fingers spread over the glass so the light is very dim. You may wish to carry a more powerful light if there is a special need. (See activities 13-18 below.)

What to do on a night hike:

1. Discuss the various changes that occur after the sun goes down and as night falls. If campers can't respond, mention the difference in light, that temperature becomes cooler, moisture increases, and wind decreases. Thus, scent does not carry as readily.

2. Many animals take advantage of these changes to feed, move about, and hunt prey. Some feel safer at night, since visual cues decrease. Discuss which animals are active at night (nocturnal)—skunks, foxes, raccoons, opossum, some squirrels, mice, spiders, owls, many insects such as fireflies and crickets. Talk about the kinds of activities they may be engaging in, e.g., owls hunt for food, voles and mice feed on seeds and plants under cover of darkness, spiders spin webs and catch insects, crickets and katydids call to establish territory or to seek mates, fireflies also flash to attract mates.

3. Talk about how visual humans are. Our eyes are located in front of our heads (so are owls') and vision has evolved to be the major way humans receive sensory information. Vision requires light, thus most humans sleep at night, or seek artificial daylight.

4. Nevertheless, humans can probably see more at night than they think they can. That is why you should aim for a non-flashlight night hike to demonstrate this potential. It just takes time to get used to less illumination and to get over the discomfort of not relying so much on the visual. Point out the need for increased awareness of tactile senses—your feet can feel, even through shoes, if you concentrate on what you're doing.

5. Demonstrate how to look at objects in subdued light. Have the campers look directly at some object, such as the top of a particular tree. If you are looking right at it, it should disappear from view. Explain that this occurs because the center of the eye contains a concentration of the cones which see only in color. The rods, which are located away from the center, ''see'' better in the dark. Thus, looking indirectly, from one side, will be more effective in the darkness.

6. Listen for animal sounds. The group must be quiet or they won't hear anything. Have campers cup their ears to enhance any sound. Tell them that is why nocturnal animals have large, upstanding ears. If you begin your hike near a meadow in August, listen for the insect musicians—crickets, katydids, grasshoppers. Try to differentiate the sounds made by various species. Insect

sounds are available on records and tapes. Try the library or nature center for these. You may wish to bring a tape recorder with you to record the night sounds to re-play on a cold night in winter to remind you of summer! If you can discern the chirps of the snowy cricket (steady, evenly spaced), count how many you hear in fifteen seconds, add forty to get the temperature (°F). Kids will love to do this because it really works since the cricket's actions are governed by temperature, slowing down with cold, speeding up as it gets warmer. The katydid says its name. Rustling sounds in the trees may be made by squirrels; birds, except for owls, are usually asleep. You may hear and see bats; they are active just as darkness settles. To locate prey, they emit sounds some of which are audible to humns, others are in a frequency too high for our ears. Look for zig-zag flying against the darkening sky.

7. Are you or your campers aware of any subtle smells? Most humans have a poorly developed olfactory sense, but you should talk about this with the hikers. Some flowers do release their scent at night, presumably to attract night-flying insects. The evening primorse is one of these flowers; so is jasmine. Perhaps there'll be skunk odor (far away, hopefully). This topic makes for interesting conversation while walking. You might use the occasion to point out the warning coloration of a skunk. That white stripe is visible even in the dark. Have them observe how much easier it is for them to see the white or light-colored clothes.

8. To demonstrate the principle that earth and rocks retain heat longer than the surrounding air, have the participants feel a large rock or stone wall and the ground. Wait until the air temperature drops a bit so that the difference will be more apparent.

9. If you are walking on a wooded trail or path, or if you just sense your campers would be more comfortable, even on a road, have them join hands, one in front, one behind. If they meet an obstacle (roots, stones, puddles), they must relay this information to the person behind them. Make sure this is done in quiet tones, or else the walk will be too noisy, destroying one of the purposes of a night hike. If the feet are lifted off the ground, very slightly, between steps, then there is more control and tactile sensation through the feet.

10. Talk about native Americans and their ability to stalk prey and enemies in darkness by utilizing and sharpening their senses.

11. The most exciting event that can be carried on during a night hike is the calling down of owls. Since owls are territorial, they will respond to imitations (or recordings) of their species' specific calls. Mastering owl calls is quite difficult but worth any effort expended. A handy substitute for the owl imitation is to use a recorded version of the call. Record on a tape recorder that is battery-operated and not too heavy. You may have to raise the volume for the owl to hear and respond. Put each owl's call on its own cassette and record it over and over, filling up the tape, so you won't need to rewind or have to

locate the place you need in the dark. If you don't know if any owl or what kind of owl resides in the woods you'll be hiking through, try one call at a time, for at least ten minutes. (You might want to do this on your own several successive nights beforehand to determine which owl(s) live there.) It sounds like a great deal of time and effort; but, if you are successful, you'll be rewarded with a dramatic experience and doing it with a group of children (or adults) will provide them with an exciting night they'll never forget. Sometimes more than one owl will respond; sometimes one or more will get so close that you will be able to flash a beam of light on them. Or, you may just get a glimpse of the great bird as he flies down to investigate on silent wings. Look for the silhouette against the sky because you won't hear the flutter of his wings.

12. Seek out the luminescent plants or animals. Look at fireflies, most active just after dusk. Count the time lapse between flashes. See if you can differentiate the types of flashes of various species. Perhaps you might see two firefly-lovers find each other. Look for Foxfire, the luminescent fungi that grows on some rotting wood. Its luminescence increases when it is moved. Also look for glowworms in various larval or pupal stages; you may find these in leaf litter, in the soil.

The rest of the activities requires the use of flashlights. Perhaps you may want to do these on the way back from the hike so that night vision is not affected.

13. Try to catch the reflective eyes of animals by very slowly shining a good light around. You might pick up a pair (or several!) of red, glowing eyes. Raccoons, opossums, cats and other animals' eyes will reflect light shone on them. So will the wolf spider; its eyes look like tiny glowing diamonds when light bounces off them.

14. Try to find the crickets or grasshoppers who are responsible for the sounds. Follow the sound, then flash the light on it.

15. If your walk takes you near a pond, shine the light beams into the water to see all the activity taking place; there are many active eaters at night. A neat trick is to seal a light into a glass jar and submerge the jar illuminating the water and its inhabitants.

16. As you start the hike, you can paint a tree trunk with an overripe banana or other sugary mixture such as pancake syrup. Then, on your way back, see what's been feeding on the mixture.

17. See *OBIS* "White Sheet Trick." Set up an old white sheet with a light shining on it, or behind it. See what the light has brought.

18. Look for a spider building its web. Shine the light on it and observe the mini-engineer as it constructs its food-catcher. Look in corners of building where roof and porch beams meet, or in a hole in a tree. The orb weaver creates the most intricate and beautiful of the spiders' webs.

Nature at night can be just as fascinating as nature in the daytime. An exciting night hike might inspire poetry, or a good article for the camp newspaper.

All-Day Nature Hikes

As camp season winds down, there may be days of loose programming. A rewarding experience is the all day hike, devoted to nature exploration further afield than a more structured program permits. There are two ways to run this:

1. You may take out an entire group with their counselors and group head. More than twenty-five children is an unwieldy number, however, and not too effective in terms of a nature hike.
2. You may select a few (five to seven) campers who are really into nature and take them by yourself. I call these kids nature "nuts" and commemorate the occasion by rewarding them with walnuts or pecans made into little people. (It became so popular, I was unable to accommodate all who wanted to go, and I had to abandon the idea.)

Pack a picnic lunch and carry nets, guide books, lenses and the other nature paraphernalia. You should, naturally,

"Nature nuts"

have already scouted the route you take. If you need to pass on private property, be sure to clear it with the owners. Let the camp director know you're planning this to make sure it presents no problems for the camp in its dealing with its neighbors.

You might have a goal—the fossil quarry, the waterfall, another lake, a hilltop lookout. Watch the weather; if it promises to be hot, bring suits and find a place to cool off. Better still, reserve these hikes for cooler days when heat will not exhaust the hikers.

Remember, it's a nature hike, not one for endurance. If you're attempting to seek mileage records, you'll miss the nature explorations which require stopping and looking. Hikes for mileage are fun, too, but they can be taken without a nature specialist.

Free or Optional Periods

Your camp may have free play and/or optional periods. Campers who choose to go to nature program will be there because they want to be there. You will therefore have a more interested group and you can do things with them you might not try during regular activity period (e.g., dissections). The optional period should also be less structured than when a regular group is assigned. You may also find times when less than a complete group is present.

Suggested activities for free/optional periods:

1. Using filmstrip viewer with cassette
2. Using micro-viewers
3. Feeding and caring for animals; possible simple animal experiments, such as learning of mazes.
4. Jigsaw puzzles
5. Games—Animalia, Predator, Lotto, Yotta, Old Maid, Concentration
6. Work on natural weaving or dyeing
7. Listening to Audible Audubon or Bird records

Computer Programs

With advances in technology, computers are finding their places in camps. If your camp has a computer, software programs are available with nature/environmental themes and concepts. Some are tutorial or drill types which teach and/or reinforce specific concepts. Other programs are of the simulation or game type. The drill type with a question and answer format can be fun if the graphics are effective. However, they tend to be more school-oriented and less recreational. The game-type programs, which are more open-ended, goal-oriented and allow for greater interaction, would seem to be more suitable for camp.

Certainly, youngsters of today are very much at ease with computer games, yet still sufficiently intrigued to play them. Thus, the video game with an environmental message can be an attractive tool in motivating kids. Since the computer and programs are relatively expensive, any software should be carefully screened by the purchaser.

Computers do not lend themselvs to use by groups; most are used by one or a few people at time. This, therefore, limits their use to optional periods or rainy days so that kids can take turns. In more advanced or elaborate computer setups, the machine could be used for data base with information, such as species identification, programmed into the memory. But this type does not lend itself to common use for children's camps. As more and better software is produced and people become computer literate, its use as a tool may increase; but it will never replace the best nature teaching tool—the outdoors.

For suggested software distributors see Appendix V.

Record Keeping

Get a spiral or other notebook for records. Writing down specific items will help you to become more efficient, avoid repetition and/or duplication, and will jog your memory.

What kinds of records to keep

1. Group activity. Every group activity should be recorded at its completion. The entry should contain the date and a brief note about how the activity went. This will help you to keep track of what you did with each group. Comments on how it went, the pitfalls, or the problems will help you to improve the activity when you repeat it with another group.
2. Future plans.
3. List of supplies needed. Keep a shopping list for the next summer, too.

4. Achievements attained, together with the date.
5. A log, diary or chronology on which you can reflect afterward.
6. Keep a record of all your purchases and any expenses you've incurred. Paste an envelope in the back (or keep a separate file) for receipts so you will be reimbursed. Include tolls, phone calls, etc.
7. Make (or keep) a copy of the nature shack inventory. You will use this list to help you re-order materials for subsequent seasons.

Camp Newspaper

If there is a camp newspaper, write an article for every issue or have a camper write one about nature. Articles take very little time and are very helpful in assuring the success and acceptance of your program. It could be a "Nature News of the Week," make-believe interviews with wildlife, or guessing games. It could be a short word-search puzzle—whatever motivates campers to think about nature.

No camp newspaper? Make up one of your own and distribute at mealtime. The entire paper could be devoted to nature; make it short enough so it will be read. Mention campers by name.

The End of Summer

As the summer draws to a close and camp winds down, you may find it necessary to shift gears. Regular programs may change and your focus may change too. The final days of camp may be devoted to finishing projects—nature weaving or dyeing, putting the flowers that were pressed earlier into a decorative arrangement under glass or clear contact. The camp garden will need to yield its final harvest; some of it can be cooked or even dried.

You can also catch those stragglers who never completed their nature achievement; or you may want to take groups on an all-day nature walk, preferably away from camp to make it a special event. Or, it may be a good time to arrange an excursion to special places—fossil hunting, berry-picking, county fair (see p. IV-87).

End of summer is also the time to tally the final results of any nature contest. Your camp may have a special awards ceremony or final campfire or similar ritual; this would be a suitable occasion for presenting nature awards. Some camps present certificates, plaques, or trophies for achievement or improvement. If nature is not already among the areas so recognized (like swimming or athletics), try to convince those who make policy that achievement in nature merits recognition also. The award can take a variety of forms—perhaps a plaster animal figurine or pin, or clear cast plastic, or a nutty owl perched on piece of bark—something you prepare as a token. It should be something a camper can retain—to wear, hang up or put on a shelf. This way, it serves as a reminder of the nature program. If you chose, you can prepare a printed certificate, decorated with nature symbols. Or, pressed flower bookmarks are a lovely memento.

End of summer also is the time to dispose of the animals you've kept all season (refer to page 15 in Section II). If you

are so inclined, you might use the time to prepare stuffed study skins to use in the future.

You might prepare a final article for the camp newspaper. Try to sum up what was accomplished—name names; feature the special nature happenings of the summer, the rainbow, the chicken hatch, the orphaned bird the children fed and released, the caterpillar that turned into a butterfly. (Consult the records you've kept.)

Your nature shack will have to be dismantled. It should be done in a way that will protect the materials from damage and prove most convenient for the following year. Most camp facilities are uninsulated and are closed for the winter. Depending on location, you'll need to protect the things in your shack from freezing, dampness, mice, squirrels and insects. Many expensive items, if not cared for properly, can be destroyed by rust, mildew, clothes; moths, beetles, rodents, etc. It's interesting to observe the habits of these creatures—but when you lose a chart or poster that's no longer in print, or a prized specimen or collection that took years to acquire, you realize that some defensive measures must be taken.

Therefore, see to it that all charts and posters are dry and either rolled in tubes or piled flat. Use heavy-duty plastic bags for valuable specimens. All glassware should be thoroughly washed and dried. Seal the materials in boxes, using masking tape. Sprinkle moth flakes or balls into boxes to discourage the insects. Use plastic tubs or containers with tight-fighting seals. Try to pack the materials so that when they are unpacked they will be in some kind of order for ease in setting up again next summer.

Some things need to be protected from freezing and should be packed separately for removal and storage in a place where the temperature is controlled by a thermostat that does not allow it to go below freezing. For example, white glue loses its stickiness if it freezes; frozen plaster of Paris will also not set.

The camp director may also wish to make arrangements to store valuable equipment—telescope, mircoscopes, binoculars, projectors—in a secure place to protect from vandalism or theft. Naturally, any item you've borrowed or brought from home, will have to be shipped or taken back. Account for all books borrowed from libraries. If kids have borrowed cages, nets, books—these must be collected.

Some camps require that the supplies be inventoried and a list of items on hand be submitted. While so doing, make a shopping list of items consumed or needed so that you can purchase the needed materials before next season. Once you get to camp, shopping is more difficult.

You might also want to request that certain repairs be made during the year—the extra electrical outlet, the roof leak. Be sure to get the full name and address of the year-round caretaker if you expect to set up a camp garden, since you'll want to have the seeds sent before camp starts next summer.

Be sure to wash or clean the shack, sweep the floor, stack the boxes and leave the facility neat. After all, you may be the person who comes back to the shack next summer, ready to begin a fresh program for another season.

APPENDIX A
Glossary of Ecological Terms

Adaptation—Any characteristic which helps an organism to survive in its particular environment.

Animal—Any living thing that gets its food from plants or other animals, living or dead; *most* animals are mobile.

Balance in Nature—Tendency of living things to maintain a dynamic equilibrium between themselves and their environment.

Biome—Climate, plants, and animals in a broad region, e.g. tundra, desert, deciduous forest.

Carnivore—Any animal that feeds on animal matter; a secondary consumer.

Chlorophyll—Green coloring matter in plants; essential in process of photosynthesis.

Climate—Average of weather conditions over a long period of time in a large geographical area, as determined by air pressure, heat, wind, and moisture.

Community—An interrelated and interdependent group of plants and animals.

Conservation—Wise use of the environment.

Consumer—In the food chain all organisms other than green plants.

Decay—Reduction of the materials of plant or animal bodies to simple compounds through the action of bacteria or other decomposers.

Decomposers—Organisms that break down tissues and excretion of other organisms into simpler forms; bacteria, yeast, mold, and other fungi, etc.

Ecology—Study of the relationship of living things (including man) to each other and to their environment.

Energy—The ability to do work.

Environment—All of the biological and physical components of a given place.

Erosion—Loss of soil caused by the action of wind and water.

Food Chain—Transfer of energy through an ecosystem through the action of food producers, food consumers, and decomposers.

Habitat—The place where a plant or animal can find the right food, shelter, water, temperature, and other things it needs to live.

Herbivore—A plant-eating animal; a primary consumer.

Humus—Organic material in soil produced by plant and animal decomposition.

Interrelationship—The interaction between plants and animals and their environment.

Mammal—A warm-blooded animal with hair or fur; born alive; suckle their young.

Niche—The "job" a living thing does; its relation to the environment.

Photosynthesis—The process by which green plants, using light energy, combine carbon dioxide and water to produce basic food substance and oxygen.

Pollution—Defilement of the environment by people.

Predator—An animal that preys on other animals.

Producer—In the food chain green plants; the only organisms capable of making food.

Respiration—Oxidation of food and the release of energy involving the exchange of gases (oxygen in, carbon dioxide out) between living cells (plant and animal) and the environment.

Transpiration—Loss of water from plants into the surrounding atmosphere.

Water Cycle—Continuous movement of water, in its various forms, between earth and air.

Weather—Condition of the atmosphere, determined by air pressure, heat, wind and water.

(Audubon-Greenwich Center Staff. Used by permission.)

APPENDIX B

Field Guides and Keys
Amphibians and Reptiles

Vertebrate cold-blooded animals (body temperature controlled by surroundings)

	AMPHIBIANS	REPTILES
Skin	either moist and smooth or dry and warty, no scales	dry, scales
Eggs	usually laid in water	laid on land (some snakes bear living young)
Young	different shape from adults, except salamanders	same shape as adults
Breathe	with gills when young (usually) with lungs when adult (usually)	with lungs at all times
Claws	none	all except snakes
Examples	TOADS, FROGS, SALAMANDERS	SNAKES, TURTLES, CHAMELEONS, LIZARDS, CROCODILES, ALLIGATORS

Most of these animals are harmless; however, the jaws of a large snapping turtle are dangerous. Only two species of poisonous snakes, the copperhead and rattlesnake, are found in Massachusetts, and these are rare. The bites of other snakes are not dangerous unless the wound becomes infected.

Salamanders are often called lizards but actually they are more like frogs with tails. (Lizards have dry and scaly skin and the skin of a salamander is moist and smooth.) They eat mostly insects and other small invertebrates.

Although adult frogs and salamanders usually have lungs they also breathe through their skin, so must be kept moist at all times. In hibernation they breathe entirely this way.

Frogs eat primarily land or water insects. They have moist smooth skin. Their slipperiness and their ability to jump enable them to escape their enemies. They are much better jumpers than toads. Frogs' eggs are laid singly or in clusters.

Toads eat mainly insects and earthworms. They have a dry warty skin, but people cannot get warts from handling them. Toads lay their eggs in a chain-like formation.

Snakes are very useful animals which should not be killed. The small ones live largely on soft-bodied animals, earthworms, slugs, and some insects. The larger ones eat mice and other small vertebrates, frogs, toads, etc. A snake swallows its prey whole, holding it with teeth which curve back, while the top and bottom jaws move alternately to work the prey down. The hinged jawbones and the elasticity of the skin and stomach allow it to eat animals bigger around than itself. A snake sleeps with its eyes open since it has no moveable eyelids. Its forked tongue is not a stinger but aids the snake in smelling, tasting, and feeling objects.

Turtles are among the best protected of animals due to their shell which is like a hard suit of armor. The backbone of turtles is attached to the upper shell and the breastbone to the lower shell. A full-grown turtle has few enemies, but the eggs are often dug up and eaten by skunks or raccoons and the young turtles are often eaten by larger turtles and other water animals. They all lay their leathery-shelled eggs on land, usually digging a hole for them. Some turtles live on land and some in the water.

Crocodiles and *alligators* are not found wild in Massachusetts. One *lizard,* the Five-lined Skink, may occur in Massachusetts but there is no authentic record. The pet store "chameleon" is really an anole lizard which is common in Florida. A true *chameleon* is found only in the old world.

(Used by permission of the Massachusetts Audubon Society, Lincoln, MA 01773.)

KEY TO

Land and Freshwater Turtles

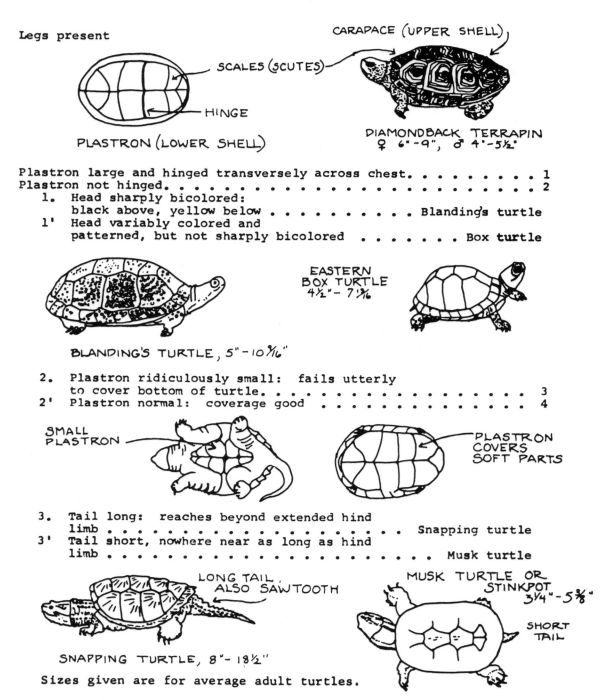

Legs present

CARAPACE (UPPER SHELL)

SCALES (SCUTES)

HINGE

PLASTRON (LOWER SHELL)

DIAMONDBACK TERRAPIN
♀ 6"–9", ♂ 4"–5½"

Plastron large and hinged transversely across chest. 1
Plastron not hinged. 2
   1. Head sharply bicolored:
      black above, yellow below . . . . Blanding's turtle
   1' Head variably colored and
      patterned, but not sharply bicolored . . . . Box turtle

EASTERN
BOX TURTLE
4½"–7¹⁵⁄₁₆

BLANDING'S TURTLE, 5"–10⁵⁄₁₆"

   2. Plastron ridiculously small: fails utterly
      to cover bottom of turtle. 3
   2' Plastron normal: coverage good 4

SMALL
PLASTRON

PLASTRON
COVERS
SOFT PARTS

   3. Tail long: reaches beyond extended hind
      limb . . . . Snapping turtle
   3' Tail short, nowhere near as long as hind
      limb . . . . Musk turtle

LONG TAIL,
ALSO SAWTOOTH

MUSK TURTLE OR
STINKPOT
3¼"–5⅜"

SHORT
TAIL

SNAPPING TURTLE, 8"–18½"

Sizes given are for average adult turtles.

4. Hind feet large, webbed paddles 5
4' Hind feet not large, webbed paddles 7

5. Head and neck longitudinally striped with
    yellow 6
5' Head and neck not striped, but grey or
    spotted with gray. found in salt marshes
    and brackish water of Cape Cod. Scarce. .Diamondback terrapin

6. Large yellow bar behind eye: plastron
    predominantly yellow . . . . Painted turtle
6' Only narrow yellow lines on head: plastron
    rosy or reddish.
                                Rare. . . . .Red-bellied turtle

PAINTED
TURTLE,
4½"-7⅝"

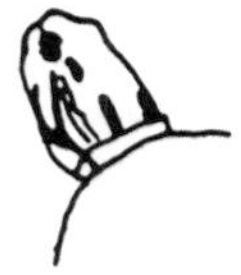

RED-BELLIED
TURTLE,
10" - 15 ¾"

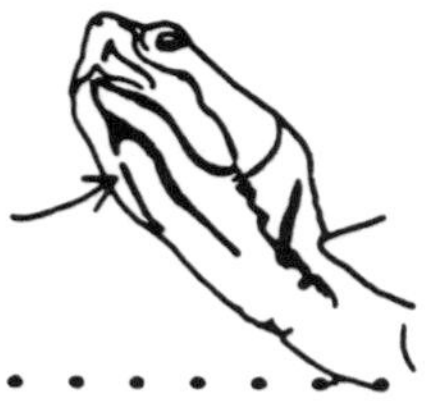

NARROW
LINES

7. Carapace fairly smooth; orange or yellow
    spots on head and/or limbs 8
7' Carapace rough; each scute showing
    concentric laminations; an orange wash on
    head and limbs . . . . Wood turtle

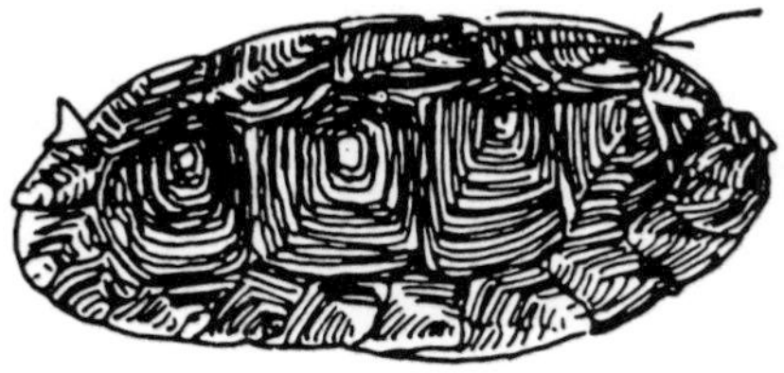

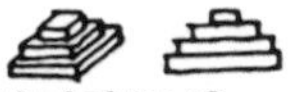

CONCENTRIC LAMINATIONS
ON SCUTES OF
WOOD TURTLE, 5½"-9"

8. Bright yellow polka dots on carapace . . . . . Spotted turtle
8' Carapace virtually uniform in color.
            Very rare. . . . . . . Bog (Muhlenburg's) turtle

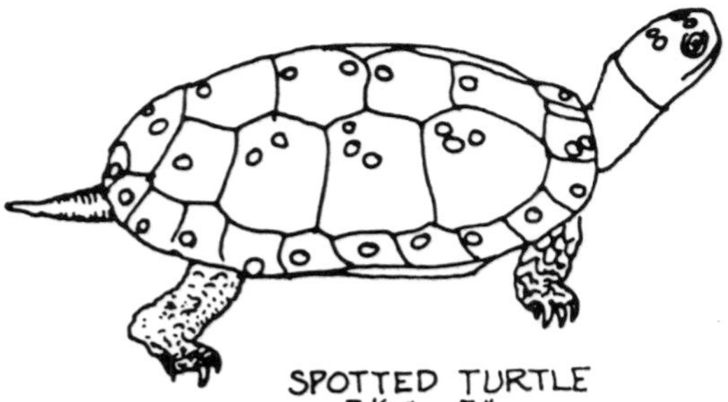

SPOTTED TURTLE
3½"-5"

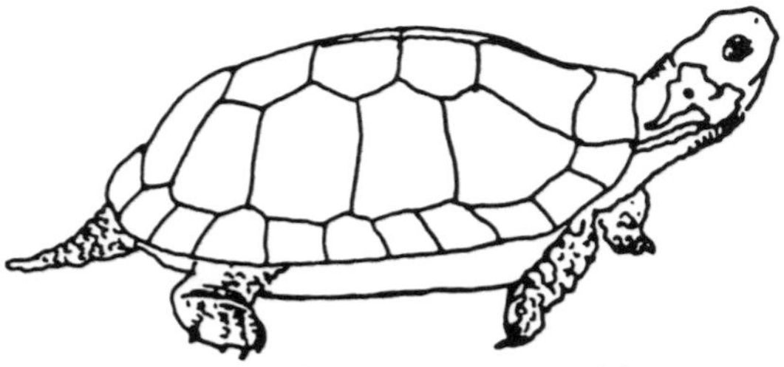

BOG (MUHLENBURG'S) TURTLE
3"-4½"

References:
A Field Guide to Reptiles and Amphibians, Roger Conant,
Houghton Mifflin Co., Boston

Reptiles & Amphibians in Massachusetts, James D. Lazell, Jr.,
Massachusetts Audubon Society, Lincoln, Ma. 01773, 1974

Turtles and Their Care, John Hoke, Franklin Watts, Inc., 1970

APPENDIX B
Field Guides and Keys
Birds: Parts

WHAT BIRD DID YOU SEE?
LOOK AT

SIZE Bigger or Smaller than
Sparrow
Robin
Crow

SHAPE

of **HEAD**
Beak

Crest?

of **WINGS**

of **TAIL**

COLOR & FIELD MARKS

FILL IN THE BOXES
AND **LEARN THESE PARTS**

BACK   SIDE   FEET
RUMP   BELLY   WING
CHEEK   TAIL
BREAST
CROWN
BILL

THE PARTS OF A BIRD

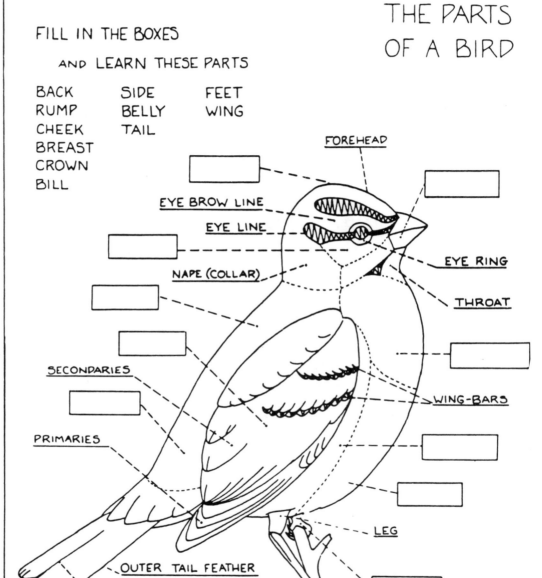

FOREHEAD

EYE BROW LINE

EYE LINE

EYE RING

NAPE (COLLAR)

THROAT

SECONDARIES

WING-BARS

PRIMARIES

LEG

OUTER TAIL FEATHER

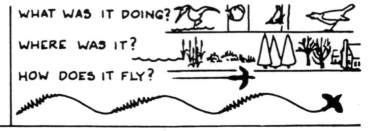

WHAT WAS IT DOING?

WHERE WAS IT?

HOW DOES IT FLY?

APPENDIX B
Field Guides and Keys
Birds: Silhouettes

(From Field Guide to the Birds by Roger Tory Peterson. Used by permission of Houghton Mifflin Company, Boston, MA.)

APPENDIX B
Field Guides and Keys
Birds: Flight Silhouettes

Flight Silhouettes

1 BARN SWALLOW
2 CLIFF SWALLOW
3 PURPLE MARTIN
4 CHIMNEY SWIFT
5 STARLING
6 GRACKLE
7 RED-WING
8 BLUEBIRD
9 ROBIN
10 GOLDFINCH
11 HOUSE SPARROW
12 KINGFISHER
13 BLUE JAY
14 FLICKER
15 MOURNING DOVE
16 MEADOWLARK
17 BOB-WHITE
18 RUFFED GROUSE
19 PHEASANT
20 NIGHTHAWK
21 CROW
22 SHARP-SHINNED HAWK
23 SPARROW HAWK
24 KILLDEER
25 WILSON'S SNIPE
26 WOODCOCK

(From Field Guide to the Birds by Roger Tory Peterson. Used by permission of Houghton Mifflin Company, Boston, MA.)

APPENDIX B
Field Guides and Keys:
Birds: Shore Silhouettes

Shore Silhouettes

1 COMMON TERN
2 BLACK TERN
3 HERRING GULL
4 CORMORANT
5 BLACK SKIMMER
6 GREAT BLUE HERON
7 BLACK DUCK
8 PIED-BILLED GREBE
9 MARBLED GODWIT
10 GREATER YELLOW-LEGS
11 DOWITCHER
12 CLAPPER RAIL
13 HUDSONIAN CURLEW
14 BLACK-BELLIED PLOVER
15 RUDDY TURNSTONE
16 NIGHT HERON
17 PHALAROPE
18 LEAST SANDPIPER
19 SEMIPALMATED PLOVER
20 SANDERLING
21 SPOTTED SANDPIPER
22 KILLDEER
23 GREEN HERON

From a "Field Guide to the Birds" by Roger Tory Peterson. Houghton Mifflin Co., Boston, 1947.

BIRD STUDY FIELD SHEET

As you see a bird, observe the following:

* Size and shape of body

head _____

_____

beak _____

_____

feathers _____

_____

legs _____

_____

feet _____

_____

* Colors and markings

unusual designs on body _____

_____

color on head _____

_____

wings _____

_____

body feathers _____

_____

* Sounds (chattering, warbling, singing, other sounds)

_____

_____

_____

* Movements

On ground (hopping, strutting, jumping) _____

_____

in flight (flappings, wings, soaring) _____

_____

* Nests

location (on ground, in a dead tree, low bush, eaves, buildings)

_____

materials used in building a nest _____

_____

* Surroundings

location (field, forest, city, water) _____

_____

travel (alone, with others)

_____

area (wet or dry) _____

_____

tracks made _____

_____

* Food _____

_____

* Other observations _____

_____

Possible identity:

APPENDIX B
Field Guides and Keys
Conifer Key

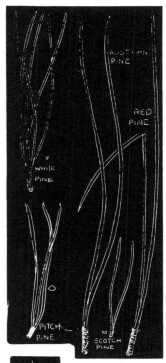

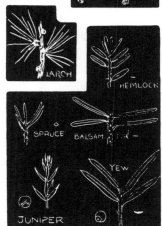

CONIFER KEY

I. LEAVES NEEDLE-LIKE

A. *Leaves in bundles*

  1. Leaves evergreen

    a. Five leaves in a bundle. . . . . *White Pine*

    b. Three leaves in a bundle . . . . *Pitch Pine*

    c. Two leaves in a bundle

      1) Leaves 2″ to 3″ long, twisted, blue-green . . . . *Scotch Pine**

      2) Leaves 3″ to 6″ long, stiff, do not break when bent . . *Austrian Pine**

      3) Leaves 4″ to 6″ long, break easily. . . . . Red Pine

  2. Leaves deciduous (dropped in fall)

    a. Many leaves in a bundle, twigs knobby . . . . Larch

B. *Leaves single*

  1. Leaves flat, tips do *not* feel prickly

    a. Leaves ½″ or less, on tiny stems, 2 white bands below;
      twigs rough after leaves fall . . . .*Hemlock*

    b. Leaves ¾″ to 1″, *no* stems; silver-white bands below;
      twigs smooth after leaves fall . . . . Balsam Fir

    c. Leaves dark green above, yellow-green below;
      fruit red, berry-like; a shrub . . . . *Yew*

  2. Leaves not flat, grow all around twig, tips prickly

    a. Leaves usually 4-sided; can be rolled in fingers;
      twigs rough after leaves fall . . . . *Spruce*

    b. Leaves ¼″ to ½″, one side gray-white, the other side green;
      fruit blue, berry-like, a shrub . . . . *Pasture Juniper*

II. LEAVES SCALE-LIKE

A. Branchlets flattened, fan-like sprays; cones ½″ long,
  oblong. . . . .*Arbor Vitae*

B. Branchlets not flattened; young leaf tips feel prickly,
  old ones do not; fruit blue, berry-like. . . . . *Red Cedar*

(*Introduced species)

(Used with the permission of the Massachusetts Audubon Society, Lincoln, MA 01773.)

V.

APPENDIX B
Field Guides and Keys
Flowers

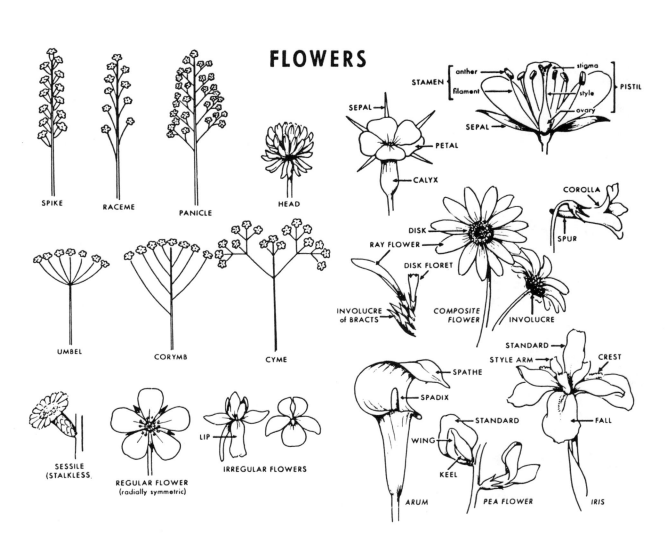

From Field Guide to Wildflowers by Roger Tory Peterson and Margaret McKenny, Houghton Mifflin Co., Boston, 1968

=APPENDIX B=
Field Guides and Keys
Galls, Common

GALL
MIDGE

SPRUCE
CONE
GALL

WILLOW
PINE CONE
GALL

GALL
WASP

OAK
APPLE

OAK
BULLET
GALL

GOUTY
OAK GALL

GOLDENROD
BALL GALL

ELLIPTICAL
GOLDENROD
GALL

SOME COMMON GALLS AND THEIR INDUCERS

A. Those easily found in winter.

1. <u>Spruce Cone Gall</u> – cone-like swelling on Norway spruce. Induced by an aphid.

2. <u>Pine Cone Willow Gall</u> – on tips of willow buds. Resembles a small pine cone. Induced by a gall midge.

3. <u>Oak Apple</u> – on twigs or fallen brown leaves of oak. 1" in diameter or more, fibrous inside. Induced by a gall wasp.

4. <u>Oak Bullet Gall</u> – small hard round swelling on oak twigs. May occur singly or in groups. Induced by a gall wasp.

5. <u>Gouty Oak Gall</u> – irregular dark swelling on oak twigs. Many exit holes. Induced by a gall wasp.

6. <u>Goldenrod Ball Gall</u> – round swelling on goldenrod stem. Pithy interior. Induced by gall fly.

7. <u>Elliptical Goldenrod Gall</u> – spindle shaped swelling on goldenrod stem. Smooth interior. Induced by caterpillar of a moth.

B. Those easily found in summer.

1. <u>Poplar Petiole Gall</u> – round swelling at base of leaf, on poplars and aspens- often numerous. Induced by an aphid.

2. <u>Hedgehog Gall on Oak</u> – small spiny galls on midribs of white oak leaves. Induced by a gall wasp.

3. <u>Maple Leaf Spot Gall</u> – yellow spots with red margins on maple leaves. Induced by a gall midge.

4. <u>Cherry Leaf Gall</u> – slender, tube-like growths on cherry leaves. Green or red, may be very numerous. Induced by a gall mite.

5. <u>Goldenrod Bunch Gall</u> – ball of deformed leaves at tip of stalk. Induced by a gall midge.

6. <u>Poplar Vagabond Gall</u> – looks like an ear. Induced by an aphid.

APHID

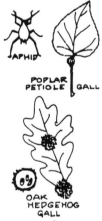

POPLAR
PETIOLE GALL

OAK
HEDGEHOG
GALL

MAPLE LEAF
SPOT GALL

GALL
MITE

CHERRY
LEAF GALL

GOLDENROD
BUNCH GALL

POPLAR
VAGABOND
GALL

(Used by permission of the Massachusetts Audubon Society, Lincoln, MA 01773.)

APPENDIX B
Field Guides and Keys
Insects: Ten Common Orders

COMPLETE METAMORPHOSIS

TEN COMMON INSECT ORDERS

ORDERS	METAMORPHOSIS (change during growth)	MOUTH	FIELD MARKS	EXAMPLES
ORTHOPTERA "Straight-winged"	Gradual change Three stages	Chewing	FW leathery	Grasshoppers Crickets Cockroaches Mantids
HEMIPTERA "Half-winged"; two suborders as follows:				
HETEROPTERA "Varied-winged"	Gradual change Three stages	Piercing-sucking	FW leathery at base, thinner at extremities.	Stink & Squash Bugs Boatmen Backswimmers
HOMOPTERA "Wings-alike"	Gradual change Three stages	Piercing-sucking	Wings clear or leathery. FW form roof over HW.	Cicadas Aphids, Leaf & Tree Hoppers Spittlebugs
EPHEMEROPTERA "Ephemera-winged"	Gradual change Three stages	Non-functioning in adults	Wings delicate, many cross veins; nymphs aquatic.	Mayflies
ODONATA "Toothed" (mouth parts)	Gradual change Three stages	Chewing	Long, slinder insects with long, clear wings. Nymphs aquatic.	Dameselflies Dragonflies
NEUROPTERA "Nerve-winged"	Complete change Four stages	Chewing	Wings equal in size with many fine veins. Clear	Ant-lions Lace-wing flies.
TRICHOPTERA "Hairy winged"	Complete change Four stages	Sucking Larva: chewing	Wings covered with long hairs; Larvae aquatic, often in cases.	Caddisflies
LEPIDOPTERA "Scaly-winged"	Complete change Four stages	Siphon-sucking Larva: chewing	Wings covered with scales.	Moths Skippers Butterflies
COLEOPTERA "Sheath-winged"	Complete change Four stages	Chewing	FW horny, meeting in straight line down back over HW.	Potato & Lady Beetles Fireflies
HYMENOPTERA "Membrane-winged"	Complete change Four stages	Chewing Lapping Sucking	FW larger, HW often hooked to FW or no wings.	Wasps Ants Bees
DIPTERA "Two-winged"	Complete change Four stages	Piercing-sucking or Sucking	One pair of thin transparent wings.	Gnats Flies Mosquitoes Craneflies
			FW—Front wings	HW—Hind wings

GRADUAL METAMORPHOSIS

A) Young do not resemble adults

B) Young resemble adults

(Used with the permission of Massachusetts Audubon Society, Lincoln, MA 01773.)

APPENDIX B

Field Guides and Keys
Insects: Common Pond Insects

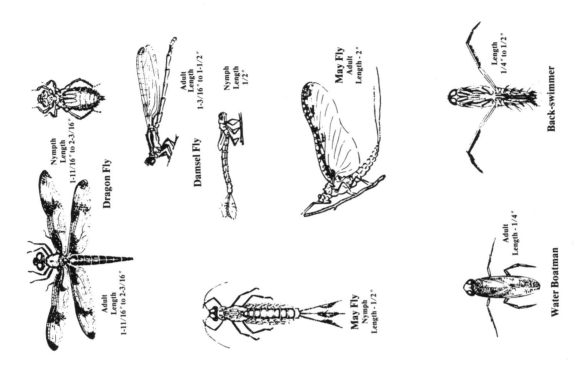

COMMON POND INSECTS

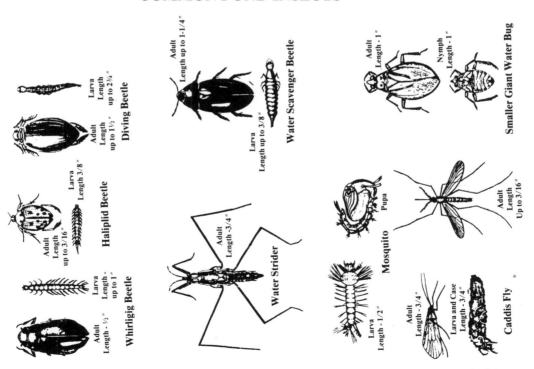

(Used by permission of Verne N. Rockcastle, Cornell Science Leaflet, Volume 60, No. 2.)

APPENDIX B

Field Guides and Keys
Insects: Creepy Crawler Guide

CREEPY CRAWLER GUIDE

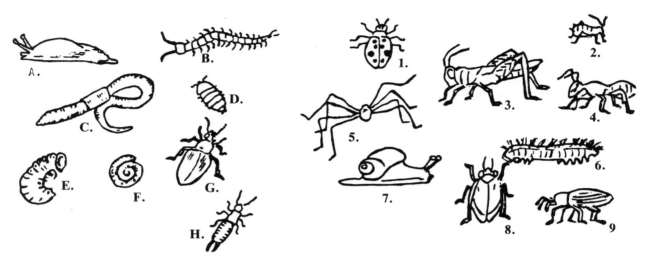

Critters Found Under Rocks

Critters Found on Plants

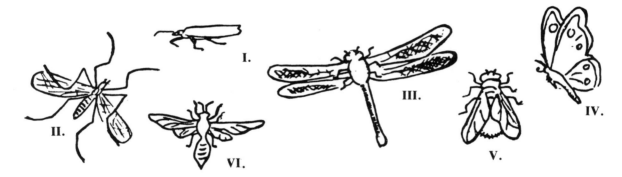

Critters Found in the Air

KEY

Critters Under rocks:

A. Slug
B. Centipede
C. Earthworm
D. Isopod
E. Beetle larva (grub)
F. Millipede
G. Ground Beetle
H. Earwigs

Critters on Plants:

1. Lady Bug
2. Aphid
3. Grasshopper
4. Ant
5. Daddy-long-legs (spider)
6. Caterpillar
7. Land Snail
8. Leaf Hopper
9. Weevil

Critters in the Air:

I. Lawn Moth
II. Crane Fly
III. Dragonfly
IV. Butterfly
V. Housefly or Horsefly
VI. Wasp or Hornet

*From a Guide created by Mary Vorndan for use
at the Helmer Nature Center. Used by permission.*

LEAVES

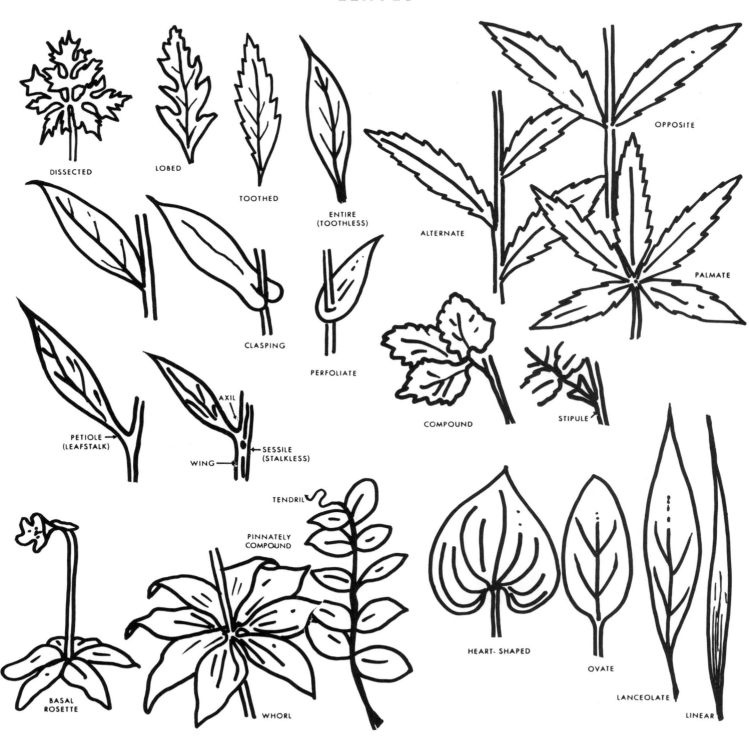

DISSECTED

LOBED

TOOTHED

ENTIRE (TOOTHLESS)

OPPOSITE

ALTERNATE

PALMATE

CLASPING

PERFOLIATE

COMPOUND

STIPULE

PETIOLE (LEAFSTALK)

AXIL

WING

SESSILE (STALKLESS)

TENDRIL

PINNATELY COMPOUND

HEART-SHAPED

OVATE

LANCEOLATE

LINEAR

BASAL ROSETTE

WHORL

From *Field Guide to Wildflowers* by Roger Tory Peterson and Margaret McKenny, Houghton Mifflin Co., Boston, 1968

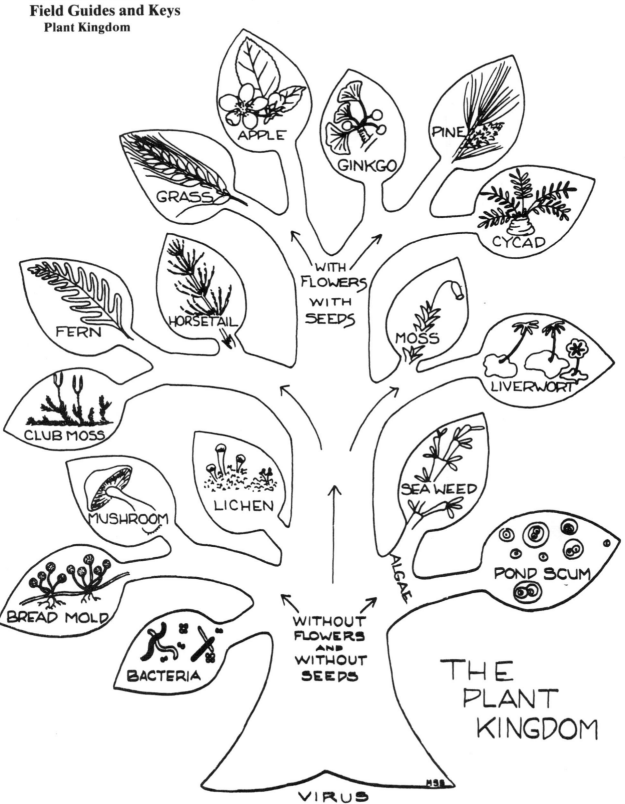

Tooth and jaw structure tell us so much about the eating habits of mammals that a good student can tell by the skull alone what animal it belongs to. Each species has its characteristic dentition ("arrangement of teeth," cf. "dentist"): combinations of the following:

INCISOR
(cutting)

CANINE
(tearing)

MOLAR
(grinding)

SKULLDUGGERY
AMONG THE MAMMALS
or Food Getting Adaptations

The teeth of mammals are adapted in different ways to get food.

HERBIVOROUS

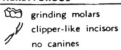 grinding molars
clipper-like incisors
no canines

INSECTIVOROUS

All teeth sharp-pointed, suitable for catching, holding and cutting prey.

CARNIVOROUS

 sharp molars for tearing and cutting,
canines for slashing.

OMNIVOROUS

Such animals as **opossums, skunks, coons,** and **man** are omnivorous; literally eating anything. This broad diet is reflected in the teeth which are less specialized than in most mammals.

Gnawers of seeds, roots, and stems. **Rodents, Field Mice** and **woodchucks,** like all rodents, have long incisors, and a space between the incisors and molars. The chewing area can be closed off by a fold of skin for food storage.

Insect Eaters. Insectivores
Insects are attracted to plants of the fields and grasslands, and they, in turn, attract **moles** and **shrews.** These animals have a battery of small teeth useful in seizing and crunching hardshell beetles and other small fry.

Meat Eaters. Carnivores
Field mice, moles, and shrews attract **foxes,** who feed on them and on rabbits, abundant in grassy meadows. Foxes have teeth equipped to handle meat. The canine teeth help seize and tear prey.

Stem croppers. Ungulates ("having hoofs")

Cows and **deer** have no upper incisors. They tear grass with lower teeth and lips against the upper roof plate. **Sheep** and **goats** have similar dentition, but crop the grass closer as their jaws are narrower, and lips thinner. Sheep are not popular on cattle ranches!

Horses bite grass stems. They have both upper and lower front teeth.

Dentition is expressed in a dental formula. The example given means that in one-half of man's jaw, from front to back, there are 2 upper and 2 lower incisors, 1 upper and 1 lower canine, 2 upper and 2 lower pre-molars, and 3 upper and 3 lower molars.

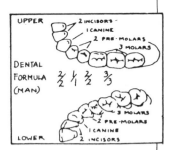

UPPER — 2 INCISORS, 1 CANINE, 2 PRE-MOLARS, 3 MOLARS

DENTAL FORMULA (MAN) $\frac{2}{2} \frac{1}{1} \frac{2}{2} \frac{3}{3}$

3 MOLARS, 2 PRE-MOLARS, 1 CANINE, 2 INCISORS — LOWER

(Used by permission of Massachusetts Audubon Society, Lincoln, MA 01773.)

ANIMAL TRACKS

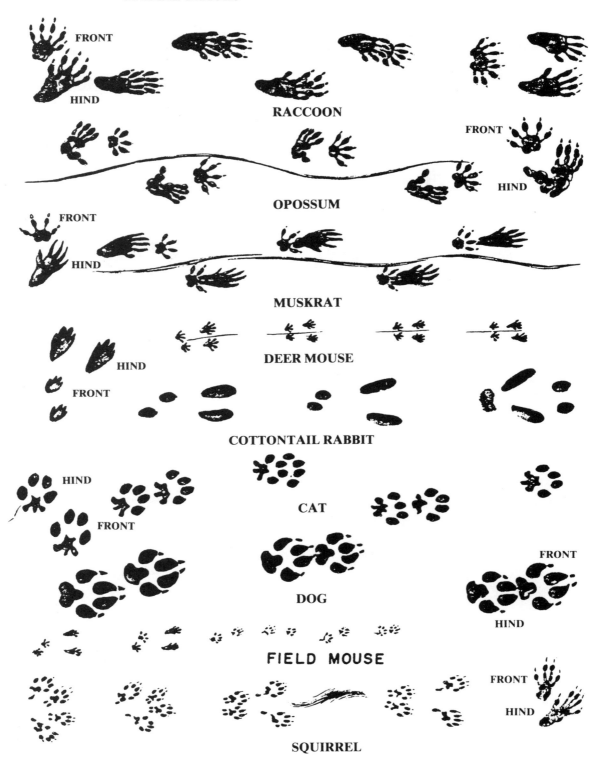

RACCOON

OPOSSUM

MUSKRAT

DEER MOUSE

COTTONTAIL RABBIT

CAT

DOG

FIELD MOUSE

SQUIRREL

APPENDIX B
Field Guides and Keys
Tracks

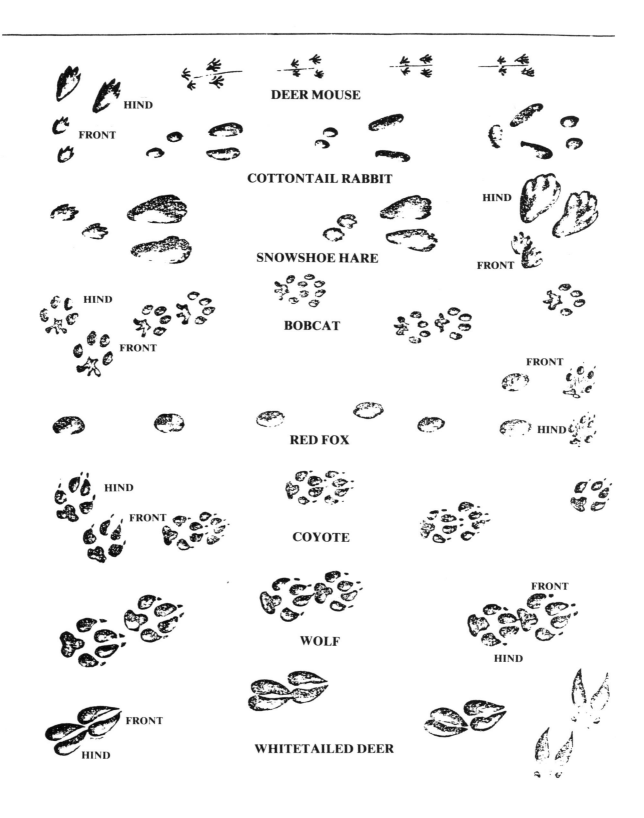

DEER MOUSE

COTTONTAIL RABBIT

HIND
FRONT

SNOWSHOE HARE

HIND
FRONT

HIND
FRONT

BOBCAT

FRONT
HIND

RED FOX

HIND
FRONT

COYOTE

WOLF

FRONT
HIND

FRONT
HIND

WHITETAILED DEER

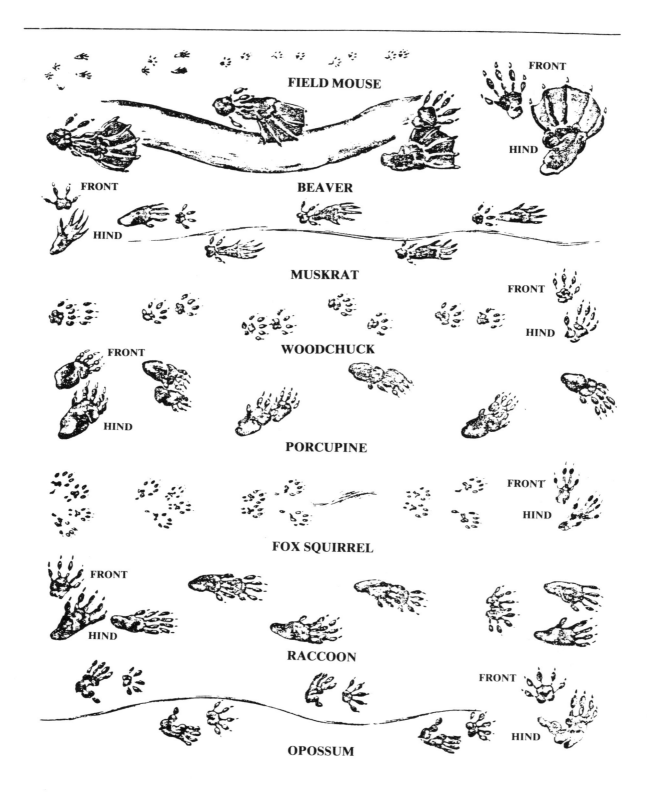

FIELD MOUSE

FRONT

HIND

FRONT

BEAVER

HIND

MUSKRAT

FRONT

HIND

FRONT

WOODCHUCK

HIND

PORCUPINE

FRONT

HIND

FOX SQUIRREL

FRONT

HIND

RACCOON

FRONT

HIND

OPOSSUM

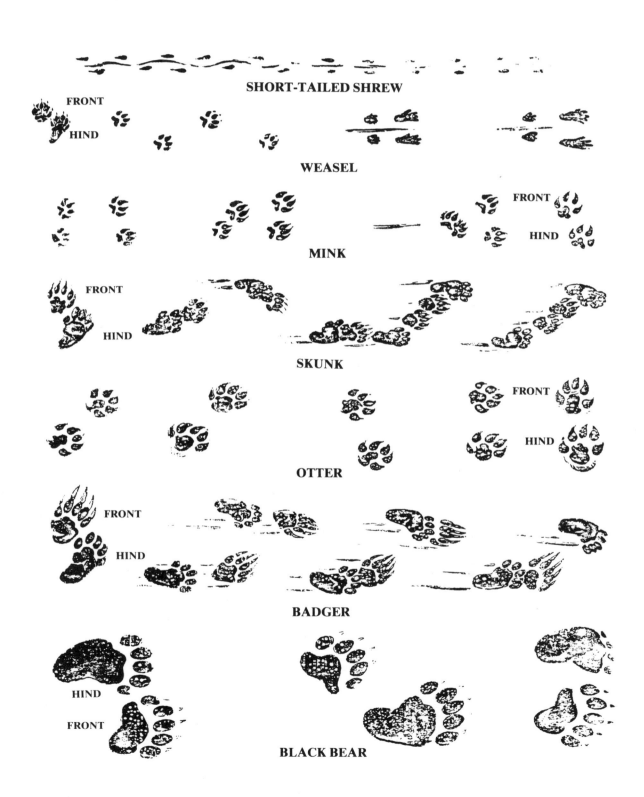

SHORT-TAILED SHREW

WEASEL

MINK

SKUNK

OTTER

BADGER

BLACK BEAR

APPENDIX B
Field Guides and Keys
Trees: Aid to Identification

TREES — AN AID TO IDENTIFICATION

Trees may be identified by shape, bark, leaf, flower and fruit
(and in winter by their characteristic buds and leaf scars).

A. <u>SHAPE</u> of the tree, growing in the open,   and   ANGLE OF BRANCHES

Red Cedar   Fir or Spruce   White Oak   Maple   Red Oak   White Oak   Pin Oak   Elm

B. <u>BARK</u> – an expert can tell trees by their bark. Examples easy to identify are:
   Shaggy, in long, loose strips – Shagbark Hickory   White, peeling – White Birch
   Gray, mottled with yellow – Sycamore   Light gray, smooth – American Beech

C. <u>LEAF</u>
   1. Shape – notice the edge as well as the whole shape.

   Pine   Maple   Elm   Gray Birch   Oaks

   White Oak group – rounded lobes

   Red & Black Oak group – bristle-tipped lobes

   2. Texture
      Leathery – Wild Black Cherry   Rough – Elm
      Crisp, like a new dollar bill – Beech

   3. Structure – to distinguish a simple leaf from a leaflet on a compound leaf, look for the new bud at the base of the leaf stem.

   SWEET GUM   GINKGO   (like a hand) palmately compound   HORSE CHESTNUT   (like a feather) pinnately compound

      a. Simple leaf, single leaf on a stem.   b. Compound leaf, several leaflets on a stem.

   4. Manner of growth on twig

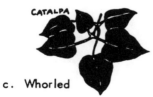

   Only 4 common trees have opposite leaves and twigs: Maple, Ash, Dogwood, <u>HORSE</u> Chestnut

   CATALPA

      a. Alternate   b. Opposite   (Remember MAD HORSE)   c. Whorled

D. <u>FLOWER</u> – all trees have flowers.
      Conspicuous flowers – fruit trees and Magnolia
      Lacking petals, harder to see – Elms and some Maples
      Catkins – Alders, Birches, Oaks and nut trees
      Many small flowers surrounded by white or colored bracts – Dogwood

E. <u>FRUIT</u> – the structure which follows the flower and contains the seeds.
      Fleshy fruit – Apple, Cherry, Pear   Cone – Conifer   Acorn – Oak
      Winged fruit – Maple, Elm, HopTree   Nut – Beech, Hickory

Ref. George A. Petrides, <u>A Field Guide to Trees and Shrubs</u>, Houghton Mifflin Co., 1958

BASIC LEAF FORMS

DECIDUOUS TREES:

TREES THAT LOSE THEIR LEAVES IN THE FALL.

1. **Arrangement of the Veins**—this helps give the leaf its shape.

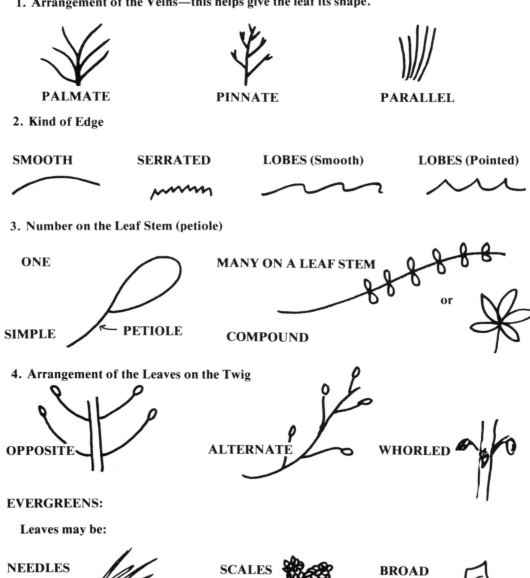

PALMATE   **PINNATE**   **PARALLEL**

2. **Kind of Edge**

SMOOTH   **SERRATED**   **LOBES (Smooth)**   **LOBES (Pointed)**

3. **Number on the Leaf Stem (petiole)**

ONE   **MANY ON A LEAF STEM**

SIMPLE   ← **PETIOLE**   **COMPOUND**   **or**

4. **Arrangement of the Leaves on the Twig**

OPPOSITE   **ALTERNATE**   **WHORLED**

EVERGREENS:

Leaves may be:

NEEDLES   **SCALES**   **BROAD**

APPENDIX B
Field Guides and Keys
Trees: Tree Designs Worksheet

TREE DESIGNS WORKSHEET

The pictures below show several different designs found on trees.
Each row of pictures shows a different part of the tree. Circle the pattern
in each row that best shows your tree design. If none of the pictures look
like your tree design, draw in your own in the empty space provided.

						Other	6. Location
1. Tree Silhouettes	Round	Spreading	Pyramidal	Pyramidal/ Evergreen	Narrow		
2. Bark Patterns	Horizontal	Vertical	Smooth	Combination			7. Name of Tree
3. Patterns Of Buds	Opposite	Alternate	Whorl				
4. Fruits	Winged Seed	Cone	Berries	Nut			
5. Leaf Patterns	Simple	Compound	Compound	Long Needles	Short Needles		

(From: City, Trees, Country Trees. Original concept.
Used by permission of Thomas B. Wolfe, NYS, D.E.C.)

══════APPENDIX C══════

How to Make:
    Accordion Fold Guide
    Ant/Earthworm Houses
    Berlese Funnel

Accordion-Fold Guide

A handy graphic reference device to use as an aid when identifying wildflowers is the accordion-fold guide. It rapidly and readily illustrates the classification appearance of flowers using the terminology in field guides. To make this pocket-held folding booklet, first duplicate the drawings and examples on the next three pages. Cut them out on the lines and cover with clear contact paper (or laminate) on cardboard or index cards. Pressed live specimens may also be used.

Reinforce the seams between each with strips of clear contact or transparent tape. Fold accordion-style, so that when you open it, it opens outward with one movement and closes easily and compactly, and slips into a pocket or field bag.

May be adapted for other field uses, for example: insect families, beach and marine forms, bird shapes, etc.

(Courtesy: Win and Pam Carter, based on ideas of Maria Montessori.)

Ant House (or Earthworm House)

Ants or earthworms may be kept in glass houses. Ants' homes can be narrower (1/2 by 3/4 inches) than earthworms (1 inch). Use two panes of window glass. Have blocks of wood cut to the dimension of the glass. Glue the glass to the wood, using an adhesive that is suitable. (Read the label. Silicone cement will be good.) Glue two small pieces of wood crosswise on the bottom to act as a supporting base.

For ants, fill halfway with soil. Introduce ants and add more soil. The ants can be found under rocks or logs and in other places. Cover top loosely with fourth piece of wood. Feed and place wet cotton ball on top.

For earthworms, fill halfway with soil. Introduce worms. Add a bit more soil and lots of leaf litter. Both homes should be covered with a dark paper curtain on both sides for maximum activity. It can be lifted when viewing.

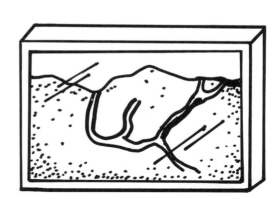

Berlese Funnel

Animals that live in the soil shun the light. The light also dries the soil. To force these creatures out of the soil where they may be identified, create a funnel that leads into an alcohol-filled jar. The spout of the funnel and the jar should be a light-tight container, like a coffee can. Place the entire set up under a lightbulb. Allow it to stay for two or three days, then lift up the funnel and examine the creatures that have dropped into the alcohol and are now preserved in it. You may see many more if you use the microscope (10X).

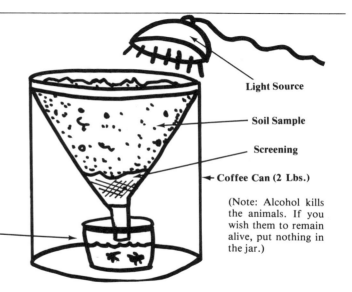

Light Source

Soil Sample

Screening

← **Coffee Can (2 Lbs.)**

(Note: Alcohol kills the animals. If you wish them to remain alive, put nothing in the jar.)

Small Jar with Alcohol

Kinds Of

Inflorescence

PAM + WIN CARTER /AUDUBON

flower

regular

flower

- lip

irregular

<u>Examples</u>: clover,
dandelion, composites

a group of flowers joined
together in a short, dense
terminal cluster.

head

APPENDIX C
How to Make
Accordian Fold Guide

Examples: yarrow,
pearly everlasting

a flat-topped or convex
branched flower cluster,
branching _alternate_.

corymb

Examples: ragweed,
enchanter's nightshade

an elongated flower
cluster - flowers that are
stalked arranged along
a central stem.

raceme

Examples: wild parsnip,
Queen Anne's Lace

a flower cluster in
which all flower stalks
radiate from the same
point, like an umbrella.

umbel

Examples: vervains,
common mullein,

an elongated flower
cluster with _stalkless_
flowers on a central stem.

spike

APPENDIX C
How to Make
Accordion Fold Guide

EXAMPLES: motherwort, whorled loosestrife

arranged in a circle around a central point.

WHORLS

EXAMPLES: panic grass, panicled aster, jewel weed

an elongated, branched flower cluster.

PANICLE

EXAMPLES: arrow arum, jack-in-the-pulpit, skunk cabbage

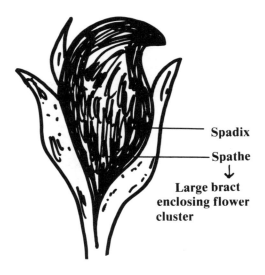

Spadix

Spathe

↓

Large bract enclosing flower cluster

spadix—fleshy spike of flowers

EXAMPLES: chickweek, flat-topped aster

a more or less flat-topped branched flower cluster in which the branching is opposite.

CYME

APPENDIX C
How to Make
Bird Feeders

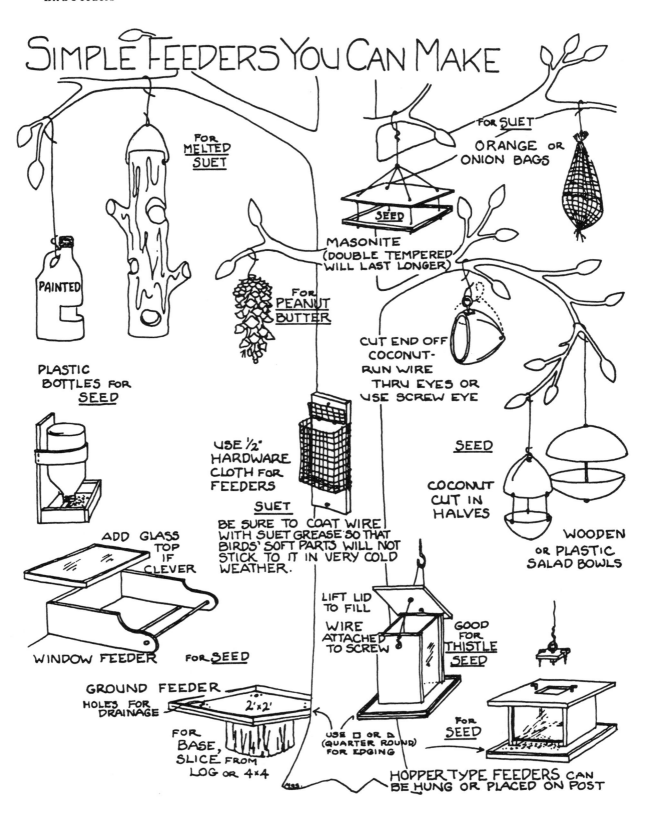

SIMPLE FEEDERS YOU CAN MAKE

FOR MELTED SUET

FOR SUET
ORANGE OR ONION BAGS

PAINTED

MASONITE (DOUBLE TEMPERED WILL LAST LONGER)

PLASTIC BOTTLES FOR SEED

FOR PEANUT BUTTER

CUT END OFF COCONUT- RUN WIRE THRU EYES OR USE SCREW EYE

SEED

USE ½" HARDWARE CLOTH FOR FEEDERS

SUET
BE SURE TO COAT WIRE WITH SUET GREASE SO THAT BIRDS' SOFT PARTS WILL NOT STICK TO IT IN VERY COLD WEATHER.

COCONUT CUT IN HALVES

WOODEN OR PLASTIC SALAD BOWLS

ADD GLASS TOP IF CLEVER

WINDOW FEEDER   FOR SEED

LIFT LID TO FILL
WIRE ATTACHED TO SCREW

GOOD FOR THISTLE SEED

GROUND FEEDER
HOLES FOR DRAINAGE

2'x2'

FOR BASE, SLICE FROM LOG OR 4x4

USE □ OR ◿ (QUARTER ROUND) FOR EDGING

FOR SEED

HOPPER TYPE FEEDERS CAN BE HUNG OR PLACED ON POST

(Used by permission of Massachusetts Audubon Society, Lincoln, MA 01773.)

MORE IDEAS FOR FEEDING BIRDS

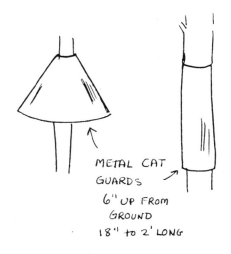

METAL CAT
GUARDS
6" UP FROM
GROUND
18" to 2' LONG

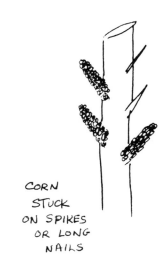

CORN
STUCK
ON SPIKES
OR LONG
NAILS

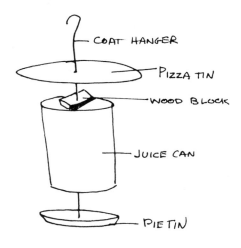

COAT HANGER

PIZZA TIN

WOOD BLOCK

JUICE CAN

PIE TIN

TO HAND-TAME BIRDS,
DRESS A DUMMY IN COAT
AND HAT. WHEN BIRDS
LEARN TO FEED FROM ITS
HAND, EXCHANGE PLACES
AND CLOTHES WITH DUMMY

APPENDIX C

How to Make
Chick Brooders
Electrical Games

Chick Brooder

Make a large wooden box, about 16-18″ high and big enough to hold the number of baby chicks you'll be hatching. For 12-24 chicks, box can be about 4′ x 2½′. You must have a source of heat, a lamp with a 75-100 watt bulb is fine. The bulb must be kept on day and night—temperature must be maintained at 90° F. It should have a screen cover and the cover should be placed on whenever it is unattended. No predators can get in; and, later, chicks can't get out. Line bottom with many layers of newspaper. Wood shavings may be used, too.

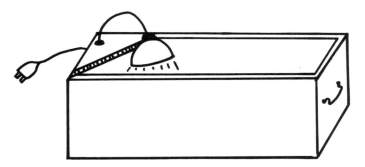

Electrical Games

Games that buzz or light when the answer selected is correct, are very popular with children of all ages. You may need assistance from the craft or maintenance shop, preparing and cutting wood, making the holes, soldering wire, etc. Electrically wired games are of two types:

1. The wires may be placed so that only the correct match will complete the circuit.

2. The wires may be placed to offer two choices, e.g., YES/NO, TRUE/FALSE. (See the wiring diagram on the next page.)

Both types, however, should have changeable questions, or things to match, i.e., some means of replacing the ques-

tions. Therefore, do not write directly on the wood, since your major work will be the preparation of the board itself and its wiring. Then, when the children tire of it or have learned all they can from the game, you just switch cards or questions.

The matching type of board lends itself to topics like tree, bird, wildflower or mammal identification. The sets of Audubon cards are well-suited for this use. The "either-or" type of board lends itself to single topics. Example: *Birds.* Ten questions about birds, answerable by TRUE or FALSE. 1) All birds have feathers. 2) All birds fly. 3) All birds lay eggs. 4) All birds migrate, etc. Be sure to re-wire a few when you change the questions, so that kids don't just memorize by position. Keep books available for looking up correct answers.

For complete directions and other electrical game suggestions, order the pamphlet *Nature Quiz: Electric Nature Games* by Dorothy A. Treat, from National Audubon. The Audubon Tree and Bird Study Programs are also good sources for TRUE/FALSE questions.

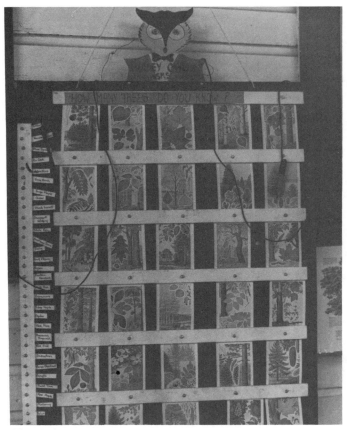

Electrical games

MATCHING—TYPE BOARD

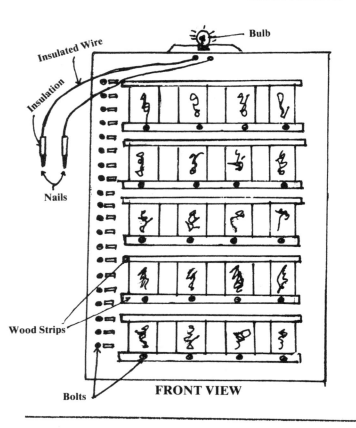

FRONT VIEW

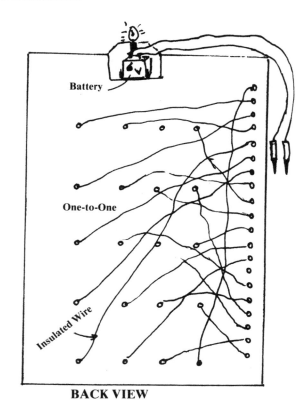

BACK VIEW

EITHER/OR—TYPE BOARD

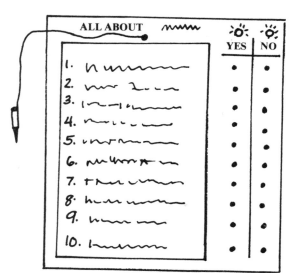

FRONT VIEW

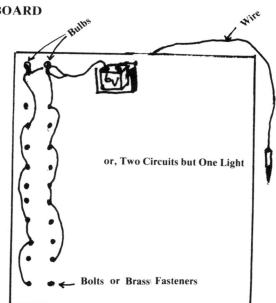

or, Two Circuits but One Light

BACK VIEW

APPENDIX C

How to Make
Feely Boxes
Insect Cages

Feely Boxes

A very popular display and lesson motivator is the Feely Box. Made by cutting the top off an old sock and stretching and glueing on an oatmeal or other round box, the Feely Box resists looking and encourages only using the fingers.

Suggested items:

1. evergreen cones
2. snake skin
3. acorn, other nuts
4. seed pods
5. bird feathers
6. twig
7. bark
8. leaf or sprig
9. rock (smooth)
10. rock (rough)
11. sweet gum ball (prickly warnings)
12. sycamore ball
13. peanut
14. lima bean
15. shell (clam)
16. bone
17. snail
18. starfish
19. evergreen sprig
20. nest (small)

Change items in the Feely Box every third or fourth day. Use the items to initiate discussion. If you wish, you may have more than one Feely Box, but avoid repetition. A variation is the stationary Feely Box that is affixed behind a wall or table and children put their hand in when they pass by.

Children may have an odd reaction to Feely Boxes, at first. They are very reluctant to put their hands in, questioning if there is something in there that will bite or hurt them or that feels disgusting. They need to be reassured; be certain you don't put anything prickly inside so as not to reinforce this fear.

Insect Cage (Large)

This cage is suitable for raising moths and butterflies from egg to adulthood.

Materials:

Two round bleach containers, ½ gallon or gallon size, or any circular plastic bottle (like large soda bottle), sharp knife (mat knife), wire screening, plaster of Paris, waxed paper cup.

Procedure:

Cut the bottoms from two plastic bottles of the same size. Cut wire screening about 12-14″ tall x an inch or more than the circumference of the bottles. Roll the screening into a cylinder the size of the bottle; overlap an inch or so. Pull off some wires from the cut end and use that to sew the edges together. Make sure sharp wire edges are folded inward toward each other so they do not cut anyone.

Mix and pour plaster of Paris into one bottle bottom as a base. Put a paper cut into the center and set the rolled screen into the base. Allow the plaster to harden. The other bottle bottom serves as a top. The cup may now be filled with water to keep alive whatever plant the insect is feeding on. The cup may be pulled out and replaced when a fresh one is needed.

When placing plant in cup with water, stick the stem through a hole in a piece of cardboard first. Then, stick the stem in water. The cardboard prevents the caterpillar from drowning in the water.

(Olivia Hansen High Rock Park, Staten Island, NY. Used by permission.)

Insect cage

APPENDIX C

How to Make
  Insect House
  Insect Net

Insect House

If screening is not available, here is an alternative Bug House. Obtain a half-gallon milk carton and cut windows in two sides. Slip the entire carton into a nylon stocking and knot the top.

Children love to catch insects and observe them. Here is an alternative to glass jars which are dangerous and do not provide the right environment for keeping specimens.

Note:

1. Insects suitable for class observation are: caterpillars, beetles, ants, moths, butterflies, crickets, flies.
2. As many different insects as possible should be brought to class for observation.
3. Pick up some of the grass or leaves they are living on—these will supply both food and water.
4. Harmless insects should be released after observations are concluded, into the environment from which they came.

(Source: Ira Kanis)

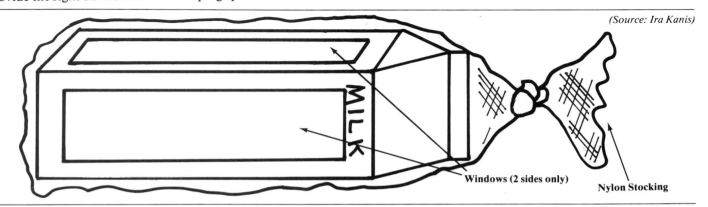

Windows (2 sides only)   **Nylon Stocking**

Homemade Insect Net

You'll need dowels or old broom handles, wire hangers, wire cutters, fine bridal veil netting and needle and thread, strong tape (cloth). Open the wire hanger and try to make it into a circle. Use wire cutters to cut ends of hanger off. Cut a rectangle of netting; fold and machine or hand stitch the long side and one end. Fold the other end over the wire circle and stitch down. Secure ends of wire to dowel with strong tape.

Note: Insect nets are easily torn. Instead of throwing them out when they tear, both homemade nets and those ordered from a supply house may be patched. Even when they can no longer be patched, cut off the old net, use it as a pattern, make a new net, and sew it on to the existing frame. When you cut off the old net, leave the fabric part where the wire goes through. Then you can sew it more easily.

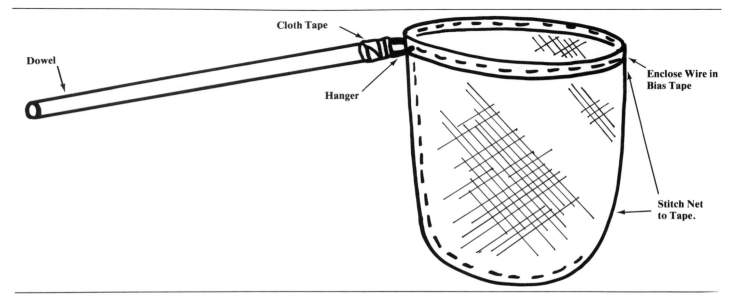

Cloth Tape

Dowel

Hanger

Enclose Wire in Bias Tape

Stitch Net to Tape.

APPENDIX C
How to
Raise Butterflies and Moths

HOW TO RAISE BUTTERFLIES AND MOTHS
by Colleen Seeley

The ability to raise butterflies and moths is a great aid in getting perfect specimens to round out a collection. More than that, it is a rewarding side hobby, particularly for the young, because it sharpens the eye and gives an intimate knowledge of the lepidoptera.

Knowledge of trees and plants is a big aid in rearing butterflies and recognition of plants is essential. Adult butterflies are very selective and will lay their eggs only on the plant on which the larvae will feed. Last spring we watched a female black swallowtail flying along the little creek behind our home. She flew down in the weeds, then up again, paused and then flew on. I watched closer and she stopped not on flowers but on the foliage of Queen Anne's lace. Then I knew what she was doing. I followed her and collected a few of the eggs she had laid, one at a time, on different plants. I could never have found them if I hadn't seen her place them. This is one method of gathering eggs, but rather slow if any large number are to be obtained. Sometimes one just happens to find eggs, but then one is not sure what they are.

Butterflies

I have experimented with several different ways for raising butterflies with some satisfying results. Here are some of the practical methods that really work.

Catch a female (the female can be told by the coloring, even at a distance) and place her in a nylon sack over a branch of the plant food she prefers and tie the bottom (4); or in a screen cage with plant food growing in it (2); or on a bouquet of plant food set in a bottle of water (1); or in a plastic box with picked leaves in it (3). You will obtain from a few to perhaps a hundred or so eggs. The female may be released after three days.

There are several ways to rear larvae. The best is to leave them in the sack or cage, changing the foliage if neded. If there are only a few eggs, remove the leaf with the eggs on it to a small plastic box. Most butterfly eggs take be-

tween five and seven days to hatch (monarchs take seven). The larvae must have a constant supply of food and must be kept clean. After the first week, cheesecloth over the top of the plastic box is better. It takes about two weeks for the larvae to become full size, then they will form chrysalises on the netting.

Bring the chrysalises into the house, where the expected butterflies will have room to expand their wings. I usually hang them on the bamboo drapes in our studio where I can watch them; the color changes and the wings can be seen through the chrysalises twelve hours before emergence.

With butterflies that have two or more broods a year, the butterfly will come out about the seventh day; in those having a single brood only, the butterfly will not emerge until the next spring. Let the butterfly fully expand. Put it in the killing jar just before it flies. In this way you will have a perfect specimen for your collection.

Moths

Rearing moths is quite different. One can start anywhere in the life cycle. Some start by finding a larva; I plan on raising those for which I have the plant or tree on which the larvae feed. If a female is caught outside it is assumed that she has already been bred. Ordinarily, the female moth does not fly until she is ready to lay eggs. If a female moth emerges in the house, a male must be put in with her or she can be tied outside. The moth should be tied out in the evening after she emerges from the cocoon and left all night (this is the German method). Tie the moth with strong thread, around the thorax, crossing and around the abdomen. The thread should be loose enough not to hurt the moth and tight enough so she won't escape. Tie the thread ends through a piece of screen and hang out of doors (5). Male moths will find her; sometimes nighthawks will, too.

To get eggs is easy. Simplest way is to put the female in a large paper sack, close the top by folding it over, holding it shut with a paper clip (6). Keep her in the sack from one to three days. Some moths, as the polyphemus, glue their eggs to the sack; the Virgo's eggs will resemble sugar in the bottom of the sack. If the eggs are glued to the sack, cut around them, put them in a plastic container with proper food and cover.

Hatching time varies. The polyphemus takes seven days. When they hatch, they usually eat the eggshell; prometheas do not. Then the little larvae must have their choice of leaves. I grew polyphemus on white birch and maple, though neither leaf was listed as their food. Birch leaves grew giant moths. I grew lunas on shagbark hickory, prometheas and cecropias on cherry, virgos and cajas on dandelion.

The larvae must be kept clean and without too much moisture. It is easier to raise a small number. If a glass jar is used, only two or three should be put in it. More satisfactory is a netting sack (I use nylon curtain material) over a branch of a tree with twenty or more larvae in it. This will have to be changed from time to time. Cut off the whole branch, put the sack over a fresh branch and put the larvae in it. The larger they grow, the more space and food they need.

Sphinx moths pupate in the ground. So after the last molt, feed them in a box or large can with two inches or so of peat moss in the container. The larvae will crawl down into the moss. These can be left right in the moss until they emerge. Most of the large moths spin cocoons on the branches. The cocoons are gathered and put in a coool place until time for emergence. Bring the moth cocoons in the house in the spring. A screened cage one foot, by 18 inches, by one foot, is ideal (7). The moth can crawl up and hang from the top to stretch its wings. If you have missed the big event, the moth will still be perfect. Watch the cocoons closely; some get wet on one end an hour or more before the moth comes out. The polyphemus does this.

If a screened cage isn't available, glue cheese cloth or netting on the inside of a cardboard box, stand it on end, and cover the front with plastic. The box must be bigger than the expanded moth will be. The netting gives the moth a foothold. If a moth has no place from which to hang to expand, he will not develop fully. Allow the moth to hang several hours before killing it so the wings will be hard enough to spread easily.

The polyphemus is the easiest to raise. I raised over fifty by the sack-on-tree method. I've raised lunas, cecropias and prometheas by the bouquet method. Great tigers and virgos were raised in plastic boxes. Good luck!

APPENDIX C

How to
Raise Butterflies and Moths

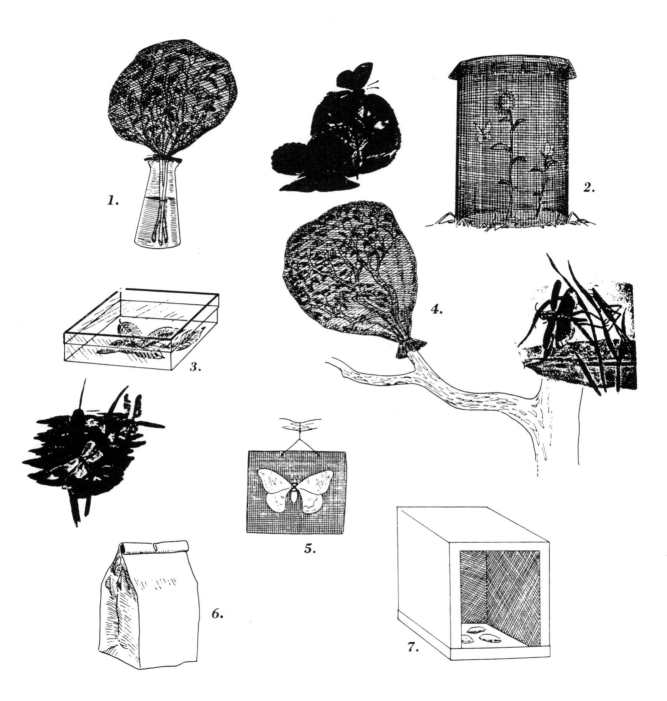

(From the New York State Conservationist, April/May 1963. Used by permission.)

APPENDIX C

How to
Spread Mount
Butterflies and Moths

HOW TO MOUNT BUTTERFLIES

You should have a spreading board, relaxing fluid, insect pins and a round-ended tweezer. The purpose of these materials is to enable you to soften dried and fragile butterfiles so that you can handle them without breakage and to position where you want to. Before you begin, please read through these instructions carefully. Remember, dried butterflies are very fragile and delicate in their dried state. Do not try to move the wings or handle or you will break them.

Dilute package of relaxing fluid with three parts of water to each package of fluid. Take any container which can be covered—coffee can, metal cookie box with lid, plastic container with lid, etc. Line the container with three layers of paper toweling. Saturate with the diluted relaxing fluid so that the paper is damp, not soaking wet. Place butterfly (in envelope) in container and cover with another layer of dampened paper towel. Close container tightly and leave for 24 hours to soften. See Ill. A

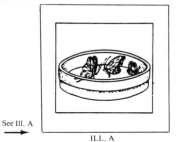

ILL. A

Remove butterfly from envelope. ALWAYS HOLD THE SPECIMEN BY THE BODY, NOT THE WINGS. Hold the thorax, squeeze gently and blow into wings. If properly softened, the wings will separate. If not soft enough, replace specimen in relaxing container between damp paper for another few hours. See illustration B.

ILL. B

With left hand squeezing thorax and by blowing gently between wings, wings will separate. Carefully insert black insect pin through the thorax, using your right hand. Be careful. Insert so that about 1/2 of pin protrudes through bottom. Place body of butterfly in grove of spreading board and push pin down into board, at the same time pressing body of butterfly gently down into groove. See illustration C.

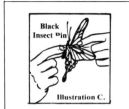

Illustration C.

Place a small ball of cotton between wings to hold in an open position. Use as much cotton as you wish to separate the wings in a V position according to your taste. Allow to stand and dry for a few hours. Place in a warm dry place to speed up drying process. Illustration No. D.

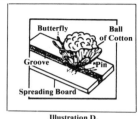

Illustration D.

When dry, carefully remove cotton. Remove pinned butterfly from board with pin still through specimen. Wings are now dried in a proper V position. Place a lump of glue on the top of the branch and glue on the bottom of the butterfly body. Carefully set butterfly on top of branch and gently push pin into branch to hold butterfly in place. Allow to dry. Carefully remove any excess glue from butterfly and/or branch. See Illustration E.

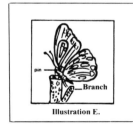

Illustration E.

Note: Although the butterfly will look more natural with the wings in a V position, some people may prefer to simply set the butterfly with closed wings. If you want to do this, soften the butterfly as instructed above. Place a lump of glue on branch. Apply glue to bottom of butterfly body. Allow to stand for a few minutes until glue becomes tacky. Press butterfly gently on branch and hold for a few minutes until the two parts hold together. Allow to dry.

A SUGGESTED DISPLAY FOR BUTTERFLIES

1. Glue branch near center of platform. Make sure there are no branches protruding over the edge of the board.
2. Glue moss all around the branch, covering cardboard completely. Stretch moss if necessary.
3. Glue pine cone to moss in any convenient place. Glue fern along pine cone or branch.   See Ill. C

4. Prepare butterflies for mounting. Glue butterflies on pine cone and/or branch. Save a large butterfly for the top of the branch. Make sure that this butterfly does not extend higher than the glass dome when set into position. Glue beetle into place on the moss, or wherever you prefer it. See Illustration F.

5. Transfer the completed arrangement to the base, with a few drops of glue under the cardboard. To keep the arrangement fresh, sprinkle a few crystals of para flakes (crushed moth balls) onto moss. Repeat this every 6 months. See Ill. G.

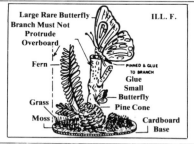

MOUNTING INSTRUCTIONS

1. Holding the pinned insect, place the body in the groove of the spreading board and force the pin into the groove. This will hold the butterfly in place. Place cardboard strip between wing and push wings down and pin as shown in figure 6. Repeat for other wings.

2. Lift one end of strip and with the other hand place pin in the heavy vein of the forewing. Pull the wing up until the bottom edge is at right angle to the body. Move bottom wing up so that just a little space shows at the outside edges of the top and bottom wings. When wing is in position pin cardboard strip close to the inner edges of the wings (near the body) using glass head pins. See illus. 6 and 68. Repeat for other side.

3. Next to thin strips, pin large strip of cardboard. Make sure this strip is large enough to cover wings.

4. Allow to dry on board for 24 hours. Remove pins and strips carefully. For picture of completely mounted butterfly, see figure 9.

The Butterfly Co., Rockaway, NY (212) 945-5400

===APPENDIX C===

How to Make
Plankton Net

Materials:

A. Small jar
B. Auto hose clamp
C. Shirt sleeve or nylon stocking
D. Sleeve is hemmed around loop from wire coat hanger
E. Nylon fishing line—36″ or more
F. Swivel to prevent lines from tangling
G. Tow rope—20 feet

Procedure:

1. Cut off shirt sleeve evenly at shoulder.
2. Sew ½ inch hem.
3. Cut small hole, ½″ in length in one side of hem. Run straightened hanger through hem to form circular opening and twist ends together. Cut off any excess wire.
4. Puncture cloth just below hanger at three even points around the circumference. Attach three 12″ lengths of fishing line at holes. Join free ends at swivel.
5. Cut off cuff of sleeve leaving one inch of doubled material.
6. Attach jar using auto hose clamp.

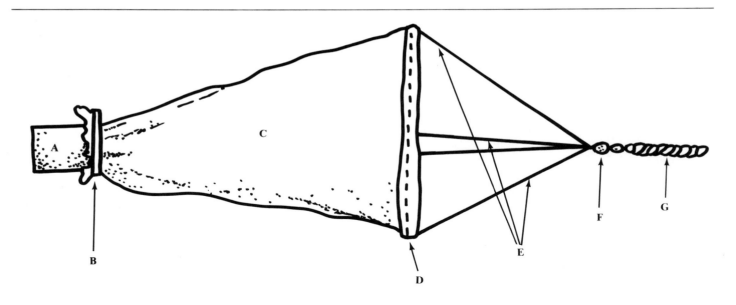

Silhouettes

Several activities call for pre-cut silhouettes of animals:

Sun prints	Habitats
Saran aquaria	Spatter prints
Flannel boards	

Children and adults are often frustrated by their inability to reproduce identifiable likenesses of animals, yet want to incorporate these likenesses in their art work. Use the following pages as an aid for preparing silhouettes. Duplicate, or use carbon paper to trace on shirt cardboard. Careful cutting with a small scissors is necessary to bring out the fine details. A coat or two of spray paint will provide greater durability for the delicate and intricate appendages. Make a few of the popular ones so you'll have enough to go around. Combine with plants or think up uses of your own for these.

APPENDIX C

How to Make
Silhouettes of Animals

APPENDIX C
How to Make
Silhouettes of Animals

Horned Owl

Hawk

Meadowlark

Canada Goose

Pintail Duck

Warbler

Great Horned Owl

Kingfisher

Heron

Grosbeak

Mallard

Owl

Barn Swallow

Cardinal

APPENDIX C

How to Make
Silhouettes of Animals

=**APPENDIX C**=

How to Make
Silhouettes of Animals

Chipmunk

Butterfly
in
Profile

Rabbit

Grasshopper

Turtle

Amanita

Barn Swallow

Mushroom

APPENDIX C

How to Make
Silhouettes of Animals

Woodchuck

Chipmunk

Beaver

Deer

WORM

Weasel

Fox

Dragonfly

River Otter

Frog

Frog

Squirrel

V.

Toad

Box Turtle

Water Snake

Garter Snake

Turtle

Salamander

Damselfly

Snail

Turtle

Beaver

Frog

Bat

Appendix C
How to Make
Smell Jars
Tree Bingo

Smell Jars

Aim:

To use another sense to discover the world of nature; in addition, the scents you will be bottling are all derived from plants, so we can point out that plant oils, herbs, spices make our own lives more interesting.

Materials:

Empty baby food jars, plaster of Paris, various spices, herbs, essential oils (bought in supermarket spice section or health food store or in store that sells supplies for candle-making). Some you might find: cinnamon, nutmeg, clove, peppermint, rosemary, lavendar, etc. NOTE: Do not use anything that is not or that may be an irritant to the nose. Show drawings or pictures of the plants from which they come.

Preparation:

Spray paint the tops of the baby food jars (optional—but it looks nice). When dry, use a hammer and nail to make holes in the tops. Mix and pour about ¼″-½″ of plaster in bottom of jars. When dry, that will act to absorb the scent. Some of the powdery spices will have to be ground with water in a mortar and pestle, or crushed with the back of a spoon in water. You do not want the children to inhale the materials. As an alternative, put the spices in the jars and cover the tops with fine netting so that the scent can come through, but not the powdered spice. Just use a small amount, as these things may be expensive and they'll need occasional replenishment. You can turn it into a guessing game; number each jar and write the names (or the picture) of the spice you've used. Have them match the number with the name. Or just for display, use lift up tabs to match the name with the number. Check for mold occasionally, and for dissipation of the scent. Do as many as your budget (and number of jars) will allow. Or do five each week, changing the spices to maintain interest.

Use the display as a motivator for activities or discussions about the olfactory sense in animals (and people).

Tree Bingo

Materials:

Access to a duplicating machine or copier, thirty to fifty shirt cardboards, clear contact paper (or laminating machine), paper cutter, colored dots (or marker).

Procedure:

1. Make thirty to fifty copies of each of the sheets with the drawings of the tree leaves and fruits.
2. Use one of each sheet as a *master* and identify each of the objects, writing the name of each tree on *only that* copy.
3. Rule horizontal and vertical lines on another sheet to act as cutting guides.
4. Spread out on a large surface in preparation for cutting and setting up the playing cards.
5. Use a paper cutter to cut apart the sheets into individual pictures; be sure to keep each picture in its own pile.
6. You will then have twenty-eight to forty-eight piles of forty-eight pictures; each pile is one picture.
7. Keep the master sheet in view (tape it with masking tape?) because you may have to refer to it.
8. Cut the contact paper *with backing still on* to the exact size of the cardboard. (If laminating, this step is not necessary).
9. Make the easy version first. Use half of your cardboards. You can fit twelve pictures on a cardboard. Select sixteen to twenty of the pictures you will use.
10. Spread all the boards out and randomly place the pictures on the boards, trying to vary their placement with each board.
11. Keep repeating, until all twelves spaces are filled. Remember, not all the boards will have all of the easy pictures, so skip some.
12. Adjust and switch the places so that each board is somewhat different. Check to see that all pictures are different.
13. Finally, peel the backing off the contact paper and seal the pictures onto the cardboard—or feed into laminator.

*****

14. Now, do the "hard" versions. Try to get sixteen of these pictures by cutting and overlapping since you want to use up the entire forty-eight and make it more of a challenge.
15. Repeat steps 10-13.
16. Make the calling cards. Contact seal one of each of the forty-eight pictures onto smaller pieces of cardboard. On the back, write the name of the tree and its part, and its distinguishing feature. This will enable you to teach it effectively. Example: White pine leaf—five long needles. Use colored dots or a marker to color code the easy and hard cards on the back since the easy cards get mixed in for the hard version and this allows you to separate them quickly.

Appendix C
How to Make
Tree Bingo

(Game and drawings used by permission. C. Pessino/B. Neill, Alexander M. White Natural Science Center, American Museum of Natural History.)

Appendix C
How to Make
Tree Bingo

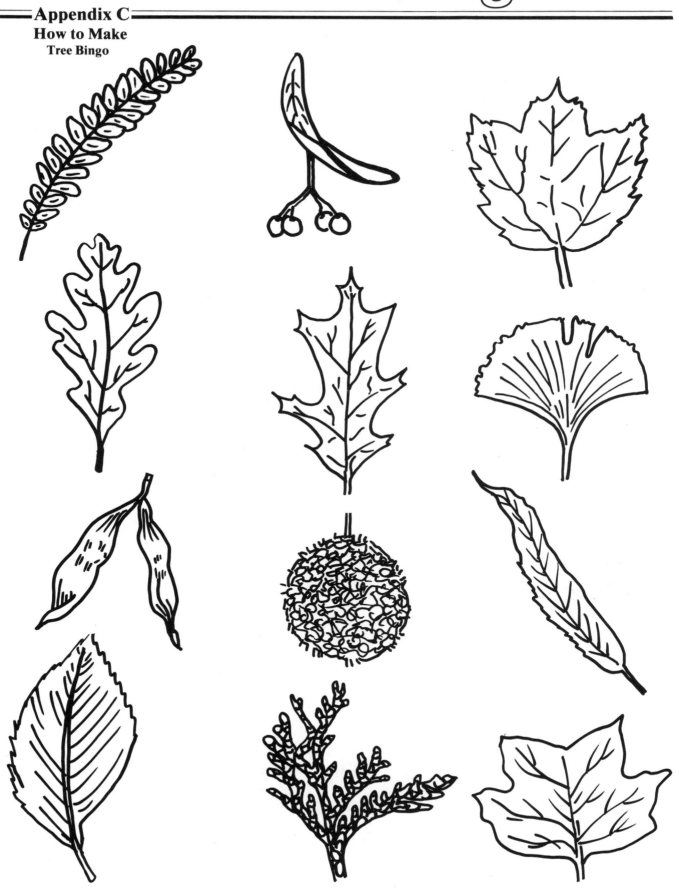

V.

Appendix C
How to Make
Tree Bingo

Appendix C
How to Make
Tree Bingo

Key to Tree Bingo Pictures

1. Page 140

Norway Maple Fruit (Seed)	Sassafras (Leaf)	Horse Chestnut Leaf
Sweet Gum Leaf	White Pine Leaves	Hemlock (Cone) Fruit
Oak Acorn Fruit (Seed)	Grey or White Birch	Sweet Gum Fruit (Seed pod)
Basswood Linden Leaf	Ailanthus Tree of Heaven (Leaf)	London Plane (Leaf)

2. Page 141

Honey Locust Leaf	Linden Basswood Fruit	Red Maple Leaf
White Oak Leaf	Black Oak Leaf	Gingko Leaf
Ailanthus (Fruit)	London Plane (Fruit)	Willow Leaf
Elm Leaf	Cedar (Arbor Vitae) (Leaf)	Tulip Leaf

3. Page 142

Beech Leaf	Catalpa Leaf	Mulberry Leaf
White Pine Fruit (Cone)	Osage Orange Fruit	Ash Fruit (Seeds)
Honey Locust Fruit (Seed pod)	Tulip Fruit	Catalpa Fruit (Seed pod)
Holly Leaf	Spruce Leaves	Dogwood Leaf

4. Page 143

Norway Maple Leaf	Shagbark Hickory Fruit	Elm Fruit
Balsam Fir Fruit (Cone)	Buckeye Leaf	Horse Chestnut Fruit
Ash (Leaf)	Hackberry Leaf	Apple Fruit
Birch Seeds	Mulberry Fruit	Hemlock Leaves

Appendix C

How to Make
Water-Scope
Wildflower Holder

WATER-SCOPE

To look below the surface of a pond, lake, or stream, a homemade waterscope provides a special glimpse into that wet world. Make several.

Materials:

A long plastic container, such as a quart take-out container or well-washed empty bleach or soda bottle, heavy duty clear plastic (such as a food storage bag), strong rubber bands, knife.

Procedure:

Cut off the closed bottom of the container with a good knife. If the resulting edge is ragged, cover with masking tape since that part will be held to the face and used for looking. Cover the open end with the clear plastic bag, pulling it as taut as possible. Secure the plastic around the opening with rubber band(s). If you wish, you can open the bag and pull it up, securing it at the top and bottom.

To use, while wading or leaning over the edge of the lake, push the plastic-covered end down under the water's surface. Peer through the cut end.

For a longer scope that will go a bit deeper, use a 2-liter plastic soda bottle. Cut off both ends. You may have to sand or file the edges so that they do not cut into the plastic.

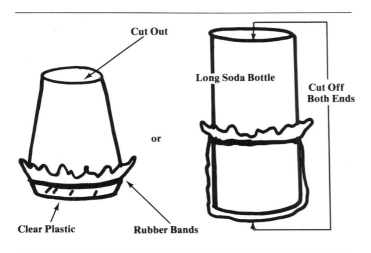

Cut Out

Long Soda Bottle

Cut Off Both Ends

or

Clear Plastic

Rubber Bands

WILDFLOWER HOLDER

An attractive way to display wildflowers is with a base made from a log or driftwood and with test-tubes or glass cigar holders for the flowers. Have the log planed, if necessary, so that it doesn't roll. Holes must be drilled that are *exactly* the diameter of the test tube or a fraction bigger; too small, the tubes won't fit in, too big, they'll topple. Space them about two to three inches apart. The holes should be at least an inch deep so the tube fits securely. If needed, use paper towels to wedge them in. (Sometimes, the log still has its insect inhabitants and the "sawdust" they produce becomes another lesson.)

The floral display should be looked at daily and should contain as many wildflowers as possible. The display should be as colorful as the flowers nature paints. Beneath each tube, shoot a staple or two from the staple gun, right into the log. This will form a little ledge on which small labels with the names of the flowers can perch. If you want to use this for testing flower identification, remove the name labels. Also, each flower has its season; what is plentiful early in July will be replaced by other wildflowers as the season progresses. If you print all the names on index cards first, cover the card with clear contact, then cut into small sizes, they will last longer.

It is best to change the water with a pitcher after dumping the discolored water out.

Wildflower holder

APPENDIX D

How to Care for Injured Birds

How to Care for Injured Birds

OUR RESPONSIBILITY

If baby bird is fully feathered, has short tail feathers and hops but doesn't fly . . .

Leave Him. His parents will return and take care of him (even if he has been handled by human hands!). You can best help by removing dogs and cats from the area.

IF you are POSITIVE that the baby bird is an orphan . . .

Baby Bird Headquarters

—Use a strawberry box for a nest and fill with paper towels and tissue. (Do not use old nest.)

—Temperature in "nest" should be 95° to 100°. Use outdoor thermometer as guide. Heating pad, hot water bottle or table lamp could be used.

—Using a blunt toothpick, feed baby bird formula *every ½ hour* during daylight hours.

—Place food *far* down throat when mouth is open, using blunt toothpick.

—When baby bird is too big for "nest" place him in cardboard box—see "temporary home for injured."

BASIC WILD BIRD FORMULA
(for most baby birds and injured adults)

1/4 lb. raw chopped beef
1 hardboiled egg yolk
1 tsp. wheat germ
1/8 tsp. garden soil

—sprinkle with vitamins
—moisten with water
—mix
—place in dish or serve on a blunt toothpick

Dry dog food moistened with water till soft is a convenient substitute for worms and bugs, or for above formula.

Slices of orange, banana, or peeled, chopped grapes and apples for older birds.

If possible, adult birds should be offered foods they eat in the wild.

If adult bird still will not pick uo food after 6 hours . . . *he may have to be forced fed.*

—Hold bird on towel in your lap facing away from you.

—Gently but firmly press on corners of jaw, slipping fingernail between upper and lower bill.

—Insert food as far down throat as possible—wait until bird swallows.

—For a robin size bird, feed ½ to 1 tsp. three times daily.

—*Never* force water or liquid down throat of any bird. With fingertip, place drops of water on the tip of the bill.

—Usually after two or three feedings the bird will start eating and drinking from a shallow dish or jar lid.

SHOCK—CONCUSSIONS

Put bird in small covered box with air holes.

Leave in quiet warm place for two hours. Release.

Or

Place bird in protected bush in sunny spot. Go away.

FIRST AID FOR INJURED BIRDS

—Clean cuts with Hydrogen Peroxide
—Apply first aid cream
—For broken or weak wing . . . wrap masking tape (NOT adhesive) around body and bad wing, using body as a support for folded wing. Remember to leave good wing free.
—Remove tape in three weeks

TEMPORARY HOME
FOR AN INJURED BIRD

Use a cardboard carton covered with a grate or screen. Do not use a parakeet cage.

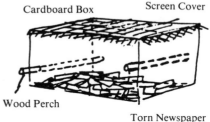

Cardboard Box   Screen Cover

Wood Perch   Torn Newspaper

Use wood perches of varying sizes.

Place torn newspaper or paper towel on floor.

Suggested Reading

Care of Wild, Feathered and Furred— Hickman and Guy

Bird Ambulance
Mockingbird Trio—Arline Thomas

My Orphans of the Wild—Collett

Wild Orphan Babies—Weber

(Used by permission. Sallie Ruppert, Volunteers for Wildlife, E. Norwich, NY 11732.)

APPENDIX D
Topography of a Bird

TOPOGRAPHY OF A BIRD

Locate the following:

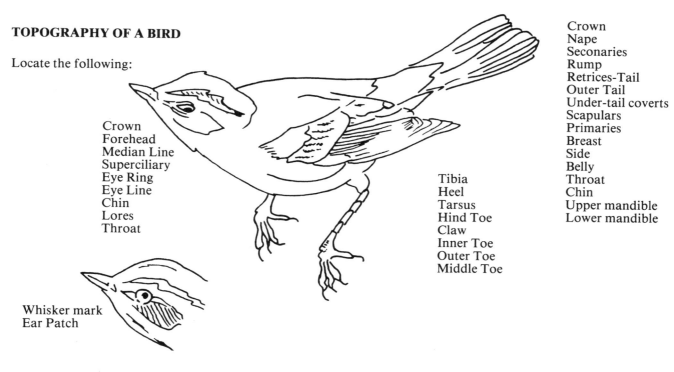

Crown
Forehead
Median Line
Superciliary
Eye Ring
Eye Line
Chin
Lores
Throat

Whisker mark
Ear Patch

Tibia
Heel
Tarsus
Hind Toe
Claw
Inner Toe
Outer Toe
Middle Toe

Crown
Nape
Seconaries
Rump
Retrices-Tail
Outer Tail
Under-tail coverts
Scapulars
Primaries
Breast
Side
Belly
Throat
Chin
Upper mandible
Lower mandible

FIRST BIRD WALK: See how many you are able to recognize already.

An old-timer took me on my first bird walk one morning. A House _____ flew up as we started down the path. On the lawn, a short-tailed, shiny black _____ waddled about near where a _____ was standing, head cocked, listening for worms.

A crested _____ shrieked in the oak tree up which a Downy _____ was hitching its way. In contrast, a Brown _____ spiraled up the neighboring tree where our _____ Owl was looking out of its hole. Overhead a _____ cawed and a _____ was flying from the bay or lake to its favorite garbage dump. From a thicket came the vigorous scratching of a _____ and from a branch above, we saw and heard the unoiled squeak of the Brown-headed _____. Nearby, on the feeder, a Black-capped _____, a White-breasted _____ and a Redwinged _____ were busy eating.

Over the garden, a black and yellow _____ bounced in characteristic flight calling "potato-chip." An orange and black _____ piped its treetop welcome to spring with loud whistles. From the barn door, a fork-tailed _____ whizzed out. On a dead apple tree perched that harbinger of spring, the _____.

From the distant creek came the rattle of a _____ flying to its lookout perch over the water. Near at hand from a maple, I heard the dry trill of the Chipping _____.

My first half-hour in the field that first walk taught me how easy it was to recognize twenty species of birds.

American Goldfinch	Chickadee	Herring Gull	Finch, Sparrow, Wren
Barn Swallow	Creeper	Nuthatch	Sparrow
Blackbird	Cowbird	Baltimore Oriole	Starling
Belted Kingfisher	Crow	Robin	Towhee
Bluebird	Blue Jay	Screech	Woodpecker

(Used by permission of Jack Padalino.)

APPENDIX D
What They Eat

YOU CAN TELL WHAT THEY EAT BY THEIR BILLS AND THEIR FEET

On this page are some wild foods (numbers 1-7) and some implements (bills and feet lettered A-G). If you were a bird, which implements would you need to collect each type of food?

Not to Scale

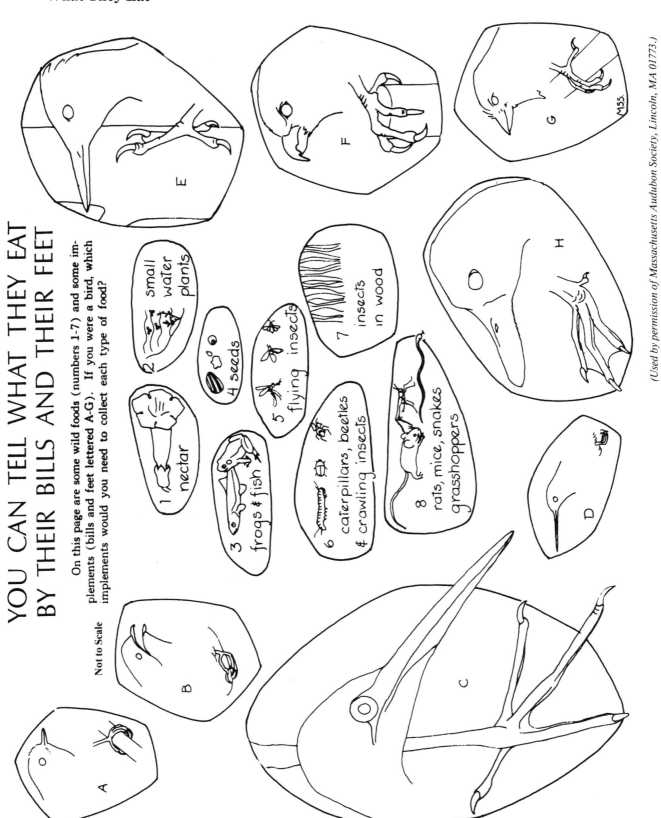

1 nectar
2 small water plants
3 frogs & fish
4 seeds
5 flying insects
6 caterpillars, beetles & crawling insects
7 insects in wood
8 rats, mice, snakes grasshoppers

(Used by permission of Massachusetts Audubon Society, Lincoln, MA 01773.)

APPENDIX D

How to Care for Injured Birds
  What They Eat

ANSWERS TO:

YOU CAN TELL WHAT THEY EAT
BY THEIR BILLS AND THEIR FEET

A.

6. caterpillars, beetles & crawling insects

F.

E.

insects 7. in wood

B.

5.

flying insects

8. rats, mice, snakes & grasshoppers

H.

small water plants

2.

C.

3. frogs & fish

not to scale

nss/m.as

1. nectar

D.

G.

4. seeds

(Used by permission of Massachusetts Audubon Society, Lincoln, MA 01773.)

APPENDIX E
Puzzles, Games, Word Searches

Word Search Puzzle #1

How many names of trees can you find in this puzzle? There are 34.

```
S  M  O  E  R  A  M  A  C  Y  S  O  Y

C  M  L  A  P  A  T  E  L  P  P  A  T

Y  M  F  I  G  U  E  R  Y  X  B  I  U

P  O  N  T  N  M  A  P  L  E  M  O  N

R  E  R  L  J  D  W  S  E  Z  W  U  T

E  P  A  O  E  O  E  C  H  H  A  Q  S

S  W  L  C  U  G  H  N  I  L  S  E  E

S  P  P  U  H  W  E  C  U  R  P  S  H

S  E  O  S  M  O  K  Y  R  R  E  H  C

C  C  P  T  A  O  G  O  V  I  N  S  Z

Y  A  Z  K  R  D  V  R  S  F  B  S  Y

O  N  A  Y  N  A  B  W  O  L  L  I  W
```

Apple	Cherry	Linden	Pine
Ash	Cypress	Locust	Plum
Aspen	Dogwood	Maple	Poplar
Banyan	Elm	Oak	Sequoia
Bay	Fig	Palm	Spruce
Beech	Fir	Peach	Sycamore
Birch	Hickory	Pear	Walnut
Cedar	Lemon	Pecan	Willow
Chesnut			Yew

Tree Puzzle #2 - These names are not in straight lines, but the letters must be adjoining each other, even diagonally (like in the game BOGGLE).

```
M A S H I
U P B D L
O L E A B
M H C R I
W E Y F G
```

Find the names of these trees: cherry   alder   beech   elm
ash   pear   pepper plum
larch   yew   hop   peach
mulberry fig   cedar
crab   apple   fir   birch

Tree Word Search #3

```
L B T Q A C O R N C E L M M C
I C R S E E D R L E A V E S O
M N E E V E R G R E E N P D L
B U E F S Y C A M O R E I L O
G T S A V D B R A N C H N O R
H P I U M W J O A K N Q E G S
R L B T A C F J F R U I T X K
O A R U P O A N A T U R E K Y
O N O M L N L A S H L W O O D
T T W N E E L N Z S P R U C E
P B N L B E E C H P T R U N K
```

Find these:

sycamore   nut   fruit   cone   spruce   log
trees   leaves   autumn   acorn   colors   nature
oak   brown   wood   plant   seed   beech
ash   fall   elm   root   branch   maple
limb   trunk   pine   evergreen

Ron Larson '75

Predator the food chain game
© COPYRIGHT 1973 AMPERSAND PRESS. OAKLAND. CALI'

(Used by permission of The Ampersand Company, Oakland, CA.)

Predator the food chain game
© Copyright 1973 Ampersand Press, Oakland, California

The Food Chain Game

On the preceding page, is a depiction of some of the plants and animals featured in the commercially available card game Predator, by Ampersand Press. The drawing of the various organisms can be used by itself, for younger children. Some suggestions for use follow:

1. The children can color and name all the animals. While they're coloring, talk about what the animal eats, to emphasize that all animals must eat plants or other animals (only living things are food for other living things).
2. Children can make up stories about what eats what.
3. They can color-code the producers, primary consumers, secondary consumers, decomposers.
4. They can draw the lines that connect the animal with its food source(s). They can then consider what would happen to some animals when others are threatened with extinction or when land is lost.
5. You could help them dramatize the picture, with each child assuming a specific role as shown in the drawing.
6. You could create a contest around the drawing, perhaps encompassing the idea of a food pyramid.
7. Present the drawing to youngsters and see what ideas THEY come up with!

APPENDIX E
Puzzles, Games, Word Searches

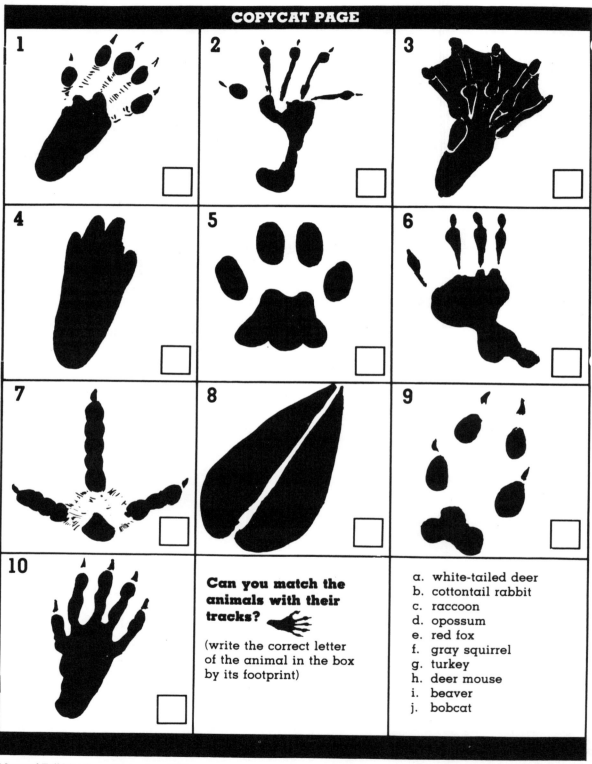

COPYCAT PAGE

Can you match the animals with their tracks?

(write the correct letter of the animal in the box by its footprint)

a. white-tailed deer
b. cottontail rabbit
c. raccoon
d. opossum
e. red fox
f. gray squirrel
g. turkey
h. deer mouse
i. beaver
j. bobcat

Mammal Tail Match-up, September, 1982
Bird Box Puzzle, May, 1983
Ant Maze, September, 1981

Tracks, January 1981
Bird Silhouettes, January, 1982
The Food Web Game, March, 1982
Classifying Animals, May, 1982

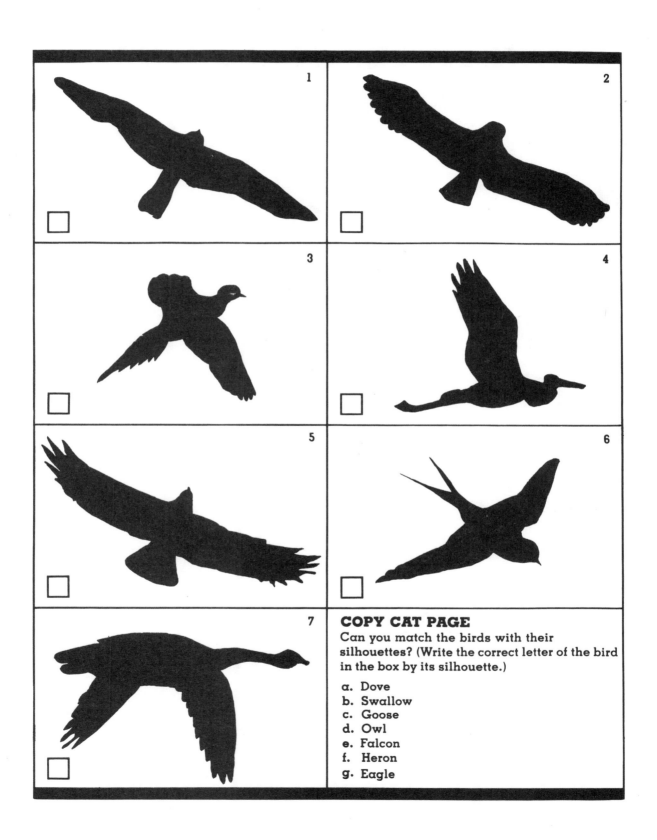

COPY CAT PAGE

Can you match the birds with their silhouettes? (Write the correct letter of the bird in the box by its silhouette.)

a. Dove
b. Swallow
c. Goose
d. Owl
e. Falcon
f. Heron
g. Eagle

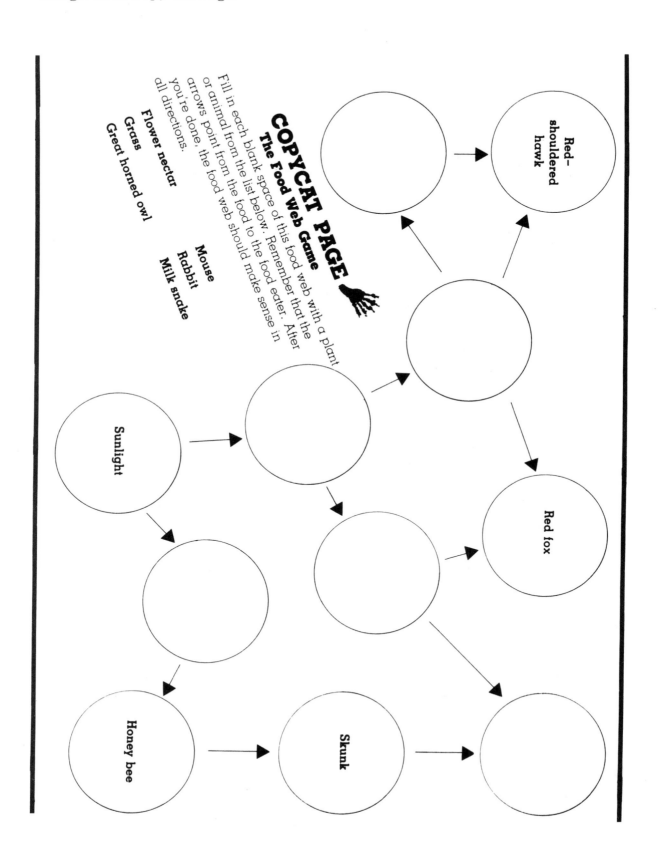

COPYCAT PAGE
The Food Web Game

Fill in each blank space of this food web with a plant or animal from the list below. Remember that the arrows point from the food to the food eater. After you're done, the food web should make sense in all directions.

Flower nectar
Grass
Great horned owl

Mouse
Rabbit
Milk snake

Red-shouldered hawk

Red fox

Sunlight

Honey bee

Skunk

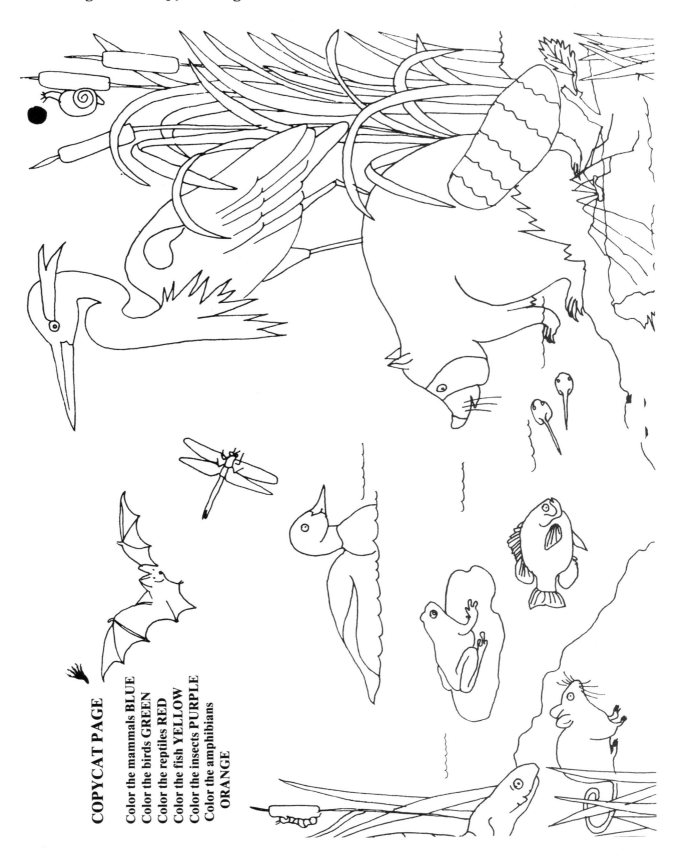

COPYCAT PAGE

Color the mammals BLUE
Color the birds GREEN
Color the reptiles RED
Color the fish YELLOW
Color the insects PURPLE
Color the amphibians
ORANGE

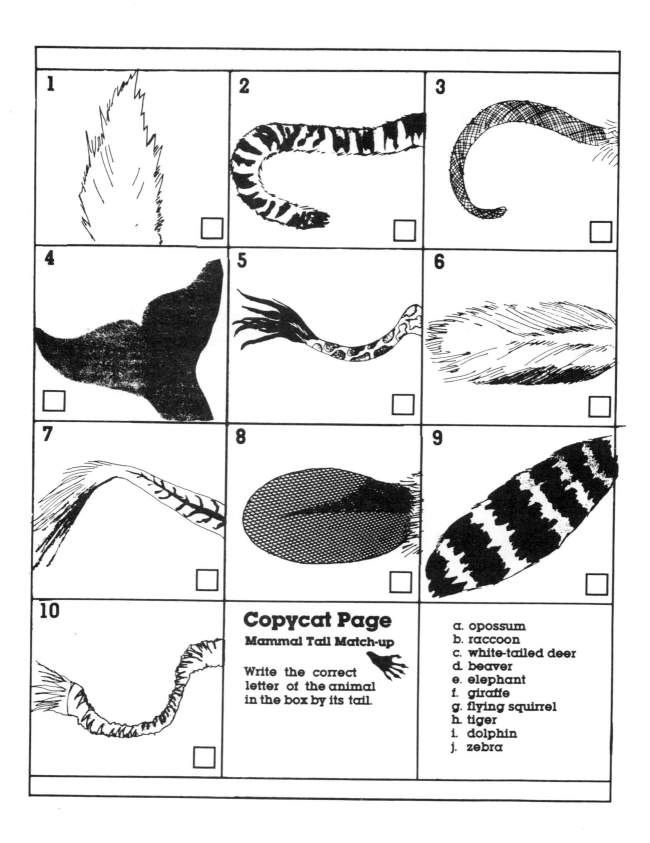

1

2

3

4

5

6

7

8

9

10

Copycat Page
Mammal Tail Match-up

Write the correct letter of the animal in the box by its tail.

a. opossum
b. raccoon
c. white-tailed deer
d. beaver
e. elephant
f. giraffe
g. flying squirrel
h. tiger
i. dolphin
j. zebra

Copycat Page

Bird Box Puzzle Write the name of each bird in each space. Find the one letter that all four birds in each row share and print it in the blank box at the end of each row. If your answers are correct, you will spell the name of another bird from top to bottom.

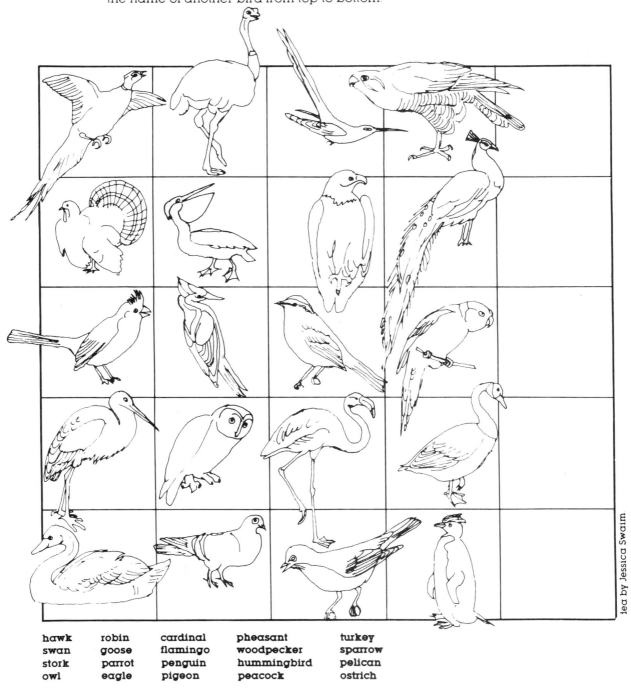

hawk	robin	cardinal	pheasant	turkey
swan	goose	flamingo	woodpecker	sparrow
stork	parrot	penguin	hummingbird	pelican
owl	eagle	pigeon	peacock	ostrich

COPYCAT PAGE

This little ant needs to bring food to the queen! Help her find her way to the "food room" <u>and then</u> to the queen.

FOOD ROOM

QUEEN

APPENDIX G
Things to Carry in Your Field Bag

APPENDIX H
The Nature Library

Things to Carry in Your Field Bag

1. Binoculars or scope, small
2. Bug boxes, clear plastic with lenses
3. Field guides—small, pocket size
4. Clipboard—small one with paper. (Make one from a piece of masonite and a squeeze clip.)
5. Hand lenses
6. Hand mirror, magnified on one side
7. Paper cups
8. Paper towels
9. Pencils
10. Plastic baggies, small sandwich size and larger sizes with twistems to close them
11. Pill bottles with lids; assorted sizes, for small specimens.
12. Plastic containers with lids, for larger specimens.
13. Pocket knife
14. String
15. Tape measure
16. Thermometer
17. Tissues
18. Trowel or tablespoon

The Nature Library

The nature library is an important adjunct to a successful nature program. The amount of knowledge about the natural world is staggering and much of this knowledge is available in books and other publications. Few people are totally expert at identifying all organisms; even the experts consult the field guides. Children also enjoy reading about nature and looking at pictures. You will also expand your own knowledge by referring to available resources. Reading material is available at all reading levels, and a variety of these levels should be represented in your camp collection.

Where to Get Books

Books may be obtained by the following means:

1. Cumulative purchases made by camp. Each summer add three or four.
2. School libraries are an excellent source of children's nature books.
3. Public libraries. Inquire about vacation lending policy (not all books, nor all libraries). Check the children's section for the most suitable selections.
4. Your own personal collection.
5. Used book stores often have great nature books.

Be certain to inventory all the books at the beginning and end of summer so you can keep track of them and know where each book must be returned.

Both hard covered books and paperbacks are utilized. The most useful books are the small, lightweight pocket guides; they are less expensive and more convenient than other kinds.

In the list that follows, books and other materials that I have found particularly useful and suitable for camp, are marked with an asterisk (*) and should be included in every camp nature library.

I. Field Guides

1. *The Golden Nature Guides,* Herbert Zim, et al.
    Birds
    Butterflies and Moths
    Flowers
    *Insects
    *Non-Flowering Plants
    *Pond Life
    Reptiles and Amphibians
    Sky Observer's Guide
    *Spiders and Their Kin
    Trees
    Weeds
2. *Nature Study Guild Pocket Finders,* Ma Theilgaard Watts, et al.
    Fern Finder
    Flower Finder
    Track Finder
    *Tree Finder
3. *The Peterson Field Guide Series,* by Roger T. Peterson, et al.
    Birds
    Butterflies
    Trees and Shrubs
    *Wildflowers
4. *Audubon Society Field Guides*
    North American Wildflowers, Eastern Region
    Birds
5. *Fruit Key and Twig Key,* William Harlow
6. *Name That Fern,* Elliott Blaustein
7. *Birds of North America,* Chandler S. Robbins, et al.
8. *Trees of the Eastern and Central United States,* William M. Harlow
9. *The Stars,* H. A. Rey
10. *Pocket Key to Common Wildflowers,* Lawrence Newcomb
11. *Spotter's Guide Series*
    Birds
    Rocks and Minerals
    Shells
    Trees
    Wild Flowers

II. References

1. *Aquatic Life*
   Beginner's Guide to Fresh Water Life, Hausman
   Life in a Drop of Water, P. Schwartz
   Life in a Pond, Robinson
   Life in Ponds, Gorvett
   *Pond Life, Cornell Science Leaflet
   Trip to a Pond, Hofman

2. *Birds*
   *A Chick Hatches, Joanna Cole and Jerome Wexler
   Boy Scouts of America Handbook—Bird Study
   From Egg to Chick, M. Selsam
   How and Why Wonder Book: Birds
   How to Know the Birds, R. T. Peterson

3. *Crafts*
   Fun with Naturecraft, Nagle and Leeming
   Nature Crafts, Johnson and Pearson

4. *Gardening* (catalogs and seed companies)
   *A Child's Garden, available from Chevron/Ortho
   Catalogs from seed companies (see the list in this section)

5. *Insects and Spiders*
   Adventures with Insects, Headstrom
   Aquatic Insects and How They Live, R. McClung
   Kinds of Bees, D. Shuttlesworth
   Ants, Epple
   Bees, Edwin Way Teale
   Bees, Bugs and Beetles
   Beginning Knowledge Book of Ants
   Beginning Knowledge Book of Bees and Wasps, Heatlin
   Boy Scouts of America Handbook—Insect Life
   Caddis Insects, R. Hutchins
   Caterpillars, D. Sterling
   Collecting Cocoons, Hussey
   Catching, Rearing Moths & Butterflies, Dirig-Cornell
   Dragonflies, H. Simon
   First Guide to Insects
   Galls and Gall Insects, R. Hutchins
   How and Why Wonder Books
      Ants and Bees
      Butterflies and Moths
      Insects
   Honeybees, by S. Russell
   Insect Pets, by Stevens
   Insects and the Homes They Build, Conklin
   Insects and Their Young, R. Hutchins
   Insects Build Their Homes, Conklin
   Junior Book of Insects, Edwin Way Teale
   Our Six-legged Friends and Allies, H. Simon
   Story of Ants, Shuttlesworth
   Story of Flies, Shuttlesworth
   Story of Spiders, Shuttlesworth
   Wonders of the Spider World, Lavine

6. *Nature Games*
   A Leader's Guide to Nature-Oriented Activities, Betty van der Smissen and Oswald H. Goering
   American Folk Toys, Dick Schnacke
   Curriculum Enrichment Outdoors, John W. Hug and Phyllis J. Wilson
   Folk Toys Around the World, Joan Joseph
   Games of the North American Indians, Stewart Cullin
   Great Indoor Games from Trash and Other Things, Judith Conaway
   Learning About Nature Through Games, Virginia Musselman
   101 Best Educational Games, Muriel Mandell
   101 Best Nature Games and Projects

7. *Reptiles, Amphibians, Earthworms*
   Beginning Knowledge Book of Snakes, Loundes
   Discovering What Earthworms Do, Seymour Simon
   How and Why Wonder Book of Reptiles and Amphibians
   Reptiles, Carr
   Reptiles and Amphibians, Bevans
   Snakes, Herbert Zim

8. *Trees and Plants, Flowering and Non-Flowering, including Fungi*
   Ferns, Plants Without Flowers, B. Kohn
   First Book of Tree Identification, by P. Rogers
   Fun with Fungi, Cornell Science Leaflet
   How and Why Wonder Books:
      Mushrooms, Ferns and Mosses
      Trees
   *How to Know the Wildflowers, Mrs. William Starr Dana
   Leaves, P. Caulfield
   *Plants of Woodland and Wayside, Swain
   Plants without Leaves, R. Hutchins
   Story of Mosses, Ferns and Mushrooms, by D. Sterling
   This Is A Tree, by R. Hutchins
   Wondrous World of Seedless Plants

9. *Miscellaneous*
   Animal Architects, Friedman
   Animal Partnerships, Burton
   Animal Sounds, Mason
   Animals That Hide, Imitate and Bluff, Hess
   Animal Tracks, Mason
   *Animal Traces, Cornell Science Leaflet
   Bird Feeders and Shelters You Can Make, Ted Peltit

=APPENDIX H=
The Nature Library

APPENDIX I
Sources of Supplies
Computer Software

*Caring for Gerbils and Other Small Pets, Shuttlesworth
*Cornell Nature Study Leaflets
*Complete Care of Orphaned Animals, Spaulding
Discovering the Outdoors, Pringle
Experiments with a Microscope, Beeler and Branley
Exploring with a Microscope, P. Simon
Fun with Nature Hobbies, Hillcourt
Green Fun, Maryanne Gjersvik
*Handbook of Nature Study, A. B. Comstock
*How Animals Communicate, Gilbert
*How to Explore the Secret Worlds of Nature, Brown
How to Make a Home Nature Museum, Brown
*Insect Pets, Stevens
Joy of Signing, Lottie Rickerhof
Natural Partnerships
Nature with Children of All Ages, Sisson
*Odd Pets, Hess and Hagner
Practical Guide for the Amateur Naturalist, Gerald Durrell
Shelf Pets, Riccuitti
Small Pets from Woods and Field, Buck
*The Lorax, Dr. Seuss

10. *Environmental Discovery Series,* available from
    National Wildlife Federation
    1412 16th Street N.W.
    Washington, D.C. 20036

Change in a Small Ecosystem	#79187
Differences in Living Things	#70925
Fish and Water Temperature	#79090
Nature Hunt	#79105
Nature's Part in Art	#79178
Oaks, Acorns, Climate and Squirrels	#79089

Outdoor Fun for Students	#79230
Plant Puzzles	#79150
Shadows	#79034
Soil	#79132
Stream Profiles	#79203
Wind	#79043

Ranger Rick Activity Guides and their new publication, Naturescope, also available from National Wildlife Federation.

III. Magazines

National Wildlife
Naturescope
International Wildlife
Ranger Rick
    Available from:
        National Wildlife Federation
        1412 16th Street, N.W.
        Washington, D.C. 20036

Audubon
    Available from:
        National Audubon Society

Conservationist
    Available from:
        New York State Department
          of Environmental Conservation
        P.O. Box 1500
        Latham, NY 12110

Contact your state department of environmental conservation to find out if they publish a magazine.

IV. *Sources of Supplies*

Write to the address given for catalogs of various types of supplies which can be used in a nature program. No official endorsement of any of the suppliers is intended or implied.

  1. *Computer Software* (Manufacturers and Distributors of Educational Software)

CBS Software
Greenwich, CT 06836

Computer Skill Builders
Department EE
P.O. Box 42050
Tucson, AZ 85733

Earthware Computer Service
P.O. Box 30039
Eugene, OR 97403

Edu-Soft
CA
1-800-227-2778

Educational Computing
Oakton, VA 22124

Krell Software
1320 Stony Brook Road
Stony Brook, NY 11790

Learning Arts
Department EE
P.O. Box 179
Wichita, KS 67201

Micro Center
Box 6
Pleasantville, NY 10570

V.

═══**APPENDIX I**═══

Source of Supplies
Computer Software
Gardening Aids
Gardening Seeds

Micro Ed
P.O. Box 444005
Eden Prairie, MN 55344

2. *Gardening Aids*

Cornell Cooperative Extension
Gardening Program
11 Park Place, Suite 1016
New York, NY 10007
    Various publications

Kings
24 Yost Avenue
Sp. City, PA 19475
    Biological pest control

Necessary Trading Company
367 Main Street
New Castle, VA 24127
    Chemical-free gardener's guide

New England Insect Traps
P.O. Box 938
Amherst, MA 01004
    Natural (non-toxic) pesticides, biological pest control

Ortho/Chevron Chemical Company
Public Affairs Department
P.O. Box 3744
San Francisco, CA 94119
    "A Child's Garden," "Trees for a More Liveable Environment," "Learning on the Light Side."

Rincon-Vita
P.O. Box 96
Oakview, CA 93022
    Biological pest control

3. *Gardening Seeds*

(List by courtesy of Brooklyn Cooperative Extension.)

Agway, Inc.
Route 4, Zeager Road
Elizabeth Town, PA 17022

Burgess Seed Plant Company
P.O. Box 218
Galesburg, MI 49053

Charles Hart Seed Company
Wethersfield, CT 06109

George W. Park Seed Company
Greenwood, SC 29646

Gurney Seed and Nursery Company
Yankton, SD 57078

Henry Field Seed Company
Shenandoah, IA 51602

J. A. Demonchaux Company
225 Jackson Street
Topeka, KS 66603

J. L. Hudson Seedsman
P. O. Box 1058
Redwood City, CA 94064

Jackson and Perkins Company
Medford, OR 97501

Johnny's Selected Seeds
Albion, ME 04910

Joseph Harris Company
Moreton Farm
Rochester, NY 14624

Le Jardin du Gormet
Dirt Road
West Dansville, VT 05873

R. L. Holmes Seed Company
2125 46th Street, N.W.
Canton, OH 44709

Seedway
Quality Seeds, Inc.
Hall, NY 14463

Steel Plant Company
Gleason, TN 38229

Stokes Seeds, Inc.
Box 548, Main P.O.
Buffalo, NY 14240

Thompson and Morgan, Inc.
P.O. Box 24
Somerdale, NJ 08083

Twilley Seed Company
P.O. Box 65
Trevose, PA 19047

Vermont Bean Seed Company
Garden Lane
Bomoseen, VT 05732

APPENDIX I
Sources of Supplies
Gardening Seeds
General Scientific Supply
Nature Supplies
Reprints, Graphics, Posters

W. Atlee Burpee Company
Box 6929
Philadelphia, PA 19132

4. *General Scientific Supply*

Carolina Biological Supply
2700 York Road
Burlington, NC 27215

Cenco
11222 Melrose Avenue
Franklyn Park
Chicago, IL 60131

Connecticut Valley Biological Supply
Valley Road
Southampton, MA 01073
    Source for live specimens: books providing infor-
    mation and culture methods

Edmund Scientific
101 East Gloucester Pike
Barrington, NJ 08007

Fisher Scientific Company
1-800-621-4769

Frey Scientific Company
905 Hickory Lane
Mansfield, OH 44905

Kuhl Company
Flemington, NJ 08822
    Makers of Educational Chick Incubator
    (Hovabator)

Lab-Aids, Inc.
130 Wilbur Place
Bohemia, NY 11716
    Supplies, kits

NASCO
Fort Atkinson, WI 53538
    Biotips

National Teaching Aids
120 Fulton Avenue
Garden City Park, NY 11040
    Makers of microviewers

School Masters
745 State Circle
Ann Arbor, MI 48104

Sargent-Welch
35 Stern Avenue
Springfield, NJ 07081
    Microscopes, information cards

Turtox/Cambosco
MacMillan Science Company
8200 South Hoyne Avenue
Chicago, IL 60620
    Science Leaflets

Wards
P.O. Box 1712
Rochester, NY 14603
    Booklet, How to Assemble an Animal Kingdom
    Survey Collection; other aids

Warner Scientific
1-800-523-0267

5. *Nature Suppliers*

Biological Resource Development Company
1750 Wooten Road
Beaumont, TX 77707
    Styrofoam display boxes

Butterfly Company
51-17 Rockaway Beach Boulevard
Far Rockaway, NY 11691

Creative Dimensions
Box 1393
Bellingham, WA 98225
    Owl pellets

Havahart Trap
P.O. Box 551
Ossining, NY 10562
    Live traps

Insect Lore Products
P.O. Box 1535
Shafter, CA 93263

Learning Spectrum
1390 Westridge
Portola Valley, CA 94025
    Inexpensive student microscope; other materials

Museum Products
3175 Gold Star Highway
Mystic, CT 06355
    Catalog

6. *Reprints, Graphics, Posters*

Argus Communications
One DLM Park
Allen, TX 75002

===APPENDIX I===

Sources of Supplies
Reprints, Graphics, Posters
Suggestions, Teaching Tips

Forest Service
U.S. Department of Agriculture
P.O. Box 2417
Washington, D.C. 20013
   "What We Get From Trees" poster and others

Information Division
Agricultural Resource Service
U.S. Department of Agriculture
Washington, D.C. 20256
   Science study aids

John Wiessinger
Lakeshore Curriculum Materials
2695 E. Dominguez Street
P.O. Box 6291
Carson, CA 90749

North American Bluebird Society
Box 6295
Silver Springs, MD 20906

St. Regis Paper Company
150 East 47th Street
New York, NY 10017
   "Life in the Forest," "The Forest Community,"
   others

SVE
2750 North Wayne Avenue
Chicago, IL 60614
   Posters

Pennsylvania Game Commission
P.O. Box 1567
Harrisburg, PA 17120
   Display material

Roy G. Scarfo, Inc.
P.O. Box 217
Thorndale, PA 19372

7. *Suggestions, Teaching Tips*

American Humane Association
5351 South Roslyn Street
Englewood, CO 80111
   Animal care

Ampersand Press
691 26th Street
Oakland, CA 94612
   Makers of "Predator/Prey" and other ecology
   games

Ann Arbor Publications
P.O. Box 388
Worthington, OH 43085
   Exploring Our Environment, book

Book Nest
Richardson Bay Audubon Center
376 Greenwood Beach Road
Tiburon, CA 94920

Brooklyn Botanical Garden
1000 Washington Avenue
Brooklyn, NY 11225
   Catalog
   Booklets on plant dyes

City Garden Club of New York
355 East 72nd Street
New York, NY 10021

Crows Nest Bookstore
Laboratory of Orinthology
Cornell University
159 Sapsucker Woods Road
Ithaca, NY 14850
   Games, books, puzzles, Audible Audubon

Cornell Cooperative Extension
Publications Distribution Center
7 Research Park
Cornell University
Ithaca, NY 14850
   "The Know-How Catalog"; booklets on hatching
   eggs

Delta Education, Inc.
P.O. Box M
Nashua, NH 03061
   Publisher of OBIS, catalog of scientific materials

Dover Publications
180 Varick Street
New York, NY 10014
   Catalog of nature books and nature coloring
   books

Dynamic T-Shirts
7525 Mission Gorge Road
Suite E
San Diego, CA 92120

Education Section
Office of Public Information and Education
Ohio Department of Natural Resources
Fountain Square
Columbus, OH 43224
   Imagination Books

ERIC/SMEAC
1200 Chambers Road, 3rd Floor
Columbus, OH 43212
   Clearinghouse for environmental education

══APPENDIX I══
Sources of Supplies
Suggestions, Teaching Tips
Miscellaneous

Girl Scouts of the USA
830 Third Avenue
New York, NY 10022
 Exploring Wildlife Communities with Children,
 book

Gull Lake Environmental Ed Project
Kellogg Bird Sanctuary
Michigan State University
12685 East C Avenue
Augusta, MI 49012
 Good teaching aids

Hillside Outdoor Education Center
Gaze Road
Brewster, NY 10509
 In and Out, book

Lawrence Hall of Science
Astronomy Education Program
University of California
Berkeley, CA 94720
 Producers of "Stargazer's Gazette" and Sky Chal-
 lenger materials

Marginal Media
P.O. Box 241
Fredonia, NY 14063

Massachusetts Audubon Society
Lincoln, MA 01773
 Publishers of The Curious Naturalist and many
 other top notch materials.

National Audubon
950 3rd Avenue
New York, NY 10022
 Catalog of educational materials

National 4-H Council
150 North Wacker Drive
Suite 1950
Chicago, IL 60606
 "What's A Tree To Me"

National Geographic
Educational Services
P.O. Box 1640
Washington, D.C. 20013

National Wildlife Federation
1412 16th Street, N.W.
Washington, D.C. 20036
 Books, games, puzzles, wildlife stamps, Ranger
 Rick Activity Guides, reprints of "Wildlife in
 Your World"

Nature Impressions
1007 Leneye Place
El Cerrito, CA 94530
 Rubber stamp makers

P. A. Schiller Associates
P.O. Box 307
Chicago, IL 60690
 Activities; mini-field guides

Robatom Publications
Route 1, Box 148
Prudenville, MI 48651
 Spirit masters

Safari Ltd.
P.O. Box 630685
Ovus, FL
 Animal rummy games

Soil Conservation Society of America
N.E. Ankeny Place
Ankeny, IA 50021
 Materials in comic book format

Superintendent of Documents
U.S. Government Printing Office
Washington, D.C. 20402

Weekly Reader Books
Equity Drive
P.O. Box 16550
Columbus, OH 43216
 Illustrated Wildlife Treasury ("Safari Cards")

Yotta, Inc.
P.O. Box 36
Redmond, VA 98052
 Games

8. *Miscellaneous*

Calloway House
451 Richardson Drive
Lancaster, PA 17603
 Sturdy cardboard aids

General Supply Corporation
P.O. Box 9347
Jackson, MS 39206

Nature Company
P.O. Box 2310
Berkeley, CA 94702

OBIS

OUTDOOR BIOLOGY INSTRUCTIONAL STRATEGIES

OBIS activities were written and developed at the Lawrence Hall of Science, UCLA-Berkeley. They were field tested and are now distributed by Delta Education, Box M, Nashua, NH 03061. They consist of ninety-seven activities, each one fully described on its own plastic coated folio. I have listed some of the activities that I feel have been especially well-received and/or applicable to most camp settings. I recommend that you send for their booklet, *The OBIS Story,* which describes all ninety-seven, and provides other information.

A Better Fly Trap—Youngsters investigate the behavior of flies and construct fly traps from milk cartons.

Animal Diversity—Using sweep nets, the campers sample and compare the insects living in two different areas; a managed lawn and a weedy area.

Animal Movement in Water—The campers try to discover how aquatic animals move in water.

Animals in a Grassland—Campers use sweep nets to sample the variety of animals living in a lawn.

Ants—The campers investigate the behavior of ants.

Bean Bugs—Campers learn how to census a population of organisms too numerous to count, in this simulation activity.

Creepers and Climbers—Campers investigate specialized climbing structures and growth patterns of different vines.

Envirolopes—Fully described in Activities, III-44.

Habitats of the Pond—Teams hunt for organisms in different areas of a pond or lake.

Hopper Circus—Campers are challenged to study the behavior of hopping animals (grasshoppers, frogs, others).

Hopper Herding—Campers round up a "herd" of hopping insects to find out how many different kinds there are.

Invent an Animal—Campers design "animals" that blend into local habitats and search for other campers' animals.

Lichen Looking—Campers search for lichens and learn about their habitats, shapes and colors.

Moisture Makers—Participants test different kinds of leaves with cobalt chloride paper, comparing the amount of moisture released from the leaves.

Mystery Marauders—The campers gather evidence that plants in the site are being eaten, and then try to identify the plant eaters.

Plants Around a Building—Campers discover how the environment around a building affects the growth of a plant.

Population Game—Described fully in Activities, III-55.

Swell Homes—Campers locate galls and see what lives in them.

Water Breathers—The campers investigate the currents created by aquatic animals when they breathe and move.

Web It—Using spray misters, straws and sweep nets, campers investigate the behavior of spiders.

What Lives Here?—Campers observe and identify plants and animals that live on an aquatic site.

The activities are also organized into *modules* for a particular group or specific site. Instructions for self-made equipment are included, plus a price list of equipment you can purchase from Delta.

(The descriptions are from THE OBIS Story, used by permission. Delta Education, Inc., P.O. Box M, Nashua, NH 03061.)

INDEX

The items in italics are the names of specific activities described in the text.